How Simple
The Solution

Discourses With Master Teacher

ENDEAVOR ACADEMY
"Certum Est Quia Impossibile Est"

©1998 Endeavor Academy
How Simple The Solution - Discourses With Master Teacher

International Standard Book Number (ISBN-10): 1-890648-01-9
(ISBN-13): 978-1-890648-01-5

Published By:
Endeavor Academy
501 East Adams Street, Wisconsin Dells, WI 53965, USA
Phone: +1 608-253-1447
www.themasterteacher.tv
Email: publishing@endeavoracademy.com

Contents

NOTE

These are transcripts of recorded talks given through the revelatory mind of Master Teacher. Little editing has been done in hope of maintaining and conveying the exciting, spontaneous spiritual continuity.

.

How Simple
The Solution

Ostensibly we are teaching a program of enlightenment. Supposedly we are teaching there is a manner in which you can change your mind, and by that process, eliminate and transform the dilemma that you experience here on earth in association with yourself – with death and with time. One of the requisites to this sort of teaching would appear to be – would inevitably, finally be – that the earthling, the consciousness, is aware of his dilemma. If you want to join me with this, this would be sort of a rambling kitchen talk. There is no reason why we can't have a discussion of this, because there is no teaching that does not or cannot involve the problem in which there is an attempted solution.

But there is a problem in regard to human existence on the planet earth that's axiomatic with the beginning of his consciousness in association with his surroundings. And he's taught immediately (the human mind) to defend himself and associate himself in a form of reality that constitutes memories that his parents or his society or his species have in regard to what he is. Now, those of you who are sitting with me have obviously evolved a human pattern or a perceptual association with yourself that you define as reality. Isn't this so?

This is going to be the plaintive kitchen talk, because if you strip everything that's ever been said since the beginning of time it's going to arrive at what? The dilemma of purpose. Can I make this plainer for you? The dilemma of the reason why you are here. The dilemma of what? Of who you are. What are you? Now it's easy for your associates in the world to say, "well, I have solved that problem, I'm an accountant," or "I'm a housewife" or "I'm a doctor" or " I'm a human being" or "I'm a Methodist" or "a Shiite Muslim who is going to kill all Christians." I am not interested in what you are. Those of you who arrive at the conclusion that who you are does not satisfy you in relationship to the consciousness of eternity that you feel, will continue to what? Search for a justification for yourself. This is really basic. But it's so basic that it is inevitably true. Now to the direct extent, by whatever means, you are able to satiate your need to know who you are..., and that's arrived at, perhaps by religious motivations, perhaps by finding answers in your description of the Brazilian beetles, or in how many constellations there are in the sky, or in the construction of a master computer that can direct and ascertain more rapidly than the human brain the number of molecules in whatever, and on and on. So you find satisfaction. It doesn't sustain you, but it sustains you sufficiently until what? Until death. It sustains you within your time framework until your demise.

Well, many of you, and certainly I did very early in my life, questioned the notation that my existence or my life here on this planet was based on my annihilation, was based on the eventual succumbing. It always seemed very strange to me, it seemed crazy to me. And you could give me a "well you'll know later on" or "that's the will of God", perhaps, or "we don't know that" or "that's a door you can go through," or "you're going to be in a different place," or whatever reasons you gave me. It never satisfied me. I felt the frustration of my existence in relationship with pain. The question very early for me, for those of you who may not know who I am, it doesn't really make any difference, you won't be right, anyway. But hopefully, you'll be able to see that I am speaking to you from what could be termed a lucid or Light mind. I've been through some very dramatic experiences. You guys smile, because many of you know of my experiences and indeed are having these experiences yourself. We are going to arrive finally at the statement that the whole process that has ever been taught in the idea of a gaining of knowledge and advanced associations of perception, will involve inevitably what you would term Christian mysticism or transformation of the mind to a new range of consciousness.

We are jumping the gun here. I'd rather give you the premises by which you will seek this conclusion. It was very obvious to me, and this came very early in my philosophy of life, perhaps because of my early witnesses to mass death with the bomb and the incredible holocaust and all the things that went with the annihilation of individual consciousnesses. But it became obvious to me that there was no solution to the meaning of life if finally it was going to be associated with annihilation. But when I examined that, I found in my mind a statement – perhaps you would call it a statement of inevitability – of a wholeness, or a truth, or a God, or Love, or finally a single purpose of Love and understanding – an ontological, primordial realization of wholeness that is in all of us that could not be satisfied by associate evil-ness or associate separateness simply because finally my mind would not draw the conclusion of pain and death and sickness and greed and hatred and possession in association with love. The manners in which I saw consciousnesses love and lose seemed frustrating and unjust to me. I questioned very early why it is I always, and everyone here, loses the things they love, so that their reality finally has to be based on what? Pain and death, darn it!

Now I understand that the human condition of existence – the Master Teacher, Jesus, in the *Course in Miracles* calls this fear. He has simple statements that need examining in the *Course in Miracles* like "love is letting go of fear"– The condition of perceptual mind, I saw very early, was fearful. And this is taken for granted by the perceptual mind that identifies itself in a lack or in an existent situation. But finally somewhere within that framework, many of you began to feel the frustration of the inevitability of your own annihilation, either moment by moment, or in subsequent aging process – the process of getting old, wrinkled and ending up in the nursing home or run over by a beer truck or having your children desert you – all the things that you really don't like to look at, but all the things that must inevitably be true.

Now to the direct extent that you begin to question yourself in that association, you will seek, and did seek, an answer to the dilemma. You found somewhere along the line that there isn't any answer here. This is a big step, isn't it? Now this can manifest itself in everything from adolescent schizophrenia, where the consciousness becomes aware very early that the purpose in life is death, so he cuts his wrist and dies. But the conclusion in your own mind and the dilemma was that you can see reasonably that annihilation is not a solution, because no matter how much you can ascribe to it, you cannot but venture to declare a continuing consciousness at some state within the framework of yourself. Isn't it so? Let me hear you say yes. Now, on this then, we will formulate what? Religions. We are going to have a heaven, we're going to have reincarnation where we'll all return. And this seems very reasonable to me. But it didn't solve my dilemma. You know why? Because the question that persisted with me at that point was this: What is the reason then still for life? Why is it that if there is this love and this understanding and this kindness, and in my heartfelt certainty, this compassion for my brother, why is it that we didn't have it? Why couldn't we find it? Where was it?

This is the beginning of a real spiritual search now. Where is that satiated? Where did you individually find a relief for your existence in association with pain and death? All earth consciousnesses within the framework of time, each moment, find a relief within their perception for their existence. This is fundamental teaching. If they did not, if they stopped for just a moment and acknowledged the impossibility of their situation, I teach you that you would begin the transformative process. This is the whole teaching of the *Course in Miracles* – it is indeed the whole teaching of all processes to enlightenment, the absolute notation that there is a consciousness beyond perception.

The dilemma that arises then, is that if there is a consciousness beyond this perception that is beneficent and good and loving, how does it make allowances for the pain and death that I am experiencing? Now there literally is no solution to this question. Very basically, if you begin with the premise – and this is really fundamental, but here is the core of the problem – if you begin with the fundamental assertion that there is an all powerful, all good, force, call it God or call it Wholeness, call it Unity, call it non-conflictual Reality, call it anything you want, you are left with the dilemma that:

-If it is all good and allows the pain and death of earth to exist within its awareness, it is not all powerful and must therefore be beset by a force that can be in conflict with it.

-If it is all powerful in wholeness and recognition and allows for the terrible injustices and inevitable demise of the consciousness in association with the earth and doesn't do anything about it, it is not all good.

What you have formulated here within your own perception is a God. But in the long run you must consider your God to be unjust, because if He is true and whole, why does He allow these things to exist? This is the exact condition that Aquinas would arrive at in a discussion with another brother; that Augustine, that all religions and philosophies have faced in the dilemma of the confrontation of good and evil.

The problem is that the admission of evil at all, what you call duality, subtracts the possibility of a total good. And here is always where the conflict will come. Listen to me: There is no solution to this problem but one: That good does not know of evil. I'll go right up to it. This is the whole Buddhistic teaching – that a conceptual God is impossible. The conclusion you must arrive at is that of a non-judgmental whole thing. And you may do that in some sort of declaration of Dharma, or in the Judaic tradition, of a God that we may not speak of – a God that does not know us, a God that does not know about this at all. That's a statement of reasonable Socratic truth: Good cannot know of evil. All right, now I am sitting with that. I know that. How does that solve my problem? The idea that truth and wholeness does not know of this does not solve my problem of my association with the evil and death and all the things that are around here. Isn't that strange?

Now, very simply and logically, if there is a good and wholeness that I am able to express, it must be that I know of it in my own mind, all right? Now, if there is no conflicting force in association with the good, it must be that my mind is what is in conflict with the good. Big step here now. Why? We're into existentialism. We're into what? Subjective reality. We are making a statement that the only problem and solution is contained within my own reference – my own framework. I have brought the problem where? Into focus. This is a big step. Why? I can't blame good without the admission that good is evil, so I've subtracted that. I can't claim evil outside of me without the denial that there is a positive good, which puts me in a position of attempting to judge what's good and evil, which is exactly what the human dilemma is.

So, if I can get rid of that, that evil is not outside myself, I can accept the notation that my mind is in conflict. If that is so, then the solution to the conflict must be in my mind. Hey, we're getting it; we're very close to it. Now you begin to look around and you say "yes, there is much evidence of a transformative process of mind where I individually can find peace, can find grace, can find happiness within my own construction." Obviously, the search for that truth – and this seems strange but not if you really look at it – must be in direct association with the expression of the problem within the psychology of the individual. Isn't this so? If he doesn't feel the pain, if he has found a solution to his personality, to who he is – and I don't care how or whether it is with drugs or whether it's with children or whether it's a family or whether it's with an establishment, whether it's with just coping and hanging on to death, whether it's with Eros and going out and having a party and saying "I don't care" – he has found a solution. That consciousness really won't care about this talk, will he? He'll say, "well that's nice for you, but I have solved the problem" so he is not going to listen to a Christ Voice – this is Jesus Christ, or my awakened Voice, that proclaims to you that your kingdom is not of this world, the problem of truth cannot be solved in reciprocity or associate ideas or first covenant – the idea that you are going to give something to get something back – but only in the assertion of the wholeness of a single power that must emanate finally from your own mind.

So we're going to sit here then and ramble and tell you: Yes, in all of the history of man there has always been known a process – Jesus calls it *A Course In Miracles* – of enlightenment, an initiation, a transformation, a revelation, resurrection of the mind to the certainty of its wholeness. It's really not a secret now. Why is it, then, that those on earth do not know of it? Very simply because somewhere within the details of subjectivity, it smacks of super-mind. It smacks of a mind that could become more manipulative in its own associations. It is an expression that finally, power in perception corrupts. Actually, the whole teaching is one of the necessity, and this is the only way it can be reached, of surrender – to give up, to let go, to resist not evil, to not participate in the functioning of your own perceptual mind in association with itself. Of course, if you proceed to do that, you'll also be condemned and judged because you're not participating in the sociological death ritual. Your brothers are going to say, "come die with us. Come on, you have the responsibility of death here", and you still do.

So the solution must be and will be and is declared to be in the transformation of your mind. How that can come about and how that comes about is contained in the traditions and historic references of mystical Christianity and Sufism and occult Buddhistic and Hinduistic teachings, in everything, in astrology, in the declarations of Society of Whole Minds – a brotherhood, perhaps. To the direct extent that the world feels this pain, it solves its solutions through pacifism, to the expression of a need to come together and communicate, on up to the reaches of the certainty of whole communication in the relationships of brothers – but only through what? The transformation or the change of your mind. The declaration of perceptual existentialism reality is the beginning of enlightenment and will not be attained otherwise. The resistance, the determination of perceptual mind, to blame objectively something outside of itself for its dilemma, is pervasive because the perceptual consciousness is in association with objective reality.

We set a course then, only of transformation. Here's the big dilemma, if you care to really look at it. You have in your mind an idea of changing your mind and arriving, say, at a conclusion of truth. Since you are in body association, I make the declaration that enlightenment or transformation involves the transformation of the physical body. This is the whole treatment of *A Course In Miracles*. Consciousnesses in perception choose to separate their mind from their body with statements like "I am not a body and I can find a good mind." Obviously, if they are in association with the body in whatever framework of perception they're in, it must be the change of the whole self that brings enlightenment. It's not going to occur without it. This is where we begin our teachings. We begin our teachings with the statement that God cannot be known because He is. That I cannot know Him perceptually, but through a transformation of my mind. I may recognize that I am a part of that whole and am in fact that whole thing. This is all I teach. This is all that all initiations will teach.

The problem obviously is that it must include the relinquishment of myself in associations with the things that I heretofore have given value. Literally, I must let go and let God. I must stop pursuing the advantages of existence. Is this dying and being born again? Yes. You can say it in a million ways. And until you feel the pain of existence sufficiently, we might term it, to begin to search for a real source contained within you in association with your mind, you will continue to participate in the ritual of time, in the ritual of the beginning acknowledgment of your association with your own annihilation.

This is an advanced course. This is for consciousnesses that:

-Number 1: have seen the dilemma and

-Number 2: because of their search, have begun to feel the stirrings, through imagery – through what you would call perhaps, revelation, through individual episodes of association with death, perhaps – have felt the change that's occurring in their minds, in perhaps a mystical fashion. By whatever means. They have made that admission, and now I can declare to them, "Yes, brother, this is a going on in your mind. This is an awakening – a physical awakening in your own mind that you can find." This is the declaration of *A Course In Miracles*. *A Course In Miracles* by the consciousness Jesus Christ, out of body, is nothing but a certain declaration of the transformation of your mind to wholeness.

So we sit here and I sit here with this mind and make this declaration. I am fully aware as you will be now, in your completion of your processes, and many of you are going to go out into the world with this message, that you will be denied and attacked. Jesus makes a very simple statement in the *Course* when He says, let's face it, if you can find the Christ, you'll kill Him because the condition of your existence in limitation must be a denial of the wholeness of you. But if you will start with that premise, you will assume what you could call a defenseless posture. You will begin to practice beatitudes through love, understanding and forgiveness. You won't hold the grievance of your past time associations. Now you are into the mechanisms of the transformation of the mind. You will then begin to experience the miracle through your non-participation, through the emergence of a whole mind that transcends any limited perceptions you previously had about yourself. Isn't that glorious? That you could actually do this in your mind? Of course you can.

The most natural condition of yourself is to know who you are. If you are not yet doing the *Course In Miracles*, you might want to start doing it. We will use it as a whole frame of reference. Read Lesson 139, and you read it very carefully. It is the greatest most Socratic framework of consciousness that's ever been expressed in the world. It's a statement that it's impossible for you not to know yourself. That'll help you, especially those of you with high egos or high reasoning processes that have reached the conclusion that you somehow have satisfied yourself in relationship with yourself without addressing the fundamental problem of time versus eternity. If there is time, eternity is impossible. If eternity or wholeness is true, there is no time. This is the beginning statement of *A Course In Miracles*. Do you like that? Anything that is not forever is not real, therefore the earth is not real. That's fun. You come and join us here, make some of these statements with us and enjoy the meditation that is bringing about the transformation of the mind and body occurring now within this frame of reference.

What we're saying is that contained within what we have just said is the declaration of the initiation process of the physical transformation. You can call that the revolution of the whole consciousness, the secret wisdom, the admission of the *Philosophia Perennis*. I guess it must be hanging out there somewhere. The dilemma that you are going to have with this, if you decide it's a dilemma, it's a conflict. The notation that spirituality is physical is extremely difficult to present because it admits to the dichotomy of the association. It's one thing to declare a God in Heaven, it's another thing to declare God is you, to the recognition of your mind or that you are the only living Son of God or that consciousness is singular. This is the Gnostic tradition of direct revelation that has always been persecuted in objective reality, isn't it? It's the idea that, as Master Jesus would proclaim it, all earth establishments are false, that perception itself is false – that through non-participation in society, through nondefense, you will come by a revelatory process to behold the wholeness of the universe. That has to be attacked here because perceptual consciousness is the denial of wholeness. This is how simple this is.

The advanced notation, and the one where it goes so-called undercover, is the declaration that it is a physical process. The Workbook of *A Course In Miracles* begins and ends with the statement that through the relinquishment of the limited self, physically you will undergo a change of your mind. All of the notations in regard to facing the veil, there are moments in the text where it says this moment can be terrible, when through your meditations you have subtracted your defense mechanisms sufficiently to be confronted by the horror of your perceptual associations with death. This is the whole idea of the mystical "ring pass-not", of the presentation of yourself to the guardians of the door of death to the admission that you are undergoing a process of death, aren't you? Know ye not ye must be born again, Nicodemus? (John 3:3) All of the statements of initiation have to finally somewhere involve the admission of death. You have denied physical death. You must deny the idea of time, which is physical death. You must there make the assertion of the necessity to be born again, to undergo a process of relinquishment that will identify itself with fear, won't it? How could it not do it?

The teachings of the *Course*, as I will direct you, are to give you, through choice – that is through the elimination of temptation, as Jesus would say – to arrive at the conclusion that you have no choice in this matter. The whole idea that there is a revolution of the mind possible, the idea of evolution, must include and does include the certainty that there is a power that you are evolving to. That's a progression of the mind in the relinquishment of itself and hopefully, and now we'll go back to Master Jesus for a minute, He says we are going to shorten time by increasing the rapidity of associate experiences within the drama of your own mind to bring about more rapidly the conclusion of your own death association. This is the physical transformation of your body, if you want to look at it. Those of you who think that Christianity does not teach physical transformation are sadly mistaken. Our whole mystical notation is with the certainty of the reconstruction of the body of Christ into a whole solid unit. I don't care where you hear this.

We are teaching transformation of body/mind. Does that connect inevitably with the initiation process? Does that connect with the Eastern tradition of the awakening, of perhaps the kundalini? Of course. We are teaching a glandular revolution and this is an advanced idea. I don't need to get into it, but I would think that people in a Christian modality who are doing *Course in Miracles*, will begin to literally experience some sorts of visions, some sorts of revelations in the relinquishment of their ego, in the letting go of themselves. I don't know how you could help but do it. The whole process is nothing but to bring that about. Now we have got this hanging out a little bit here, but if you want to let it hang out, the reason that you are here is that you began to have these experiences. If you would like to get into the tradition of the awakening of the kundalini, I'd be happy to address that sometime. If you'd like to look at the mystical associations of the Apocalypse, for example, in the declaration that the glandular associations were the churches as expressed in the seven chakras in the body, we do that here. You guys want to hear about that? We do that. What we're saying is, the admission that you are undergoing a transformation of the wholeness of you from part of you to the Truth will include all of the traditions and will subtract nothing from your determination to be enlightened.

The statement of Jesus Christ in the *Course* is this, very simply: full purpose or full pursuit or full endeavor or full commitment, or full giving of yourself which is a full forgiving of yourself is what enlightenment is, and obviously this is so. A full commitment to a God would have to lead to God immediately. It could not *not*. Now this is the practice, then, that we are undergoing in the raising of this energy into our minds, and I am using "the raising of the energy" advisedly because that's the admission that you are undergoing physiological changes in your systems. Of course I'm aware of this.

There is no teaching in any tradition, and this includes the Christian one, that will not direct itself to that transformation that is occurring – the maturation of your whole mind body association. Jesus calls it the preparation of your body to be a perfect communicative device. He augments that with dramatic statements like, at no time is the body really real. It is always either thought of or anticipated so that the mechanism of meditation is the teaching of the coming into the whole mind. When addressing the body then, the teaching becomes: pay the body no mind. It will be whole, and service you absolutely sufficiently to your own enlightenment. Interestingly enough, this admission has caused many of our brothers to undergo the experience of youthfulness association, vitality, love, wholeness, healing and all of the delightful things that go with the occurrence of the transformation. What the hell – pardon me!! – What the heck. What the heaven! We are teaching love and forgiveness here.

The consciousness discovers that through the direction of his mind in determination to find this, he begins to feel the peace of absolute commitment. This is a transcendent peace, isn't it? If you finally decide that you are going to have this at any cost, you discover it costs nothing. But you can't know that until you determine to have it at any cost, which is nothing but giving up anything you value. Jesus teaches it, you can have everything you value by simply giving it away – but it requires that you give it away totally to know that you are perfect and whole in the love of God and the certainty of you in that relationship. Is that physical? Hey! Will miracles occur to sustain you with that? Oh, they're happening all around the world. There are miracles going on everywhere. It's just that your limited perception holds you in the bondage of associate sequential time. So you hold yourself in time and you get old. That's nonsense, there isn't any death.

There is no such thing as death. There is no such thing as getting old and there is no such thing as sickness. You're not overcoming anything. They don't exist. This is my fundamental teaching. This is the teachings of all awakened consciousnesses. We don't admit that you are evil coming to good, we maintain and declare that evil does not exist. Science of the mind. We are making emphatic statements, and this was earlier in the talk, that this isn't real, that this is a dream. If it has any reality at all, it would have to have all reality and then death would be real. If death is real, there is no God. How simple. Therefore, this is not real. Since I am in a condition of reality versus unreality – I am into the *Course* again – I can come to know that, through my own initiative and not in any other fashion. I cannot get it by questioning my mind's effects. I can't find it here because it isn't here. I have constructed in my mind a seal of unreality. There is literally no communication going on between reality and the associations of perceptual consciousness that is termed "earth." This is a statement of fact, that being true, you can find it. If there is a communication you can never find it because you then become the assertion of the duality. And I know this is fundamental, but the admission of that and the subsequent occurrences of the manifestations of continuing phenomena, which you call a miracle, is a very advanced teaching. I suppose, somewhere within the framework of society, it's attacked and denied because the world is associated with the need to survive and to exist.

You will now go out and proclaim, "No, dear teacher, this is you, you're the cause of this." As Jesus would say, the sole necessity of a miracle worker is to bring about the atonement in himself. That realization, the realization that the world is literally your mind construct, is all that I teach. Why should that be so difficult? Dear brother, there's a thousand million trillion zillion earths, what's wrong with this earth being your concept, or your dream of reality? The moment that you make that acknowledgment, you begin in your own mind to bring about atonement, to literally forgive yourself for your guilt associations that have caused you to deny and attack reality. I assure you that there is no war going on. The truth is absolutely beneficent, non-conflictual. Any conflict that you are feeling now in regard to what I'm saying is just the residual of karma memory in your determination to bring about your own death. You invented time. Jesus, so lovingly in the *Course*, says, choose not to die, Son of God, you made a bargain but you cannot keep it. There is no such thing, it's absurd. The idea of termination itself is the most insane absurd notion that could ever come. This may appear to be advanced teaching; it's really not. It's just ultimately, totally simple. Consciousness or beingness is whole and singular and you are that. Can you come to know that through this hatching that is going on in you? Through this metamorphosis going on? Of course! Everything that is occurring now within your framework is to bring about this simple admission.

Isn't it time that you looked at yourself within your own dream and made the declaration that you are the determiner of your own destiny in association with time? Come on, you guys. You smile at me. You feel this reference, this new frame of reference that is permeating your mind. It makes you very happy. Let those that can hear, hear. This is a positive statement that sin and death and pain and destruction and lack have no reality at all. And by your declaration of determination of faith, if you want to call it that, that there is a whole source of reality. You can come to know this through the transformation of your mind. I say that to you from a transformed mind having undergone what you would term the initiation. I teach from that frame of reference. If you can tell the difference in what we are saying here, then you will very rapidly decide to pursue this. This is a step above the perceptual admission, for example, that the *Course in Miracles* was written by Jesus Christ. This is the declaration of the transformation process itself. This is the *Course in Miracles* taught from the first page to the last. It's nothing but that.

We will always be what? Confronting the consciousness at his denial point, at the point where he continues to give himself value in association with the process that he is undergoing. I understand that the dichotomy occurs here. Our declaration is that there is finally no process. The admission of the necessity that the impossible occurred is stated very simply in the teachings of the *Course,* where it says that we are literally dealing with an impossible situation – a sleeping consciousness on the verge of his own glorious awakening. Those of you who hear this – finally, it's coming out. The brothers will be going around the world and they are going to be teaching this and more and more they will gather together in the declarations of the forgiveness of grievance associations, of the love they have for their brothers and the forgiveness that must be the beginning of the admission of their whole selves. This is what we say. So write us here or call us or come and see us. We'll be all around you now, speaking of the Aquarian conspiracies and speaking of whole minds. You look at the things that are happening in the world. Look how the world is turned upside down politically and sociologically, and this will give you an idea of the incredible happenings going on now in this unit of mind, this mutual declaration of this brotherhood. How exciting!

You can't fail. If you can get into your mind the certainty that no matter what you do, you can't fail, it will shorten your time a lot; that this is a course in relinquishment. Nobody likes the word surrender, but why not? The decision not to act through your own perceptions, the decision not to be the factoring – Master Jesus says you have an authority problem – you are not the author of the universe. If you will make that admission, the identity of the Author emerges as you in the union of your heart and mind with God; how very beautiful. You can call it anything you want. You then become whole mind and extend from you or literally create with your mind that certainty. That's exciting!! The more that these visions begin to occur to you the more you bring it all together. Everything that happens, and all these miracles going on... How exciting to find all around you the evidence of the single occurrence in your mind. You bring all of time together in this single episode of transformation. Wow! We are very happy that you have come now to join us.

I Know You
Perfectly Well

Here we have a sacred time which is a process of remembering who you are. To subtract anything is nonsense. It's real. You can come with that process to know that this is not true. It is the only method by which you will succeed. You must finally come to know that the earth is not true, by whatever method. Your transformation will not be accomplished in any other way. That's very fundamental. That's the fundamental teaching of all religions and philosophies. But it is nonetheless transformative and will not be accomplished intellectually. As far as your little consciousness, you are not capable of recognizing that you are an illusion. And therein lies the dilemma.

Self-identification is incredible — the sin of leaving the Garden, the dilemma of having to count the animals and name them. That's absurd. Animals all have one name. Everything is finally one thing. Or it is nothing. It would be pretty hard for it to be nothing.

You can feel particular energies flowing as you attempt to identify who they are, your mind goes, "Ch-ku, ch-ku, ch-ku. Who's that? Who am I? Why are we are here?" Pooooh. It's all just junk. We know who you are. You can't fool us.

Everybody's got a secret. You really think that separate from yourself, as identified in your ego, that you keep secrets from other people. That's absurd. Everybody has the same secrets. Everybody is finally afraid of the same thing. Otherwise why would you keep secrets?

Secrets are always kept because of fear. If you're afraid, you can't love. Can't love, you can't live. If you don't love, you die. That's why you die, because you can't love. You are afraid. So you keep all these secrets down inside — dirty, guilty, junky, all sorts of stuff, stuff you wouldn't tell your best friend, stuff you don't admit to yourself. It makes you feel corrupt because you are corrupt, because you're not true. When you came into this world you pretty well knew that, but you were taught that that's not so — that you do have an identity and you nurture it and mature it in duality. And you look outside yourself and defend yourself from non-existent forces.

You literally establish the illusion of self. It is not true. Hear this anywhere you want to. There is no such thing as separate personalities. That's absurd. You think there's four billion entities on this mud ball, earth? Come on. And they march by and they die and they're murdered. And 40,000 of them starved to death last night. No wonder you feel guilty. How do you handle that? We keep coming back to this. You are protecting yourself – and the heck with everybody else! "Well, I can't do anything about that." No wonder you're in hell. Boy, that's terrible. That's terrible!

You are willing to assume responsibility for some things but not everything. There is no justice on earth. You attempt to establish it by identifying yourself and then projecting from you what you think the truth is. You're not right. You're wrong. It's not so. The truth cannot be outside of you. The truth can only be *you*. Sorry. An idea never leaves its source. As you think you are, you are.

Quantum-ly, everything in the universe is finally totally subjective because there is only one thing. Do you see? And you are it! You may perceive yourself falsely as identified at this speed of consciousness, but I assure you, when you awaken your level of consciousness, you will perceive differently. You are asleep. You are dreaming. This isn't real.

Wake up! Wake up, everybody! I'm disrupting your dream.

You plug along and you say to yourself, "Something's got to be wrong with this. I don't understand it, but it doesn't seem right to me."

The need to retain self-identity is extremely intense in you because if you let it go, you will die. Or you will transform. First you will die and then you will transform. You have a need to retain selfness that keeps you at this stage of consciousness. You project out from yourself and believe that there are forces that cause you difficulty — that there are evil things outside of you. You made them up. There is nothing outside of you.

In the process of coming to know who you are, you will at different levels perceive things like clairvoyance, and other apparitions will occur and you go, "Oh, my." Miracles will happen to you, and you go, "Oh, look at this." They are all true. *You are in an awakening process, and it is the only reason that you are here.* You are here for no other purpose.

In truth, if you give value in duality you cannot awaken because you are holding on to self. You have established an identity and you hold on to it. All endeavors of transformation in religion teach detachment because unless you detach, you can't wake up. You must subtract yourself.

"Well, that's easy for you to say, but how do I go about doing that? I have to function here. After all, I have responsibilities. I'm working here. This is me. This is real. I must go out and pursue these things." Otherwise what? Otherwise you will die.

You are here on the planet because you think there is such a thing as death. You listen to me. You can't die! The only thing that can possibly die is your own self-identification, and that is not real in the first place. There is no such thing as separate personality. I'm sorry, but there isn't. You may hang on to yourself as long as you choose and go to worms and let your nose rot off. It will. But you hide from that. You say, "I don't want to look at that." We'll stick our old ladies in the nursing home and let them rot — our own parents. We'll do all of those things, but we won't acknowledge that we are going to die. Of course you're going to die. The wages of your sin are death.

The only possible sin that you can be in from a religious standpoint, the only possible sin that you can have, is separation — thinking that you're you. There's no such thing as sin.

You are in a process of awakening. The manner in which it finally comes about is genuinely not under your control. You listen. You control nothing on earth. Nothing! Reality is there; you are here. The more you come to know that, the more rapidly will be your cellular response in regard to your awakening.

Who inherits the earth? Christian, who inherits the earth? The meek. You're not meek. Who sees the kingdom of Heaven? The poor in spirit. You're not poor in spirit. You won't turn the other cheek. These are just common, ordinary things, the Beatitudes. If you did that, you wouldn't be here. Does that sound religious? It is. Re-ligious, coming back to know the truth, re-cognizing, re-turning to who you really are. You don't do those things. It's absurd. You resist evil every minute, evil being anything outside of you that you have identified as something that you participate with, and protect yourself from. The moment that you stop resisting evil, you won't be on earth. How much simpler can you say it?

The process of giving up is a process, and each time you do it in truth the energies will respond cellularly, physically. We teach physical awakening here because the awakening is physical. That's a new thought, isn't it? It's not a new thought. It's as old as man. The resurrection was physical! It wasn't something that somebody dreamed up. He was dead and He came back and rose! Of course!

The awakening doesn't occur out there. It occurs here, in you. You are you, in your body. Or it occurs nowhere, and there's nothing and this is chaos and has no purpose and you are here for no reason at all. There are a lot of people who, before the awakening process, come to the conclusion that they are here for no purpose at all — and they are correct because they have looked outside themselves for all of the reasons to justify themselves, and they always fail because everything here turns to dust and is not real. Period. Anything that is not forever is not real!

There's a whole universe, thousands and billions of stars out there, waiting for you. You limit yourself by perception. The only thing that could ever be evil, ever, ever, is limitation. You are conceiving yourself too small-ly.

Does it avail me to tell you that you are the Son of God? I'll try it with you. You are God! Good. You have to be. Now, you can say that intellectually to me. I understand that. When you come to know that that is true, you will have graduated. The process of coming to know that is true is a process of changing your energy responses. It's a moment-by-moment thing because finally there's no space/time. What I mean by that is that it's one thing to teach, "The Father and I are one." You obviously don't *know* that. I say to you that is true — that you can do anything, that you have all power in the universe, that you may do anything that you choose, that you control the universe, that you may disappear from here and never return. Finally you don't believe that in yourself. You can't at this point. It seems as though you can.

"I know that's easy for you to say, but I don't believe it." You say you do, but you don't, because when you finally come to know the truth through your own forgiveness, you will engender energies that extend from you to recognize that you and I are the same. As long as you hold me in duality, you are in failure. Of course. You participate in the illusion.

If I look at you and say, "I love you. I know that you are me," I will extend from me the truth of me. And you can see it sometimes. Now, you can handle that any way you want. You can say, "Who's this funny guy, standing up there?" It makes absolutely no difference to me. That's a little difficult.

I've got a biggie for you: Finally, since all consciousness is one, all atonement is individual and personal and has absolutely nothing to do with what you have established outside yourself.

How can the world be saved? How can this chaos that appears to be here —the death, starvation, murder in which you participate — how can it be saved? Can it be saved by carrying a placard that says, "Let's not drop bombs on people"? Nope. Not finally. Do it if you want to. Can it be saved by finding answers to all the diseases that are in the body, by living together in harmony? No. It can't be saved that way. I'm sorry. The fault of the earth is the earth. The fault of the earth is what you have made of it in your perception.

Do you want to change it? Change *yourself!* Not any other way. Are you loving, sharing, caring? Do you do the things that it says to do? No, you don't. Instead, you say, "Well, if he does it, I'll do it." That won't work. All relationships fail. It won't work unless you give 100%. If you give 100%, you don't have relationships. All you have is love. You don't have a relationship; you have a truth.

This funny looking guy and I are the same. I know perfectly well he's divine. He doesn't know it. It doesn't make any difference if he knows it, as long as I know that he is. How did I come to know that he is? I was forgiven.

You can't forgive yourself. Finally you've got to say, "I can't do this any more. Help me." "Oh, big deal. That's prayer. Sounds like prayer to me." It is. What do you think it is? Is it religious? I don't know. Do you get it in church? I don't know.

You get a cellular response in your energy through karma, through cellular memories that are in you. Everything that has ever occurred on this planet in space/time is contained genetically in your system. I positively guarantee you it is. And I don't mean reincarnation, I mean everything. You have 64 elements of the genetic code in you, which is the *I Ching*. Even the helix is the same. Even the symbol of the genetic code is the same as the *I Ching*. *I Ching* is potentiality. *I Ching* is Holy Spirit. *I Ching* is the distance between essence, which is God, and manifestation, which is you in corruption, darkness. Here it is: Potentiality. That's everything that could possibly happen. No space/time. Fabric of consciousness. It is all in you. It's hidden in your inner parts. The New Covenant. New deal. Not on a tablet that says, "Thou shalt not commit..." That's the Abraham Covenant.

Perfect yourself and you'll be perfect with everything. "That sounds like Christianity." It is. What else would it be? "That sounds like Buddhism." It is. "It sounds like everything I've ever heard." It is, dummy!

Because you're in duality, you think in a fractured manner. You identify things as separate from you. You think that this is a cup. That's okay if you're going to utilize it at this level. The next thing you do is judge it not to be perfect in some fashion because there's another cup that's a different color. "This cup is prettier than this cup." That's absurd. By what definition is it prettier? "Well, I think it's prettier." What do you mean, you think it's prettier? What are you judging? Who are you? How could you possibly judge these cups when you don't know who you are? And I assure you, you don't know who you are, because if you knew who you were you wouldn't have to judge the cups, because there would be nothing to judge them against. Do you see? Everything is perfect unto itself. This cup is absolutely perfect. I can see it. I see the cells moving in this cup. It's been formed cylindrically. It has a handle on it. It recognizes that it is perfect. It knows what it is. It doesn't know that it knows it. *You* know that. And that's what makes you different in consciousness. You are aware that you are aware.

Is this cup perfect? Of course! This cup is the Holy Grail. This cup is what you have been searching for all your life, right here, I assure you. I positively guarantee you it is. This cup is anything that you want it to be. Does that seem simple?

Instead of that, you turn back in, and in your duality you attempt to judge things. "She's better than he is." "This is better than that." "That's better than that." "They ought to lock him up and do that to him." It's absurd! The whole world goes and stands before a judge. And he says, "Well, I think it's this way," and the other guy goes, "I have an opinion it's this way." Everybody judges everything, including God. They have an opinion about God. That's ridiculous. God is not an opinion. He's an experience! That's why God doesn't have a name. How could God have a name? If you could name him, who are you? Are you separate from Him? No! You are all consciousness.

"That's easy for you to say, but in the meantime I have to deal with life. I've got to go out and do this." Why? "Well, I have to provide for my..." What? "Well, I've got a condominium I can move into when I retire until I..." What? Until you what? Die! The earth is a death planet. The conception of duality is death by definition. If you believe that you are you, you will die. So you share and commiserate Thanatos — Death — with other entities. The joke is that there is no death. You inflict this pain, it is incredible, and you're doing it all to yourself. Do you see? There's nobody outside of you harming you. You are absolutely invulnerable! I positively absolutely guarantee you, you are invulnerable. Nothing can harm you! It is your resistance to it that causes the pain in this illusion.

"Oh, that sounds like real fundamental Christianity." It is. Resist not evil. In your weakness is your strength. Total innocence is total power. First thought is all-powerful as extended from you. Deviousness will never avail because it's dual. That's pretty simple. "That's too simple. I can't believe that. There's got to be more to it than that."

Do you know what it comes down to finally, that's too difficult for you? Planet Earth? It's not whether the planet is good or bad, it is simply that it is not real. I teach in truth that you may, through a transformative process, share with me that truth. Or you would not be here. Nothing is by accident, and nothing can occur that has not already occurred. Of course. Remember, I speak in the past tense to you.

Are there hierarchies of consciousness, either lateral or superceding us at various speeds? Sure. *A Course In Miracles* is scribed at another level of consciousness. An itinerant salesman, lay minister, Edgar Cayce, scribed. As soon as he came out of his sleep or his trance, he didn't know what he was talking about. I teach that you may *integrate* rather than scribe. There are no scribers here. The next level after scribing is integration, or Christ development — avatarism. A scribe as an entity — and we do scribe automatically — as a matter of fact, what you think of as intuition, or first thought, is a scribing process in that you participate at a different level of consciousness. It's "first thought succeeds." It's coming to know that there's no failure. You can't possibly fail. Edgar Cayce utilized what you might term some astral-ism, that is, mediation in duality to suffice or to cause healing, which perpetuates the illusion and dis-truth. It doesn't make any difference but it's okay.

There's no such thing as separate personalities anyway. And that's the difficulty. You hold yourself in the illusion by belief in an akashic record. It isn't true. It's only true in provincialism. Of course, there's a record of everything that ever occurred on earth, but earth — cosmic time — has only been here five days. I mean the whole planet. Man has only been here five minutes. And your lives are, the lives that you would identify, are like this: Snap! Snap! Snap! Snap! Snap! Snap! Snap! This is the life you just led. Snap! That one.

The process is transformative, and you come to know it through a "give up" process. It appears that there is a path that you walk on to find this, that you can seek it. In truth, there isn't. In truth, you may only do it *now.* If you will come to know that, you will start to not identify in space/time. The retention of entity is caused by the belief that you actually got up this morning, and that when you leave here, you will go somewhere. That's not true. There is no truth in that. You have built a self-identity on recognition of past memories. The brain is simply a little imprint, like a facsimile, and you remember things and then you take them and project them over there. There's no truth in that. It's not so! It's not true!

You come to know that as you raise energies in you and come to the truth. It's a very gentle process; it can be. It is taught in some traditions, like in yoga, that it's Kundalini — that there is a yoga process. And that's true. There is finally no difference in a mystical experience, if you want to class it as mystical. There is no difference finally, between Sister Theresa and any other method you would use to raise your level of consciousness. I assure you that the energies in your body are real. There is a difficulty in society to allow spirituality to be physical. It's not accepted. "We would prefer to keep our God intellectual." So you see a subtraction in Christianity, for example, of the Shakers and the Glossalaliers. We have people who say, "Let's keep it intellectual, folks, so we can accomplish our purpose here on earth," which is nothing. So they retain their duality.

Everything that you do to bring about the change in you, whatever it is, has value. You can't fail in anything that you do. There is no failure. Every time you judge someone else outside yourself as being less than you or more than you or equal to you, who are you judging? All judgment is self-judgment. Period! Try it. You might like it. Every time you say anything about anything on earth, recognize that you're saying it about yourself and come to know that. That's kind of tough.

I know in truth that in your weakness is your strength, simply because as long as you participate in a dualistic society, you are dualistic. When you refuse to participate in it, by whatever method, you come to know the truth through a cellular awakening in your body. Period. It can come about gradually or suddenly, but it must come about in you, so that you can know the truth. There is no failure. You can't fail.

How could you fail in a dream? Try to recognize that you made this up, and that I'm disrupting you. I'm saying, Wake up! Wake up! You're saying, "No, no, I don't want to hear this. I have constructed this. I am attacked. I must defend myself." No, you don't. Wake up now. This is a nightmare. You can wake up. You must wake up. Never mind anything outside of you. That doesn't matter. You wake up.

Some of you have had the glorious experience of that awakening feeling. Some of you have been frightened by it. "No, I'd better not do that. Something's wrong with me. I feel all of these things coming into me." Somebody says, "Oh, you don't want to fool around with that." Why not fool around with it? What else is there but death for you?

What alternative do you have on earth but death or Heaven? What real alternative do you have but hell or Heaven, really, if you want to look at it that way? You have none. You do that by coming to know the truth, because the truth will make you whole.

But remember, the process is in you. It's not in me. It has nothing to do with me. I stand in front of you because I know that you're me. Never mind how I know that. I say to you, you may come to know that. I say to you, you *must* come to know that. You may resist that, but I don't care. See, I have the advantage. I know you're not real. Did you hear what I said? It makes absolutely no difference to me what you do.

I'm going to try it this way for you. I assure you, what I'm going to say is true. Everything that I have said to you in the last 45 minutes is either absolutely, totally true, or there is no truth in it whatsoever. Try that. That can bring you a long way. Just step away from your own judgment, which isn't worth a damn.

You couldn't judge anything in a million years. Do you really think that you can step back and say, "Well, he may be right in this regard. It sounds very familiar, what he's saying." In the past 45 minutes I've given you a taste of every possible philosophy and religion there ever could be, and they all mean nothing. You got Spinoza, you got Kant, you got Neo-Platonism, you got Buddhism, you got Christianity. Call it anything. You've got a little null-one logic, Aristotelian, singularity, Pythagoras. What else you want? Grecian. Hermes Trismegistus. Where are you, dear friends, in your frailty, in your disillusionment?

You're standing there, trying to judge things outside yourself. The *Philosophia Perennis* is a single truth. When the energies really start to flow in you, and you come to know that, you will do analogies that are spectacular. You'll begin to look at things and say, "Hey, everything's the same. There must be something in what's being said here. I will do it." Then you get on that path, and then it starts to get narrower.

And it gets narrower and narrower. And you keep pursuing it. You'll get there. You can't fail. Don't judge!

The world is insane. You remember that. There is no sanity here. There cannot be. Most of you know that. You say, "Why do people act this way?" They act that way because *you* act that way. "Well, I tried it the other way. I've tried to go out and share and be good. And I've tried to carry the message. And I would never intentionally harm anybody. And I go to Sunday school, and I raise my children, and I do the best I can, and I fail." Yes, you will always fail. Sorry. You have limited yourself. You will fail. You have mis-identified yourself. All must fail here. You can't win here.

Those dark nights of the soul that will come to you, and have come to some of you, are a very necessary process to the awakening. In quantum physics it's called dissipative forces belying the Second Law of Thermodynamics. It says that the world is winding down. It's not. The world is winding up.

Each time you come to cognition, confusion ensues, as you readjust your thinking to another level of consciousness. Got it? No pain, no gain. Same thing. You've got to have that. You've got to say, "Something's wrong with this," before you can do anything. If I say to you, "The body's not real," you will say, "The heck it's not. It's real to me." Or you will say, "If I take this knife and stab you, you'll fall dead." No, I won't. Isn't that funny? You extrapolate into time. You defend yourself in the future. Boy, that's a terrible way to be.

Oh, it's awful here. You make your little heavens here. You carve out your little niches. Never mind the bloating bodies of babies starving to death. "Never mind all those other things. I'll do what I can." And you keep dying. And you keep failing. And you keep dying. And you keep doing the same thing over and over again.

All consciousness is one. I am you.

Then you want to make it into a religious process and say, "I'm going to go to heaven or hell." No, you're not. "I was Cleopatra in a past life." No, you weren't. You were everything in a past life. You retain self-identity through some sort of pseudo-belief in reincarnation. You will do anything to hang on to yourself. You're not real! Let go.

So, be gentle and loving and caring. Be berated. Some people are going to say, "Hey, what happened to you? How come you're different? Don't you want to participate in this chaos anymore? Come on. Get into this fight. Don't you want to pursue death with the rest of us? Look at the fun we're having, dying here. Isn't this fun? We get cancer and disease, and awful things happen to us. Our nose rots off. That's okay. We'll stand up and fight for it."

You dummies, up in here, billions of stars and energies flow in the reality. You're in a hatchery. You're in a nursery. You're like grubs. You are blind, deaf and dumb. The extension of your consciousness will show to you that you really don't see with your eyes. Never mind hearing with your ears. Much more awaits you. Much more!

The idea that you are *you* should astonish you. When you're alone and you're standing there, say, "I'm me." Come into your own consciousness, it's a glorious feeling. Fear will come into you. You say, "Hm. I don't want to think about that. I'll discover who I really am. I'm free." That's why you're here. You're afraid to know the truth. Sorry, but that's the reason. You are afraid of God. You sinned and you are guilty. And I say to you, you are perfect!

Let's look at Jesus after His baptism. I'll tell this story. The devil, evil, ego, took Him out on the mountain and said, "I'm going to give you all of this. You now have the power within you to work magic. You can control the whole world. Isn't that wonderful?" And Jesus said, "What do I want with the world? I have the whole universe." Evil is limiting only, and you have limited yourself. The process of coming to know who you really are is a transformative process.

Do some of the analogies occur in music and poetry and art and philosophy and myth? Of course. When you see a beautiful sunset, what occurs to you? Do you feel union and love? Do you feel additional consciousnesses come into you and you are very joyous? Of course!

We've introduced a new element of consciousness into this room. Feel that? There's not an integration there. Here it comes. There it comes. They walk in, and all of this busyness is in you and all of this self-identification. Now you are letting it go. This can be practiced. We're going to have a quiet time here very soon. Those of you who are practicing extension, remember how beautifully it will work for you if you will have confidence in your own truth. Don't project from you what you think might be true. Come to your own truth and then extend your love from that. Then the response will be automatic. Now I extend to you. Can you feel it? You can feel it! It's very nice. That's a form of communication. There. As soon as we can teach this species to do that, all wars will end, because you will come to know the truth of me and you will realize that I would never harm you. Do you feel that?

If I am totally innocent with you, you will not harm me. It would serve you no purpose to harm me. Why would you harm me? At the worst you would say, "That's a dummy, imbecile. We better lock him up." You might do that. I don't care what you do. At what point do you finally allow yourself to be seen? At what point do you take down that mask?

I say to you that we are all the same, and there's nothing that you could do or say to me that I would not accept totally, tell you that you're forgiven, and say that it never existed. That is what total forgiveness means. It means that no sin is really possible. You stand in judgment of everything. Stop it.

This place is a school where you are learning to be God. This is a literal truth. You are practicing being a creator. Do you see that? You are allowed to fail. The reason that you fail is you have not nurtured enough in identification with energy to recognize who you really are. So in duality you think you are John Doe, and there is projected from you these things, which are corrupt because you are still corrupt in identification. You are a creator, but you project rather than extend.

A thought never leaves it source. There is only one final thought in the universe, and that's God's thought of Himself — the extension of you. Nothing can be separate from that one thing. So you make mistakes as you practice to be God. You say, "I love you very much, but I don't want anything to do with you." Now you're attacked by the other thing. You may be attacked by what you think you love. And it all caves in on you, and you're killed, and you're slaughtered, and you love, and you share, and you hate, and everything changes, and there's no stability. You're just practicing. It's not real. It isn't real! You joust with windmills.

In a vivid dream I had during my awakening, I saw hell for what it really is. Everybody's walking around choking themselves to death. And they never die. And then another person takes somebody and he chokes him. That's hell. Nobody can ever die. And they feel the rage, and the need to protect themselves and defend themselves. That's hell, folks. You won't have to do that.

Don't participate in it. Don't do it. Each time you don't do it, there will be a response in you, despite yourself, that will bring you to the truth. That's difficult, because you think you can run the show. And you can't. Grace comes through supplication and surrender, Christian. No other way. You are actually not in control of it. It is only your acquiescence to it that brings the truth. It is a process of awakening. My awakening was not spiritual. Had nothing at all to do with religion. None. Zero. Period. I discovered it was spiritual simply because anything that I can't conceive of here you may define as spiritual if you wish. Of course. It's spiritual in that sense. It's also biological. When you come to know it, you know it.

Wisdom is only remembering. You already know everything. There is nothing you can learn on earth. Nothing. Except a period of maturation requiring self-identification so that the self can be extended and expanded. That's why the ego exists in the first place, incidentally. Obviously the ego is a necessary part of the maturation. But when you remember who you are, you will grow to the truth.

I know who you are very well. I know you very well. Would there be anyone here that I wouldn't know? How absurd! There are only 12 tribes in Israel. There are only seven major rays, a chromatic scale of 12. Everything is a variation or a fractured-ism or a diffusion of a pure Light expressed in an energy fashion. You, contained in your symbiotic relationships, are combinations of energy patterns and colors and sound. I can see that in you. You are very beautiful. Each one has little different combinations, but we are all related. Unto some, some is given. Unto others, others. But it finally comes only to truth. I know you all very well, as you know me, because we are one. It could not be any other way.

You practice that in the world through the extension of yourself in truth. And it's a very real thing. And many of you are experiencing it now in your daily lives. And that's very nice. We didn't come here to repair the earth, because the earth cannot be repaired. When you awaken, you will know that what I say is true. You are beginning to discover, only through your efforts or through how you feel about yourself can you find truth outside yourself. That's true. That's a very nice thing to know, and you may bring that about.

The transformation process, the awakening process is real. Everything that you ever do as identified on this planet is to establish that pattern of awakening. There is no other reason for you to be here. You be very gentle with that. You have all power within you, but it's only through a total recognition of the inability of you, as you identify yourself, to do anything that the truth will come to you. So you sit at the end of the table.

Why would you be disturbed? What would you defend? Why would you have to defend it? Who could attack you? Nothing. You are invulnerable. You can't die.

Those of you who are now feeling that you have done this before, you've done this before. Now you're doing it again. Now you're doing it again. Now you're doing it again. The rent in the fabric of consciousness that created space/time and identity has long ago been repaired. We stand at the Omega point looking back at this. This has already all happened. That's nice to know. I assure you, you all won. If you're in a quandary about what you're doing here – there is no loss. You can't lose. There is nothing for you to lose to. There is only one consciousness, one power. How could you lose?

Earth, air, fire, and water. Get some oxygen into you here. Thank you. Come on. Breathe. Come on. That's a beautiful line. Remember that the line between sorrow and happiness is really non-existent. The incredible joy that can come as you release and come to the truth is incredible. You even love your own depressions. You like everything that's happening to you because you know it's true. If you really come to believe that you're in this process, it doesn't make any difference. You will say "thank you" to everything.

I can tell you about phenomena in the awakening process.It's going to happen despite you. But if you come to know that's true, then everything you do, you accept as part of that process. It's beautiful. It makes absolutely no difference to you then what everybody else thinks or does. You're coming to your own truth. And that's very nice.

Do you then become loving and extend yourself and begin to share? Of course! Do you want a big one? I have no alternative but to love you totally. "In the process of awakening, I ought to be able to not like somebody. I mean, look at this, the big old ex-Marine. I ought to have a right..." Some day I'll tell you the story. You want to see some ego, huh? See, the more power you have in ego, the more difficult it finally is to transcend. Unto whom much is given, much is expected. I assure you that the final awakening is very humiliating. It is totally and incredibly and awesomely degrading. It is the absolute final insult that can be applied to you, and it's much greater than that. It is the incredible, absolute, total realization that you are absolutely nothing. It's awesome and it's fearful and it's beautiful, because from that moment on you share in the reality of truth, of living.

All must come to that door. For some it's easier than others. The path is well trod. It appears that illumination, or call it whatever you want, the awakening process, is not common. I assure you it's extremely common in the universe. It's the process of going from duality to unity. As identified in duality on earth at this stage, it seems like, "Oh, boy, there's an avatar who's waking up and he's come to earth." It isn't phenomenal. I know everything there is to know in the whole universe. I assure you. Can I express that to you? So do you! I don't require any worship. People look at me and say, "Oh, you light up. Look at this. You must be God." Not any more than you are.

There are elements in all of us of worship, but in my case I am a server. And actually, I worship you. That's very difficult for you to get. But I assure you I do. I think you are absolutely divine and perfect. Of course I do. What else would I think? How may I serve you?

It seems too simple and it seems like there's more to it, but there isn't. And we share in that glory. It's really happening to you. And as it happens, you keep standing back and you say, "Boy, this can't be happening to me." It is! "I'm not entitled to this." Yes, you are! You're entitled to it. You feel guilty about it but you're entitled to anything. You're entitled to come to know the truth. If you're not entitled to it, no one in the universe is. Nothing outside of you can be entitled. Just you. Your dealings are with this, with this reality here. If it were not so, I would not tell you that it is. You cannot lose. There is no loss.

Each time that you're here and are beset with the chaos, turn and look at death. Then turn back to the Light and say, "No, I pursue the Light. I will not pursue the death of earth. I will pursue the truth of the universe." Then it will come about in you that you will become whole and remember me. You cannot lose.

We await your coming with great expectation. Therefore be ye perfect, even as your Father in heaven is perfect.

We will have a little quiet time. Nobody gets to talk except me; I get to say anything I want to. Be gentle. Listen:

It's the pearl worth any price. It is what you've always been seeking. Right there. It's right here. Move closer and listen. (Tchaikovsky's Symphony #6, Pathétique)

The universe is still with you for a moment, waiting, searching for truth. The ancient dream begins again. Rhythm for all eternity in the hearts of Heaven. A search for truth that cannot fail. Together, as brothers, we find it. I will show you where it is.

Come on home, everyone. Seek ye first the kingdom. Therefore be ye perfect, even as your Father in Heaven is perfect. Unto you all power is given. Greater things will you do than I have done. In my Father's house are many mansions. If it were not so, I would not have told you so.

You have nothing to do but give up. It requires no action or thought of any kind. Is that simple? Take your place. Be of good cheer!

What has been given you? The knowledge that you are a mind, in Mind and purely mind, sinless forever, wholly unafraid, because you were created out of Love. Nor have you left your Source, remaining as you were created. This was given you as knowledge which you cannot lose. It was given as well to every living thing, for by that knowledge only does it live.

- A Course In Miracles Workbook: Lesson 158 -

Subjective Thought

Everything is a reduction of a single state of consciousness. This is a fact. This is what, for example, all the quantum physicists and the biochemists and the philosophers are attempting to do – find an ultimate singularity or truth. It should be obvious to anyone in a state of real so-called analysis of consciousness to see that a "unified force field" is the same as God. There would ultimately be no difference in the idea of a unification of apparent objectivity to a singularity that would obviously constitute God.

Remember that in this state of consciousness everything is reduced. Historically, in that sense, Paul reduces Jesus, doesn't he? Augustinian ideas reduce Neoplatoism. Of course. Inevitably. Newton, for example, is an offspring of Aristotle, who reduced Plato. Sure. Of course. Look right at it. There is finally no difference in the notion of Newtonian logic or Newtonian science than in, say, objective deification. They are the same thing. They're the same idea. Do you see that? The idea is that unity can be established outside of you. Obviously, then, the next step beyond that would be for science to establish what? First, the idea of relativity – which is an incredible exposé of consciousness. It's fun, historically, to look at how it occurred to Einstein, how it came about. The idea of relativity involved what could be termed a mystical experience. That's a nice thing to look at. And of course, it's true. It did.

Do you have an idea what the new, young, modern minds in two generations since Einstein really are capable of constructing in their own mind? Try to get a hold of this, if you can. You go and sit with a young group sometime, that's really in states of thinking, and we're only talking 60, 70, 80 years here. I'm just going to point out the obvious so-called evolution of the consciousness. This occurred with me in a very high nature. I remember very well. I was about 12 years old, maybe younger, and I suddenly was presented with a pop version of the notion of relativity. And I'll never forget the experience that I had when I looked at it. There was a deep intuition in me that caused a flourish of energy in my head, where I was automatically able to conceive of how completely rational the notion of relativity is. The problem that my mind subsequently had with that idea was to sort out the limited definitions that were applied in attempts to communicate to me what relativity was.

If you want to see a young mind work today, watch them take, for example, the negativism of Schopenhauer, shake it out in about two minutes and come up with the truth of it. Real easy. The young minds are doing that. They may do it in the nature of an expression of Star Wars or Darth Vader. But they do it in their mind. Can you get it? Do you see what I'm saying to you? They will take a beautiful, divine notion of Spinoza and refine it in a single sentence in *A Course In Miracles* and take it right up to its truth. Do you see what happens with those minds? They are not reducing themselves to some sort of qualitative analysis of fractured-ism. They put together! And this is really what we're trying to bring about in your mind, do you see that? Can you see what we're trying to do?

Finally, the notion of Augustinian philosophy or Newtonian physics is highly regarded in a certain sagacity of limitation. For example, with the Pope who is a master of phenomenology, which is a high statement that there can be objective phenomena outside the single realization of selfness. The Pope will take it right straight up to the point of refusing to recognize that he is in fact instigating the phenomena. Do you see that? The whole basis of quantum thinking, of *Course in Miracles*, of absolute thought without object, of subjectivity, is the notion of noumena, or that you are involved in any equation in regard to your thinking. Holy mackerel, how beautiful! We can teach that. But we must teach it through a process of recognition that the occurrence is, in fact, a form of exposé.

All limited consciousness is willing to acknowledge the occurrence of an expansion or realization, generally speaking, as to music, as to art, as to philosophy, as to science, as to religion. But the inevitable tendency reduces it to a form of duality, simply because the consciousness is not capable of a notion of what you might term nonobjective existentialism. There is no truer statement in the Universe than *cogito ergo sum* – "I think therefore I am." But once you've arrived at that inevitable conclusion, the question continues to arise, "Ah, but who am I?" Whence comes this notion of my existence? Wow! What an occurrence. Yes!

Finally it comes more down to the necessity for consciousness to verify itself. All creation finally is, is unity verification or the extension of a total idea – how do you express that? This is in *A Course In Miracles.* Everybody finally only creates their own notion of themselves. Don't you see that? It falls into a limited framework of consciousness simply because they have identified themselves as separate from the single unity. Wow! What's more Newtonian than that idea? And what is more unifying than the idea of quantum, or the idea of a single force or congruity that finally has to arrive at the incredible delineation that the Universe is only consciousness? That's a simplistic thing, finally, because truth is extremely simple. It's the notion that truth has moving parts, or is somehow devious, that causes all of your concern. The requirement in coming to know that, involved in the actual process, is one of non-subtraction of the self in the relationship to everything that is apparently outside of it.

This is the process that we teach, which is nothing more than what we started out with in a conversation in *A Course In Miracles,* where we attempt to teach the consciousness to look at what is apparently objective, and not establish its reality, but rather ask it what it is. This disassociates you from your own memory patterns in association with duality – that's really what happens.

The problem that Brother Albert Einstein had with arriving at the conclusion of the unified force field, was only his inability to carry the concept of it to the inclusion of his own idea about it. He ended up with the inevitable apparent notion that God is rolling dice. And this is his expression. He said, "I can't believe that God rolls dice." Obviously, if there is such a thing as true objectivity, there is an element of chance that has to be involved. It would be inevitable, because there is no basic order in the concept of the apparent reality. Do you see? It causes futurizing automatically. It cannot *not*. Is that a little muddy, that thought? My mind is coming in too fast, I can't express it.

We may express it to you that it is impossible for you to have an original thought. You are thinking in the past tense, and any projection you do in the time/space sequencing must involve your previous connotations of yourself. You construct your future, in other words, based on your past – obviously – the consciousness, *you*, individually, the Universe.

Speaking to us now is Brother Andrew, who occasionally may appear to be some sort of antagonist, but in a very high sense presents Socratic ideas which are subsequently discussed in unlimited frameworks.

Brother Andrew: I have heard of a situation where a person was hypnotized, and given a suggestion that, at a signal, he would take off his shoe and put it on top of the fireplace mantle. When the signal was given, this occurred. When he was asked why he did it, he made up an excuse to explain the behavior which he didn't even understand himself. He said his foot was warm and he wanted to take his shoe off and he put it on the mantle because he wanted to make sure he knew where it was.

Whatever. We are looking at the idea that he had to justify the action. That's the whole dilemma.

Brother Andrew: My question pertains to behavior that you are attributing to us, that we may not be consciously responsible.

You are not, consciously. But ultimately, you are responsible for your behavior and do in fact justify it in some regard. This is the whole basis of what I teach.

Brother Andrew: But it's unconscious.

Who cares? You have forgotten God. What you can call the consciousness is limited to your idea about yourself and subsequently makes you stay within the framework. That's why I teach that it is indeed a transformative occurrence. You listen to what I'm saying. I am trying to change your mind-set in this regard. Obviously, every action must be justified or the action would not occur. The whole basis of what we teach is non-motivated action. Listen to me. I want to say this one other way for you. Obviously, the hypnotist was conveying to the other limited state of consciousness first a basic recognition of objectivity. The consciousness hypnotized did not say to the hypnotist, "What's a shoe?" I asked you to ask the hypnotist, "What's a shoe?" Do you see? Well, look at it. Obviously, the hypnotist and the one hypnotized shared a limited concept of the ability to take off a shoe, composed in some sort of relationship of energy that apparently constituted a body. All of it is objective thinking and limited.

All that you presented to me was limited. I can take it and move it up into a framework of truth for you. The justification of the necessity to remove the shoe is the justification of self-identity. It will inevitably occur within the state of consciousness. It cannot *not*.

Brother Andrew: How can we do the things that you're asking us to do when we don't even know the reasons why we're doing the things that we're doing?

Ah, but you have a perfect purpose. You have constructed an idea of unity in your head, and express it.

Brother Andrew: But I didn't do it consciously.

Of course not. Because consciously you deny it. You don't appear to, but in the state of limited consciousness, obviously, you are denying singularity. That's a fact. Now you may say to me, "I choose not to believe I am denying it." And I am perfectly willing to go along with the idea that you have not reached a metamorphic position in your so-called transformation, where you have access to a unified form of thinking. All I say to you then is, since you have constructed it in your mind, and you obviously have the capacity to bring it about, I would suggest that you do so. If you are determined to remain within a limited framework of your consciousness, we are now directly involved with what we teach, because the necessity for you to take off the shoe and put on the shoe is precisely why you're here, which is nothing more than a limited self- identification. What I say to you, in an attempt to stir you from this, is to inform you with certainty that there literally is nothing outside of your thoughts about it. If you were to look at it in that way, I would say to you everything that you think there is, is all that there is, and there is nothing but that. This will cause you deep concern because you are determined that there is a form of a discrete thinking that is occurring outside of your framework – which is exactly what Newtonian physics maintains. The quantumist has arrived at the incredible, obvious conclusion that there is no discernment between energies – that they're all finally the same thing.

The next and only final step that can be made, is that they are finally *you*. It does not matter how you constitute yourself, don't you see that? There is nothing to compare you with! You insist on comparing yourself with things that are apparently outside of you, as Jesus would teach in *A Course In Miracles*, and as it's taught by Buddha. Who taught it more emphatically than Buddha? Buddha is reduced automatically, Christ reduces to Christianity. Of course. Does Plato reduce to Aristotle? Of course. It goes on and on and on. Everything is always a reduction. But finally it reduces only to *you*!

Brother Andrew: How does Buddha exist?

In any attempt to define him, it's an automatic reduction.

The idea of the next step, or the idea of the transformation occurrence, which occurred with Jesus Christ in the establishment of the capacity of the consciousness to evolve, which is what Christianity is, and all it is, was automatically reduced, and turned out to be a process of death to find life, which has no real reality. This is all in *A Course In Miracles*; in the text it's beautifully expressed. You finally do not die to live. You never die. It's your acknowledgment of the idea of limitation that's sustaining you in this state.

You are in a state of absolute objection to the idea of eternity, because it involves time for you. It cannot *not* involve time. If I say to you that you're going to sit there forever and ever, you refute me by standing up and walking and sitting in another chair. You understood me. Good! I see the way your mind is working. Your mind is working, obviously, only in the past tense. Everything that's constructed in you is based on what apparently has already occurred. If you do that, if you really look at it, you are not really thinking about now, you're only thinking about a moment ago. Obviously, you can't think about next week or next month. What is expressed in *Course in Miracles* is that the mind of everyone on earth is actually blank. Look at it. So we attempt to bring you into the now, which is really what eternity is. Watch a human being come together in a group with an establishment in limitation and attempt to communicate. They will succeed only on a very limited level, but that is really all they ask for. They will say, "I don't require that you understand me totally, but it would certainly be nice if we would not nuke each other – that we would not kill each other, or that we could get together and have a little relationship here, or that we could certainly share a lot of common things until we have our demise, until we die."

So in reality there is absolutely no communication occurring here, except when it is transcendent. One of the high forms of communication is, if you go to the Chicago Symphony tonight and a thousand people sit in an auditorium and share an impulse of energy, a conglomeration of rhythms or patterns of sounds of the notions of the chromatic scale, they will enter in to a form of symbiosis of a very high nature. That's what communication is. Communication ultimately has nothing to do with the definition of it. If there is one thing that Jesus teaches in *Course in Miracles*, it's that experience can be unified, or that God is experiential – that is the whole basis of the Course – and can be shared because we have an absolute common denominator of reality.

Let's take that one step further. It would be very nice if I could show you that, say I go like this, "Pffss blah!" It has absolutely no significance at all. Somewhere along the line you were determined in your mind, at that moment, to give me a cause and effect relationship in regard to what you considered me to be. It's absolutely inevitable. The basis of Zen, or a koan, I believe you call it, is to bring about a shift in your consciousness where you no longer are sequential in your thinking. Do you see that? And you go, "Wow, what's he's trying to do? Why are you doing that? Don't tell me you don't have a reason for doing that. You're manipulating me." At the very most you try to wake me up.

Brother Andrew: Your analogy to people sitting in the symphony and sharing transcendental consciousness is very a propos. But as soon as you go to open your mouth and talk about it, you've entered into the rabble, attempting to solve the problem at the level of the problem, and it can never be done that way.

Sure, I know. Agreed. Therefore, you're condemned to hell forever.

Brother Andrew: No.

Well, okay, then as soon as you say no, then you allow for my insinuation of energy into you in the sharing.

Brother Andrew: I allowed that. But as soon as you open your mouth, you are out of it.

Yeah, but I can't extend without energy. I can't extend without an idea.

Brother Andrew: That's how you generate your shakti.

Sure. Of course. That's the highest form you can do. That's what God does. You're right on the mark. God generates shakti by extension of a true idea, if you want to look at it that way. Certainly. But remember, only you can do it. The tendency is to think that somehow – Jesus calls it in *A Course In Miracles* an absolute relationship of brotherhood that is inevitable in consciousness – the idea of establishment in time implies that there can be one consciousness that has arrived at a particular point within the framework, that seems to be more advanced. I am absolutely, totally aware in my awakening that there are no degrees in consciousness, that there genuinely are not hierarchies of consciousness. The idea of a hierarchy or the establishment of planes of consciousness always occurs in the limited state as it attempts to identify singularity. And in that process it has a validity because there is obviously an application of the possibility of a revolution or an evolvement to a higher state, which is contained in the basic necessity to overcome. You can't do it any other way. That is not practiced at what seems to be a lower level. Obviously, a rhinoceros does not construct ideas of future and all that. Since you have done it in your own state, the total realization that that can come about in you is a very, very necessary element. There could be, for example, no ideas of what you would call quantum physics or relativity without the fundamental notion of Newtonianism. You have to have a concept of the possibility of objectivity. That's a form of evolution.

Sure. And that all occurs within your own framework of thinking, if you care to look at it.

There are certain ideas involved in the incredible notion of non-discretion. There is a paradox that is contained in specialness – for me to convey to you the idea that you are totally unique and special – but not in regard to anything separate from you. The idea that you are unique and special is contained in all of your fundamental existentialism. It is absolutely inevitable. The only single thing that you can know is that "I am I." And we're back to that once again. Accepting the notion that it is transcendental, or theosophical, or gnostic, is a very major step.

Jesus will teach in the *Course* that all ideas of love are efforts to communicate. Finally, all communication is only self identity or an attempt to identify self. Limitedness can never convey. Jesus would teach that it projects rather than extends. It projects from it its concept of itself. This is what the fractured-ism is. The idea that is projected from the consciousness contains the whole, that is, it contains the idea of positive/negative or the idea of comparison or conception. What we attempt to do in *A Course In Miracles*, or in teaching a form of transformation, is to cause you to think without discretion, really, basically. That's what the atonement is. In the *Course* it is taught as: The limited state of consciousness in its attempts to perpetuate itself has established, in its own karma memory, patterns of resistance in order to sustain consciousness, or defiance or self-regulation. Limitation inevitably results in grievance or the idea that there is a form outside of you that could cause fear or attack or concern to you as a consciousness. The whole basis of your karma, of your memory in the schismed Universe of duality, is obviously based on self-subsistence in limitation. That isn't hard. Jesus in the *Course* says all of your thinking is what? Post schism. That is, you think in a manner that involves a continual breaking down in the limitation of your consciousness. Yes, it does, of course. But if you stop and look at it, there is contained in your fabric the idea of unity. Obviously, it is necessary that you participate in that equation.

Did you look at the chaos out there, as individual consciousnesses attempt to sustain their own identities? Wow! That's an amazing thing.

No wonder it's chaotic. All of them are indeed unique in their historic patterns. There is not one single fingerprint that's the same as any other fingerprint. That's a nice way to look at it if you want to. And there's billions of them. And they keep breaking down and breaking down. Survival of the fittest, in reality, is simply survival of the limited state at that moment of its own individual consciousness. Limitation always divides. Wow! There are 846 species of beetles within one square mile in the Brazilian jungle. Holy mackerel.

Brother Andrew: Are you saying we break down everything?

Yes. What you have done in your basic concept right there is broken yourself down from this table. You obviously consider this table to be separate from you, don't you? Why? What is that table? You're going to answer me by looking into your mind in a previous construction and informing me what that table is. If I keep asking you questions, you're screwed. There's no way you can tell me what that table is. You have absolutely no idea what it is in reality. Try it, if you want. These are just exercises. This is in the Workbook of *A Course In Miracles.* It is exactly what occurs. We can sit here forever; you never will be able to find it. You'll break it down, and you keep breaking it down, and you keep breaking it down. And you arrive at the molecules and then you will get into other divisions of it in your mind. Don't you see? Ultimately, what you do is give up and allow it to be a table and utilize it in your limited consciousness. This is what the fabric of society really is – the use of objectivity in limitation is all that we really do here. Then we'll battle each other over our ideas of what this table is. I'm very capable of killing you over my insistence that this is a particular table, or over the possession of the table, since it is outside of me and I want to hold onto it – the idea of scarcity is involved with that.

Brother Andrew: I can see it, but I can't tell you what I'm seeing. But I am experiencing that something is there. Does that mean I'm still off the mark?

You are off the mark automatically, but that's okay. Really what you have begun to do then is what? Examine your own projections or your own thoughts, which is a very necessary part of the awakening process. That's why I would teach you to look at the table and say, "What is it?" When you come into a framework of unifying in thinking, you may very well look at that table and see it as the Last Supper table, for example. You will see it as anything that you have constructed in your mind. The whole basic tenet of what we think, and you must get this, is: Conception always precedes perception. It is absolutely inevitable. Will you grant me that?

Brother Andrew: That means that I think of the table before I see it?

You must! You're sitting right on what I just talked about.

Brother Andrew: So I have the fear before the action?

You have the need to protect your own identity in your own framework of consciousness. Of course. You are only what you are. As you come out with that, as you begin to think, you construct all this variety and sustain your limited consciousness through variety rather than unity. It will never work. The dilemma of Adam having to name the animals is incredible. He ends up with a continual breakdown of species. Why? Because he's got himself separate from it. And he'll keep breaking it down and breaking it down. It's inevitable.

The way you finally teach it, however, would be simply the acceptance of your own thoughts. This is what we would teach in *Course in Miracles*. If there is only your thought about something, in other words, if you are the conceptor of the Universe, you are a creator – I assure you this is true. Since you are in duality and self-protection, you have established and delineated in your own consciousness, relative states in ideas about what constitutes your makeup. We would teach it in *A Course In Miracles* that it is impossible for you to have a thought that will ever leave you. Here's the whole dilemma of guilt. If you are attempting to establish yourself in limitation, and obviously you succeed in doing it, you have by nature the necessity to order your thoughts. You cannot *not* do it. You automatically reject or sustain some thoughts apparently in your consciousness. This is in the New Testament, this is what Jesus tries to teach. In a very real sense – I am sorry – if you think of "murderer," you are the murderer. It's absolutely inevitable. You don't want to look at that. I know that you don't want to look at that. You do not want to be responsible for your own thinking. But you are. You will do everything *but* be responsible for it. Why? Because you've constructed death. And you don't want to be responsible for death. Do you see? Can you see that one death is all deaths? If one thing dies, everything dies. Look at it. Death is limitation.

That's what we live in here. Death defines life. That means that you are basing your consciousness on the concept that there is an annihilation or a termination. Anywhere you look on earth, you have constructed a form of cyclicalness, or something that evolves. Really, it's an establishment of time and space that ultimately leads to an apparent termination. There are expressions that are not acceptable in *Course in Miracles* like: "Anything that is not forever is not real." Tell me something that is forever. You can't. Then you will attempt a concept of God. You will say to me, "God is eternal." But there can be no eternity outside your idea about it. What am I saying to you? God is your idea. Death is your idea. Look at it. Tell me about God. Tell me about truth. Tell me what truth is. You can't. You can only be it. The notion that you can have ideas is a very strange thing. Who are you, then? What do you have? You have ideas about things; you're simply separated. Can't you see that *you* are the idea?

Brother Andrew: Am I everything that I experience?

Yes. Only. Amen. You don't like that, though. You can't tell the difference between pleasure and pain, but you keep trying. There is a concept in the human mind of continuity, that we just spoke of, as a high necessity to the coming about of the realization of singularity. It occurs dramatically in the notion of reincarnation. The idea of a continuing consciousness has great validity. The problem with reincarnation is the sense of limitation involved in the obvious notions of separateness in the memory pattern. That is to say, you were nothing specific in the past, but everything in your own relationship of consciousness. I used to try to express that with the definition of the passion of the crucifixion where you were no more Peter than you were the Roman soldier. Everything is your idea about it. Now, if you have a mystical experience in reincarnation where you speak fluent Sanskrit... Of course! I have already allowed you that the configuration of your consciousness genetically not only contains all possibilities, but contains all previous occurrences in the whole schism. It is only your dream, brother.

History is not objective. History is not an occurrence of separate specific things. That is just in your mind that it is. What is history finally, except what *you* think it is, or what you arrive at in aggregate with your people at a particular time? We can arrive at a conclusion that Hitler was an evil man. And you'll get some people after 50 years to say he wasn't so bad. Isn't that funny? Everybody just keeps rewriting history. Don't you see that? History is always based on expedience of consciousness. For goodness sake! We'll rewrite it anytime you want to. What's nice to see occur in the consciousness is the taking of the allegory of duality, which is really nothing but what the process of awakening is, and having it reconstructed in your mind to a single truth. What is it you are trying to prove, when you ask these questions, but yourself in limitation? I'll accept anything that you say to me. It's time that your mind began to look at the occurrence of a fairy tale as having the reality of revelation contained within it. What's more mystical than the Battle of Waterloo? It's what you make it in your mind.

Freedom. Quite literally, what we ask you to do, say in the Workbook of *A Course In Miracles,* is to free yourself from your own limited configurations. As that begins to occur in you, it's an extremely joyous and happy and incredible occurrence because it is freedom. It begins basically with the fundamental idea that somewhere within the framework in which you are conceiving of yourself, there is contained a unity or a truth or a singularity. This is the tacit acknowledgment of duality. It is inevitable that the earth would not be here had it not somewhere, within a framework, however limited, constructed the conception of God or of truth or of wholeness. The next step that you will attempt to teach is that, since it cannot be found here, to gain the knowledge must be a form of transformation or a changing of the mind, or an enlightenment, or an "Ah-ha!" experience, or a resurrection, or a genius definition, or a symphony, or a beautiful poem, or anything that brings about a shift in your basic awareness of your relationship with what apparently is outside of you. This is the basis of everything that I teach.

We have reached, very nicely in this configuration, sociologically, the acknowledgment that gaining truth could in fact be transformative. It has always been known among esoteric circles. The whole idea of the ancient wisdom, the whole basic fundamental concept of the religion, Christianity, is based on knowledge of God being gained by a transformative occurrence or a resurrection. That is in all literature. It insinuates every possibility of the conception of man in duality. So if we are going to teach it, the ability that is inherent in the individual consciousness to conceive of itself as whole must be at least an intellectual presumption. If you come into a group, you must somehow assume, and do at some level, that you are there for what you might call a legitimate purpose: to come to know who you are. As I indicated, if you will look at this basket – this is really what's occurring in your minds now – and instead of saying, "You are a basket," you say, "What are you?" Don't tell it what it is. Ask it what it is. Do you see how simple that is? Obviously, if you tell it what it is, it simply becomes a configuration in your own state of memory or limited consciousness.

There is a very beautiful passage in one of the first 20 lessons in *A Course in Miracles* that reads something like this: I can get you to grant that the past is not now, so it's impossible for you to think about it in reality; and that the future is not now, and it's really impossible for you to construct it, so quite literally, moment by moment, on the planet earth, everybody's minds are literally blank. They are not thinking of anything! Do you see? All they do is construct the past as they have observed it, which is not now, and project it out into the future. It's a beautiful way to look at it. So we have people walking around, and nobody, quite literally, is really thinking at all. The upshot of that, or the actual reality of that, is that it is absolutely impossible for there to be any form of communication in the chaos. Why? Because everybody is simply basing what they see on their own individual concepts, on the past. It has no reality. Uh-oh! Now we are into what we really have to say about this. Quite obviously, if we have granted that there is a single source, you and I, individually and in consort with all other consciousnesses, must ultimately share that reality. And that's what we attempt to bring about in brotherhood. That's all.

The *Course in Miracles* calls it love. It has obviously nothing to do with love or attempts at communication that are fostered here in the duality, in the chaos. It couldn't. Why? Because love does not involve perception. Perception is always distinguishing. This would be taught in *Course in Miracles* as: It is impossible for you to have a neutral thought. Try to. You can't. Do you see? It's impossible not to take sides in perception because perception or conception of limited self is based on taking sides, and subsequently you have the incredible dilemma of literally rejecting, or attempting to reject some of your own discernment.

High thought coming: An idea can never leave its source. Its reality is only contained in the whole, which is another way of saying that two things cannot know each other because two-ness is constructed on duality.

So you have the apparent species, Homo Sapiens, sitting in a state of duality in a virtual attempt to sort out his own fractured-ism, or his own consciousness, and choose in preference, things to sustain his limited consciousness. Jesus in the Course tries to express it this way: Everything around you is an effect of your thought and has no reality because your thought of it has no reality. One of the nice ways to come to know that is to at least acknowledge that if there is nothing outside of you, it can only be your thoughts that are affecting you. That's a nice way to look at it. Obviously, that's true. Only your idea about something, or how you have constructed it within your own memory or karma framework, gives it any apparent validity at all. Since the whole notion of limited consciousness is based on – *again, A Course in Miracles* calls it "attack" or "defense" – you might look at it in this way: a state of consciousness, where there is apparently outside of you something that could affect you without your acquiescence to it, is what causes all pain and grievance and murder and all the other things that go with it. Obviously, this is so. We can teach you, and you have come to learn, that you are being affected by your own ideas about things. That's very nice.

Finally, the Universe is only an idea. If the idea is limited, obviously it is not universal, so that the thinker cannot stand separate from the thought. As long as you believe in your limited state of consciousness, through constructed limitation, that the thinker can be separate from his thought, you will maintain space/time. You cannot *not* do it. The whole basis of the idea that you can stand outside of your own thought is what has created space. If I stand here in front of you in a limited state and say, "I am Theodore Everybody. That is a pole over there." I have obviously constructed what? A space between myself and the pole and the time that would be involved for me to move from this space to that space. If my idea about that pole is finally only a configuration in my own consciousness, it in fact has never left my thought about it. This is high truth. This can be practiced. This is what *Course in Miracles* attempts to bring about in the Workbook in the first 50 lessons. In order to come to that, I may look at the pole and say to the pole, not, "You are a pole", but as the first lesson in the *Course* teaches, "I don't know what you are." What? Look what happened. I don't know what anything is. Wow! Look what happened. What's the next step? You look at the pole, and you say to the pole, "What are you?" What does this do, then, within your own framework of consciousness? This can really be practiced. It makes you, for that moment, come into the idea that you are extending a thought at that moment not based on your previous recognition of it. What did you begin to do? You began to think.

"Thinking" on earth has absolutely nothing to do with really thinking. This is all in the *Course in Miracles* in the first 50 lessons. That is a little disconcerting, and people who insist on grounding themselves to limited consciousness will look at me and say, "Well, that may be very true, but when my mind begins to do that, I become frightened because I am losing my identity. If this is not a lamp, I've got a very serious problem." Do you see? Yet I stand in front of you and say, "This is not a lamp." If I ask you to define it for me, you will look at it and proceed to break it up into parts in order to what? Authenticate yourself in pieces! It's amazing how your mind works. Now this group is obviously coming into a high state of what you might call aggregate consciousness. What would brotherhood or communion be but the acknowledgment first of a singleness of truth, that is to say altruistically: truth is true and nothing else is true, which belies the possibility of relativity or actual separate relationships within a true framework of consciousness. That, then, can cause us to what? Flow within our own memory patterns! Remember that since limited consciousness is based in space/time on historic schism, it is necessary that you come to know that all of your thoughts in duality are, in fact, based on limitedness. Religiously that is called evilness, or the fall. What we are really doing with your mind is bringing you – because you contain what you might term the genetic capability to conceive of truth or God, (obviously, you can do it since you have done it) – to the realization that since everything is finally only your thought about it, you must literally be the truth or God. You cannot *not* be. It's another way of saying you can't stand separate from your own ideas. This is the whole basis of the attempt in space/time at Christhood or guru-ship, or the establishment of an apparent entity who has gone through a transformative occurrence and can convey, through energy or ideas or by whatever means, a form whereby you, individually in your consciousness, can come to know that truth.

Taught at its highest level in consummation, there must be an acknowledgment on the individual consciousness' part that it is, in fact, truth unto itself. That has always been taught. *A Course In Miracles* says emphatically that this is a course in knowing yourself. It couldn't possibly be anything else but that. And everybody nods their head. "Know thyself" is one of the fundamentals. But it's much deeper than that. You must know yourself, because there is literally nothing else that you could know. Wow! The presentation in the Workbook of the *Course in Miracles,* with the immediate inevitability of that realization, places everyone in a high state of denial before they even begin. You can't even open it up and you have a problem. If you start out with some of the basic things, they're nice to look at.

Lesson 8: The past is not here. *When you think about the past or anticipate the future, your mind is actually blank.* That's what I just said. Lesson 14: Let me see somebody gobble this one up. Are you ready? *The world you see has nothing to do with reality. It is of your own making, and it does not exist.* That's a nice place to start. It starts out very nicely. *Everything you see is the result of your thoughts.* No exceptions. *No idle thoughts. A neutral thought is impossible.* Listen. Lesson 19: *Cause and effect are never separated. Thinking and its results are simultaneous.* Holy mackerel. *It is a fact that there are no private thoughts.* Oh, come now. Somewhere along the line, I'm entitled to a little privacy here. Listen to me. You are entitled to total privacy, and in fact that is all that God has – total privacy. Can't you see that? You are all able to look very much at that. Since there is nothing outside of you, you are of course totally private. What is more personal than God? What have you done with your own ideas to cause something to be outside of you that could subsequently harm you or cause you concern or bring about friction in you? There is no reality in combat or friction. There couldn't be. It is not possible. Wow. You ought to begin to teach this: *When you see separate things, you are not really seeing it at all.* That's lovely. I'm throwing in Lesson 23 because nobody wants to really look at it. The only way out of fear is to give up attack and defense. Resist not evil. Do not participate in the chaos of your own limited projections. Wow!

I wrote some strange things down this morning. I did some song titles. This is a digression. **There's no assurance without occurrence.** That's a dandy. That is, if you don't undergo a process, you can never be sure of anything. That's the way you can always tell an awakening consciousness or one that's awake. You may not be able to know what he's sure about, but you can see that he's very sure about whatever it is that you're not sure that he's sure about. That's a lovely definition. This one's for Nicky: **Try not to smile on your own denial.** That's a dandy. Somehow we admit that we're denying, and kind of take satisfaction in our own denial. Really that doesn't bring about anything. This one was designed for Nicky, too. It's a definition of tantric yoga: **Finding lasting peace through a lasting piece.** Put that as a bumper sticker for tantric yoga people. Bless their hearts.

The acknowledgment that this transformation is going on in you can bring about an incredible serenity and peace because, as you refine your own fractured past through recollection of your own perfection, you allow everything that apparently is occurring outside of you to be as it is without attempting to ascertain its historic frame of reference, through detachment. Isn't that lovely to be able to do that? Each time that you do that, when you do not apply in consciousness specific cause and effect relationships, there occurs in your own energy relationship a pitching up or a raising of the energy. This is really what we attempt to teach is happening to you. Your mind will then begin to reconfigure incredible occurrences that have happened in your past associations. You will begin to see them in a new focus or a new frame of reference where they come together finally in an incredible single acknowledgment that the whole purpose of your state of consciousness was the metamorphosis that is now occurring in you. Is that beautiful?!! You then may want to study it in books, like you may want to quickly get a comparison between the *I Ching* and the genetic code. You may find a thrill in seeing that the helix in the genetic code is the same as the symbol of the *I Ching*, or the total potential of the Universe. You go, "Oh, my!" Then, as the shift continues to occur in you, you look about and you'll see in your mind incredible connections of color and sound and thought. Art and poetry and literature will all come together in a singleness of the very, very obvious incredible consciousness allegory of space/time. It's lovely. You'll take all of the fairy tales and translate them, not through a process of intellectualizing them, but rather a high form of iconism or symbolism, into the reality that they are to demonstrate to you the occurrence of your own transformation. You will find in this process that your mind begins then to what? Do it with everything. So when we look at this basket instead of saying, "You are a basket," or the next step, "What are you?" You look at the basket and say, "I know in truth that you represent me in truth, and by my realization of your wholeness I see myself as whole."

What do we finally teach you then to do? Reject everything you apparently think is real, in order to see that finally only *you* are reality. This is what we are trying to do now in this process.

As this occurrence reaches maturity in you, you may well experience what apparently is conflict. Remember, in your attempt to stand aside from your own limited ideas, you will be in denial and finally, defiance of the constructs of the earth. From a religious standpoint, each consciousness unto itself practices on an apparent moment-by-moment basis the denial of its own true self, and establishes in limitation outside of itself constructs in order to sustain, through memory, its own limitation. The real problem that you have individually in consciousness is that you have conceived of truth and harmony and love and God, and are not yet in a state to recognize that it is in fact *you*. Perhaps the way now for you to look at it is this: Everything is perfect unto itself because everything is only itself. There can be no consciousness outside of the total identity of a state of awareness or a beingness. The zebra does not suffer pain in regard to its own identity. It is constructed within its limited framework of memory to the configuration of its establishment in duality. Finally, since you have 1% within your genetic code that is at variance with a chimpanzee, you are not a chimpanzee. The chimpanzee knows perfectly well what it is. It does not construct death in its mind. It does not bury its dead with artifacts to sustain it in its journey in consciousness. The thought has not occurred to it. But it has occurred to you. This engenders then great fear in you, doesn't it? Because apparently obliviation is God.

Actually, what you do is construct a method of coming to God, or truth, through death. Wow, what a strange thing to do. As a Christ, as an awakening consciousness, you will come into this chaos and present the limited state with the inevitability of recognition that there is no death, there is no termination, there is no obliviation, and that consciousness, individually in its own consort of apparent reality, will always be in the state in which it finds itself at this moment. In actuality most consciousnesses are not afraid of death, for they have constructed it as an escape from life which they are indeed deadly afraid of. We have come to discover that eternity is not a long time, but only this moment when we share our truth in love and in joy and in happiness.

We'll have just a little quiet time. When it's sleepy time outside. Be very gentle now. (Wow... He really had quiet times that were quiet!!) That's very lovely.

Physical Transformation and Christianity

Exchange, exchange. Exchange the yen for the dollar. We're out of gas. We're out of heat. We're out of food. We're out of fuel. We exist by exchange. What an astonishing notion! Exchange is what time is, if you would care to look at it. If there is distance between the cause and effect of things, that is what exchange is. It is the exchange of associate ideas, if you care to look at that. Survival is the accumulation of exchange. Exchange comes about through identification of need, separate from wholeness. So you exchange.

If you run into a real statement about it, say, in the *Course in Miracles*, in Lesson 76, in a sentence like this: *There are no laws but God's. Dismiss all foolish magical beliefs today, and hold your mind in silent readiness to hear the Voice That speaks the truth to you.* You can hold your mind in readiness to listen to, say, this voice. That's this voice, isn't it? Not some voice that is going to come out of the moon. Listen to this voice speak the truth to you — the one that is going to talk right now. Are you ready to hear this? *You will be listening to One Who says there is no loss under the laws of God.* Why is it that we suffer loss then? Why is it that we appear to lack? Why is it that we appear to have necessity? These are the things you should be examining. Ready? *Payment is neither given nor received.* Come on. It is impossible to give something to get something back. There is no such thing as relative value. There is no necessity to subsist at all. Are these the statements that

61

you are going to study and look at in hopes of bringing about some sort of result in your relationship with the things apparently outside yourself? I guess so. How do you feel about it?

Exchange cannot be made. It doesn't say that you can exchange and be false about it. It doesn't say that exchange is false, although, of course, it is. It says literally that *exchange cannot be made.* It says literally that if you exchange, you are exchanging what? Nothing for nothing. And that's the difficult part about the lesson. *There are no substitutes.* I bet you nobody hears that. *And nothing is replaced by something else.* You live by symbols here. You have given thought-forms a reality of their own and utilize them to bring about changes through the associations of your ideas. If I say to you, nothing substitutes for anything, how could you possibly then deal with subjective reality? If you did, you would immediately see that everything can become whole in your own mind. That's what we are trying to bring about in this. Nobody likes to read these lessons.

There are no laws except the laws of God. And you say, what are the laws of God? The single assertion that you are all mind and all power as you were created and are continuing to be created. That does not require a definition of what your creation is and certainly not a definition of who your Creator is. The whole idea of exchange is, again, the necessity for definition. It is the holding together of the relationalship thought.

There are no laws except the laws of God. This needs repeating, over and over, until you realize it applies to everything that you have made in opposition to the single wholeness of the universe. It is an amazing idea, if you look at it. *Your magic has no meaning.* It is not that it's ineffectual. It is not that it works sometimes. It just has no meaning. *What it is meant to save does not exist.* Isn't it time that you began to look at that? All of the defenses that you have put up to sustain — what do you call this? — a body, to keep this consciousness intact, that gap between the cause and the effect that you maintain is real in space/time, is literally nonexistent. Should I read it again for you? *What it is meant to save does not exist.* Do you want the hooker? *Only what it is meant to hide will save you.*

What it is meant to save does not exist. Only what it is meant to hide will save you. You want some freedom? *Think of the freedom in the recognition that you are not bound by all the strange and twisted laws you have set up to save you.* You want to know what strange and twisted laws are? Everything that you base your reality on here! Master Jesus, in the *Course in Miracles*, Lesson 76, calls them *strange and twisted laws.* Since these are the laws of the mechanisms of your mind, He calls your mind strange and twisted. And, indeed, the perceptual mind is strange and twisted. It is fluxing all the time. It's going through changes in what? Attempting to hold itself in balance, and it can't.

You really think that you would starve unless you have stacks of green paper strips and piles of metal discs. If I have to translate for you, that's money and change. Are you all aware that "green paper strips" aren't some sort of long paper mache? This is money He is speaking of. *You really think a small round pellet or some fluid pushed into your veins through a sharpened needle will ward off disease and death. You really think you are alone unless another body is with you.* It is kind of a nice sentence thrown in there for you to think about — as though somehow you could isolate yourself and then attempt through your own projections to share in the limited perspective that holds you in this dream of death.

It is insanity that thinks these things. It doesn't say that the thought is insane. Anyone want to read this? *It is insanity that thinks these things.* See, nobody really likes to read these lessons. They like to think, "Well, I'm thinking insane thoughts." So what you do is attempt, "I'm working on my insane thoughts." This isn't what it says. I will read it to you once more. *It is insanity that thinks these things. You call them laws and put them under different names in a long catalogue of rituals that have no use and serve no purpose.* All of the rituals of earth have no use and serve no purpose. Now do you see why nobody does the *Course in Miracles?* This is a statement of wholeness addressing sin or separation or need to be separate. It hasn't any reality. *You think you must obey the 'laws" of medicine, of economics, and of health. Protect the body, and you will be saved.* Are you ready?

These are not laws but madness. Now, it doesn't say that the laws are mad. Once again: It says that it is madness. It says that you are not madness. You are not real, and to think you are is mad and it includes the *you* that thinks. That's important. *The body is endangered by the mind that hurts itself. The body suffers just in order that the mind will fail to see it is the victim of itself. The body's suffering is a mask the mind holds up to hide what really suffers. It would not understand it is its own enemy; that it attacks itself and wants to die. It is from this your 'laws" would save the body. It is for this that you think you are a body.* Of course. You say, "I hurt" or "I have this..." You've given that pain outside of yourself and then refuse to see that it's only in your mind and constructed in your mind.

You want to begin your practice periods today with a review of the kind of "laws" you believe you have to obey. And sometimes enumeration in the meditation is real good. *The laws of nutrition:* Well, why am I choosing to eat all these different things? What am I doing? *...immunization, medication, the body's protection in innumerable ways.* Are you ready? You can do that, practice that. *Think further; you believe in the 'laws" of friendship, of 'good" relationships and reciprocity.* But who are you subtracting? Who are you holding out, distanced from yourself in this determination to come together in this limitation and die? *Perhaps you even think there are laws which set forth what is God's and what is yours.* Everybody does here. *Many 'religions" have been based on this. They would not save but damn in Heaven's name.* They literally take the truth of God, express it, and condemn through the power of their own observation and die. *Yet they are no more strange than other 'laws" you hold must be obeyed to make you safe.*

There are no laws but God's. Dismiss all foolish magical beliefs today; and hold your mind in silent readiness to hear the Voice That speaks the truth to you. I am under no laws but God's. (Lesson 76) That is an important thought.

Lesson 77 says, *I am entitled to miracles.* We are not going to get into that today, but I want you to look at what you're doing every moment around here as you exchange. You have identified yourself in your own dream and exchange with your own thought system. You are independent of the real source, and are utilizing the source of time which finally depreciates, which finally is used up. You take the potential of your own karma memory in your own genetic memory and literally use it up, don't you? That is the Second

Law of Thermodynamics, that somehow, eventually the universe will wind down because it started from totalness and is used. Actually the universe is winding up. It starts from the absolute potential, and as it is utilized in the friction of all creation — this would be in the dharma of your mind, what you call a quantum adventure — it comes from potential and is impregnated. This is the flux of the universe coming out and returning.

On a smaller scale, that's what's going on in your microcosm. It's going on in your body, as you use this energy; it is the purpose of consciousness. You are a whole relationship of ideas. You are memory. Consciousness is light. You are light memory, and you activate yourself in the relationship of yourself with yourself because there is nothing else. Beingness is singular.

What a lovely attitude to assume in this final motion or movement that you make with your mind/body — what you call emotion, what you call objective reality — you bring it together in a single, whole expression of you. And you what? You move right out of the false dream into reality! It doesn't have anything to do with all of these manifestations contained within the fold of what Jesus calls "the dismal alcove" you have constructed in your mind. It doesn't have anything to do with that. You are simply awakening. You are waking up and coming out of your shell into reality.

The idea that you are the savior of the world, whatever that means, doesn't mean anything except that you are examining yourself in your own false relationship. If there are a hundred thousand trillion trillion trillion earths, I don't see why there would be a problem with this one being yours. I assure you that it is. And I assure you, you can awaken from it and step out of it and the world that never was will be gone. And you're going to insist that there was a purpose for it. And as long as you are here, trying to do it, there will be a purpose. You are the purpose. If you can't get the notion that this never happened, at least get the notion that it's all over. Perhaps this will help you.

This old world was over a long time ago, and we are giving it accord in our memories for just a moment, and then the happy occurrence as we step lightly, Jesus says, into the Borderland of Reality. You guys go out and you teach the Text. You teach the Workbook of this incredible true light insinuation into chaos. I understand that the groups aren't doing this. And I understand that they are fearful of assertions of the *Course in Miracles*. Any assertion of wholeness — we just read that — is very fearful and is rejected by perceptual mind. You be tolerant of that in patience. You suffer love. Because this message is unqualified. It is absolute. And there is a great deal of fear connected to it — afraid of being whole, afraid of not being able to die, afraid of the responsibility for their own minds in association with themselves. It is the defiled altar that they are fearful of looking at. Those sentences that are contained in the Course are just not ones that they want to look at.

It is important that we look at the Text today if we are going to teach what you would term physical transformation — which, to us, if you're identified with the body, obviously the transformation of your mind must include the body, but it includes what we would term the fear threshold. There are some lovely passages in the *Course* by Jesus that direct you to this "ring pass not," to this point where you are fearful of parting the veil. We are going to read them to you directly because those of you who are doing the *Course* may well be experiencing some of the manifestations of the physical awakening, and you become fearful so you don't direct your attention to them, do you?

The *Course in Miracles* is a course in the mystical, nonperceptual transformation of your mind. It is the initiation, the expression of all man in association with the means by which he can come to know of his origin. And it has been taught since the beginning of time because it has been experienced to some degree since the beginning of time, whether in the form of a shaman vision or a description by Paul of the Damascus experience. We are all in the process of undergoing this with our own minds. This is exactly and only what the *Course in Miracles* — the course in atonement, the course in enlightenment — is designed to perform. Those of you who are having these experiences, we are looking now at the Text, and I'm going to read them to you, but finally we're not verifying this by reading the words of Master Jesus in the *Course*. We are verifying them by the experiences themselves!

This would not, then, be a bad definition of a miracle. If you begin to have these mind-expansion experiences that are validated by the certainty that you are going to become one-eyed, that you are going to express Holy Spirit, you will seek them more and more. Finally you will turn away from all the dreams of death that have held you in the bondage of your own perceptual thought.

Need you have, then, the physical experience? What you don't really see, those of you who are in the chaos, is that you are continually having the experiences! You are either translating the experience into some sort of disease or, at best, you are utilizing it as some sort of innovative idea to hold you in the continuing re-illusionment of yourself. I'm saying if you will gather these together in an at-one-ment or in the atonement through the admission of your own thoughts, they will become accumulatively transformative and bring about a physical change in your cellular relationship. Oh, dare we say that? Of course! That's what we teach — the mystical experience of reality, the revelation, the enlightenment.

Are there lessons to be learned in the associations of mental diseases — schizophrenia and manic-depression, paranoia — in this adventure of the waking of the mind? Of course! Every thought you are having is a lesson that you would learn in absolute association with your own reality. If you are indeed schizophrenic, as we would teach it, if you are two separate thoughts within yourself, the bringing together of those thoughts will appear to be an episode of re-identification of yourself which will cause some conflict in your own mind as it comes about. Be of good cheer. These are the indications that you are undergoing this metamorphosis. Through the admission of that, you will relax the tension of your determination to hold on to yourself and the conflict. Is that a form of surrender? Sure. And as you get more and more into what we would call the advanced teachings of this, this will be more and more obvious to you. You will then begin to value every experience that you have, won't you? Because you see that you have chosen, within this perceptual framework of time, to bring about this awakening through the release of yourself in association with your own death desires.

Boy, this is nice to talk about and nice to think about. How confidential, how personal we have become in the certainty of a mutual need for God – to transform. You are in a temporal, godless place, where, when you begin to broach the subject with consciousnesses, they have defense mechanisms that will say, "Well, that's all well and good, but let's not go too far with that. Let's not make too much of a commitment. The necessity is that you remain here in this framework in your limited identity and die with us." Master Jesus would say, "Let the dead bury the dead. Let the dreamers dream." So we are going to take the occurrences, for those of you doing the *Course*, where this is so importantly described in the Text and the Workbook. We will show you that finally the *Course in Miracles* is only a transformative process. If you are ready to make that step, then you will be ready to surround yourself with consciousnesses who are making this full endeavor, with the real advanced ideas in the teachings that are occurring here now.

You don't do anything for the reasons you think you do. You simply respond. You are a genetic response, right? Obviously, everybody does this in perceptual time — that is, it has an infallible mechanism of response. The problem that you have, at this range of consciousness is that it has become very varied, so that you can respond in multiple different ways. And nobody questions this. This is what human beings base intelligence on — the capacity to organize and respond to mind. That is what intelligence is, which is a form of response — Jesus calls it "defense" in the *Course*.

Perceptual communication is attack and defense. It would be very obvious if you looked at it. I am responding to you, and you are attacking — you are attacking in the sense that you are making statements within a variant framework from mine. We all have those thermostats that are set, obviously, to respond. We have no problem with that. That is obviously what human consciousness is. That is what perceptual consciousness is. Our problem would always be — and my problem now, what I was really looking at is: What is the source of the necessity to respond? Where is the fidelity of truth of consciousness in a singular response?

I have no problem with the idea that you are responding to reactions that are outside of you, just as I am responding to reactions outside of me. Where is our common denominator, though? Logically, we would have one since we have a necessity to respond to each other. That is what we're doing, isn't it? We search for a common denominator, which is exactly what perception is, the search for a common goal, a common acknowledgment. And that can occur, and does occur, in all human relationships. There isn't any problem with that. All I assert from an awakened mind is that we all come from a common denominator. And in the true sense it becomes nondenominational if it is true. Truth is true, and nothing else is true. The statement, then, does not contain requirements for denominations or identifications in separate relationships. Right? Not that you can't have them if you want to. You can have them if you want to. But if the statement is to whole mind, it must be then that the cognition being asserted by you in relative relationships contains all of the power that there is in the universe. And, of course, this is the teachings of the *Course*, of Jesus Christ, of my whole mind to you.

I have no problem in the earth at all except altruism. None. I am speaking to you the truth, the truth as Jesus or I would, anyone — as you guys come into your own — as a simple statement of wholeness. The necessity for the conflict occurs in your perceptual identification, the necessity of yourself. And that is your genetic memory. That is your thermostat that we spoke of. That is the recoil that you have in association with the idea that something is outside of you, including God and truth. That's easy. Obviously this doesn't lead anywhere particularly. Perceptual mind still organizes itself in relationship to itself, and lives within the framework of that organization of separate thought, cause and effect. It is a simple notion that I can gather thoughts, forms, organize them from previous experience, and present them in new experiences that would be advantageous to me in the retention of my existence. Boy, is that simple. And I don't think there are any social scientists or psychologists or pathologists that would deny this. Is that what life is?

What we are saying, then, is in the universe *life* is defined by the conflict of existence. This is so simple. And if the response to that is "yes," then that becomes life. Obviously, then, life is temporal, because if it exists, it is going to be terminated at some level. You make it last a long time. It is finally going to be gone. So really you live in a world of perceptual observation of yourself in association with other things in chaotic, continuing disassociations that occur with what you deal with at your own perceptual level where you are. That's a statement of life. It ends in the termination of you or your succumbing to the dis-ease of the necessity for you to hold yourself in that attraction.

Those of you who are determined that that is what life is, are saying that life is defined by death. You are saying the only way that you can know that you are alive is because you are not dead, even though you don't know what being dead is. Now, if that doesn't seem peculiar for you, you can stop reading. Just stop reading and go away. You are obviously very successful in your pursuit of the perception of your existence in relationship with the things that are around you in this little mud ball. What do I care? Now, if you are still reading after that — I can make it a little tougher than that for you if you want me to. Obviously you are very successful, apparently — or not successful, however you're gauging it — in your opportunity to continue to exist in your own death and diseased framework. Why would we dispute that?

If the consciousness is not experiencing the futility and the frustration of the necessity of the retention of the self, he is not interested in a message of divine whole revelation and truth. And he will only be interested to the direct degree that he is experiencing the frustration of the inevitability that everything he loves will desert him and he will become lonely. At most, he's going to die in his lover's arms — at best. At worst, he is going to be attacked and killed by his lover who will slit his throat. All of the other things that go with the machinations of attack and defense occur within the existence framework. If he is determined to muddle through on that until he dies, obviously he will do it. Is that it, then? Here's the difficulty. He may protest that that is not it. Yet he does not possess in his perceptual relationships the capacity for the admission of a single uncompromising truth. He can't do it because it is a loss of personal identity, which he would term existence — the ego — the self that exists separate from other selves. Since that is a closed system from the idea of a single wholeness, and the power of the retention of the limitation is possessed by the consciousness since there is only a single power, our method of presenting that, then, wholly to the consciousness is to direct him to the power of his own mind in relationship to the things that are about him. This is what the *Course in Miracles* is.

To the direct extent that he is willing to acknowledge that he is, then, what? The cause of what he perceives, he will redirect his mind into an attitude of beneficence that affords him peace and comfort. He will finally realize that his whole mind is absolutely responsible for it. Now we are teaching directly from the *Course in Miracles* or from my whole mind, if you want to consider me to have a whole mind, I assure you I do, although it's very hard for you to see that. Of course, you don't see the *Course*, either. So what's the difference? I am just presenting to you what it says, what it is. What will he do? He will shorten the apparent perceptual distance between his cause and effects, or the thought forms that he has organized within his genetic relationship. Jesus calls this the atonement, or the at-one-ment. He then presents that to an image that is outside of him who shares with him the certainty of the individual truth of their imagery, even though they really don't communicate. They acknowledge it. This, then, becomes a relationship of commitment to a single wholeness. This is Christianity in its tightening sense.

Then the only ingredient that needs to be added to all of what I have said in the philosophy of the teaching is the psychology of the necessity for the maturation of the mind through a transformation, and then he'll become whole and singular. So now we are teaching individual, singular transformation, which is what Christianity is — that you need change your mind, that that can come about, that you can have a whole mind through the relinquishment of the perceptions of the false mind that are the evil or the devil or the sin that you have organized about you and proclaim to be your reality. From any reasonable standpoint that is nonsense. Certainly life based on death at best would be horrendous. Yet you tolerate it here every moment. You will say, "Gee, that's okay, I'm going to die." This is what I mean by "until you feel this pain..."

Am I a step ahead of you in my mind? As I have told you many times, it is because I felt the pain more intensely and the fear more directly in association with my ultimate demise. When you come to know that, you will go into your life/death modality where you will keep looking at it every moment so that you can step out of time as you bring your past and future together. See how easy that is? The *Course* will be replete with the declarations that perception cannot tolerate wholeness. That is a fact, because it will lose itself if it proclaims wholeness outside of itself. It literally attacks the concept of God because God is an idea. But perception will finally attack it and degrade it by its necessity to judge it at all. Do you understand that? In other words, it obviously has a necessity to attempt to judge wholeness. Where if it judged it to be whole, in truth and love, unqualifyingly, it would immediately lose its own sense of judgment and become that which it is judging. This is the teaching.

Now, in the psychology, obviously you end up with a nonjudgmental wholeness. You end up with God who is totally just in the certainty of your own perfection. That obviously is not tolerable to the conceptual mind which is basing its reality on the negativity of death, or the possibility of an attack. It's silly. Now, if I present you with this, altruistically in the certain knowledge that my mind has been transformed, you will attack me. Not because you are attacking me individually, but because you are attacking God in the notion of a wholeness which would dissolve the conflictual perception which constitutes earth, which is in your mind, which is a dream and not real. Did I say all of the teachings of Jesus in that sentence? That is the teaching! Just in case somebody wanted to lay this out. There's a lot of fandangling going on out there in the perceptual evaluation of "high truths," "low truths," "relationships." It's all nonsense because none of it could be real. And that is the statement.

What isn't in Heaven isn't real. What is Heaven? Wholeness. Certainty of single source. That moment when you cross the bridge to your own reality. You feel responsible for your actions here and you, in what you call love, act accordingly, in order that everything within your own mind can die with you. Guilt is the responsibility for the organization of your thoughts, which gives you the authority problem of your non-admission of a single wholeness. Innocence is Heaven. Non-guilt is Heaven. What is its opposite? Hell. I will do it for you. This is the *Course*. Obviously, if you organize your thoughts you will assume responsibility. You will be guilty for them. Eventually you call it sinful, be separate, and be in hell. And that's why this is hell. But it is not real. So you have no necessity to judge your hell in relationship with Heaven. Be thankful. You don't have to worry about conflicting forces. It will always be between you and the truth. That simple.

This needs to be said over and over again until you can come to know this: that you do this but to yourself. I sound like the *Course* here. No matter how tempted you are to think that there is something out there that is causing this conflict in your own mind, this disease, this notation of what you call life, *you do this but to yourself.* And obviously, that is — and only there — is your salvation.

The practice of the relinquishment of associate ideas is the Workbook of the *Course*, as we are demonstrating here now in our form of meditation or transformation of the mind. Through the use of refined thought-forms, new life forms — we move into the mystical, now, which perception denies. Jesus calls it *miracle*. He says flat out — and we teach flat out — that if you will change your mind, everything around you will change. And that has nothing to do with whether you observe it as changing or not. That is a tough lesson. That's a high truth. Yes. Of course. In fact, it's the observation of the change more than momentarily that continues to hold you in the bondage of the magic or, Jesus calls it, the temptation to retain your own power of mind in limitation. Then you can get into the beautiful sentences like, "If you choose, you can depart the earth right now in a blaze of light." This is all in the *Course*. Of course. Why wouldn't you if all power is of your mind? Your admission of the decision to stay here simply constitutes the remaining necessity of your own memory of time, or the distance that continues between your cause-and-effect mind, which is what time is. Remember our assertion that time lasted but a moment. That's the three days. That's the going out and the coming back. That is the time it took for the response of the disclaimer of the claim of separation, which never happened and isn't true. If that's a little too difficult for you, I don't care. You are still caught in your own mind and handle it any way you want.

I tell you that you are in that gap between the apparent occurrence and the apparent solution. That is what time is. Do anything you want with it. Obviously you could live in it for a million years or for a moment. Time has to be finally an invention. Why? Because it has a beginning and an end that's apparent within the structure of the linear associations of ideas. For goodness sake. If it is an invention, it's either your invention or somebody else's. If it is somebody else's, somebody is inventing you and dreaming you in their dream. That's crazy. That will really cause you frustration. And you may do that. And you may trouble death-heaven with your bootless cries, and you can make all the sacrifices you want to this apparent power that is asserting itself on you. My teaching is for you to wake up and see that you are causing it to yourself. For goodness sake. Do you have that? Is that clear in your mind?

The Ancient Mariner. Is that in there? So this ancient mariner, with gray beard and glistening eye, "Why stoppeth thou me?" When you recall that you slay the albatross, you are in a constant need for repentance. You have the obligation as a savior to continue to present this message to you, right? You wind up with: "Water, water, everywhere, and all the boards did shrink; water, water, everywhere, and not a drop to drink." Of course not. Coleridge is very mystical, lovely. Your minds now, as they become whole, are beginning to take all of these lovely allegories and bring them into the parables of the truth of the passion of you in association with your own revelation. And that includes the crucifixion and Gesthemane and the Garden and Bethlehem. Joseph with a coat of many colors deciding, through the auspices of Moses, to cross the desert and to the mind and Jerusalem, which is... Oh, boy, is this getting good! All we are teaching is take your whole self, and all the ideas that you have, and bring them into this new range of the admission that their designation is only the re-cognition of yourself in relationship with yourself. You can do that. That's very nice.

The statement is of our individual certainties that our individual communion with truth and transformation is possible. That is a holy relationship because there would be no question, then, of any of the directions that occur in what we do here. It has nothing to do with our individual relationships. Nothing! We have accorded them individually any reality that they have. Master Jesus teaches it directly that there is no communication going on here, that everyone communicates with their own fantasy. See how easy it becomes now? Through that admission you can form very high assertions or declarations of the determination to find this truth. And that is what is being addressed here. We are carrying this message abroad and using these thoughts of this new range of singularity. Our certainty is now reflected in the glory and the light of your mind and the truth of you in your determination to bring this about. It does require a certain temerity, a certain tenacity, determination, as you express it, to put up with the uncompromising declarations of an awakened mind. Somewhere within your genetic memory there is an instruction. This is lovely in the *Course*. Jesus would teach it, and I will teach it, this way. Somewhere, obviously, within your memory is the instruction of your awakening at this time. In the *Course*: time is a sleight of hand. (Lesson 158) Everything that you do obviously has already been done because time is over. Yet it appears that you are doing it sequentially. Therefore, the moment of your transformation, since it's already over, occurs the moment that you decide it is going to occur and did occur at that time. These are nice teachings. It is getting a little more esoteric.

It did occur, and you are gone from here, and this is not real. Now, that can make you feel real good or sort of suspicious. Most likely, it will make you feel fearful. When you are fearful, you are all the fear there is. This is a fearful place. You cannot lose anymore than you have lost because your single loss was all the loss that there was. So don't be afraid. Fear not, for behold, I bring you good tidings of great joy of the Christ being born in you. In the city of David — in your own memory — is a savior who is Christ the Lord. We could do a very lovely Christmas talk on the revelations of the Christ in your own physiology. Wouldn't that be nice? That is what it is, isn't it. Transformation! What a lovely notation.

Transformation is not talking about it. It is what is occurring now, as you, in the privacy of your own relationship with yourself share the energy of this reach to light. Allow all of the images that enter and flow through your mind now to remind you in humility. There is a power in the universe that is and has asserted itself against your puny defenses so the relaxation of your guard will flood you with your own reality. Amazing! But you are asleep. Let's try that. Up and out.

All time is contained in each moment. Each moment that you come to know that is a holy instant where you are whole. All of your other sequential thinking, bringing your past in and bringing it into the future, simply covered this *now*, that you are being presented with. You literally do nothing. You just gather up confusion and fractured thoughts. Nothing is happening. These moments, now, are very valuable to you. You measure the amount of time that we saved by this surge of reality into your composition. You are the conflict; you are the resolution. You are the problem; you are the solution. Not outside of you. This will be a little fearful to you sometimes, as you feel this. We are getting into that altar part of you that you have covered up. Begin to look at that.

Don't be afraid. Nothing could ever harm you. Master Jesus would say the most extraordinary occurrence in duality is your fear of God. You are so fearful of Him, you don't even like to talk about Him. You cover that. "Let's not talk about that idea of wholeness, love and truth. Let's stay in this death." When you discover yourself in your own awakening process among the sleeping and dead ones, then the idea that you must let the dead bury the dead becomes very valuable to you. And perhaps difficult. If your condition of the maturation of your mind is in supersedence over the lower energies in time, the necessity obviously is for the emergence of a whole new mind. This is what we teach. And it begins to sound like Sri Aurobindo. The emergence of Gnostic, or superconsciousness. As this fills out in your own mind, you see that all frame of references are indications that there is this whole mind, the certainty through the possibility of the evolutionary process of man to wholeness. It is impossible that this not be true. If cause and effect are not apart, everything is true by the possibility of it. That's lovely.

This old world was over a long time ago. You but re-live it each moment. And we keep stretching down, living the dream. This is a dream. A hundred thousand trillion earths in this one universe. And all the things on it are manifestations of your mind. Be thankful. Nothing is outside of you. No idea that man has ever had in perception is separate from the whole karmic journey — your akashic assertions. Using all of the power that there is in personal consciousness, you make separate assertions that grow into this. And that's fine. But you remember, there is no death. You are not going to die. Your persistence in terminating yourself and staying within the formulation of time is nonsense. You are at a point now where you are making decisions not to do that. We are pleased, then, to welcome you to the gates of paradise, as Jesus would say. Will you be attacked for presenting this? Sure, but only because everything is attack and defense here, and lack and need to survive. This is a nightmare that you are experiencing. Time is over now. You are free. Now be free. Be free with this:

Each one peoples his world with figures from his individual past, and it is because of this that private worlds do differ. Yet the figures that he sees were never real, for they are made up only of his reaction to his brothers, and do not include their reactions to him. Therefore, he does not see he made them, and that they are not whole. For these figures have no witnesses, being perceived in one separate mind only.

It is through these strange and shadowy figures that the insane relate to their insane world. This is, incidentally, a definition of this world, for all you so-called teachers of the *Course.* All of you who were credential-seekers, you were nuts from the beginning. That's what this says. *For they see only those who remind them of these images, and it is to them that they relate. Thus do they communicate with those who are not there, it is they who answer them. And no one hears their answer save him who called upon them, and he alone believes they answered him. Projection makes perception, and you cannot see beyond it. Again and again have you attacked your brother because you saw in him a shadow figure in your private world. And thus it is you who must attack yourself first, for what you attack is not in others. Its only reality is in your own mind. And by attacking others you are literally attacking what is not there. (Text, 13:5)* For those of you who are not familiar with this, this is from the teaching of Jesus Christ, the same man from Nazareth who went through this transformation. He is at a higher level of consciousness, directing this to you. Do you believe that, brother? Not yet. Not quite. Do you believe that what I just read you is true? What a gigantic step that would be if you accepted responsibility for the certainty of the non-communication here. That would be lovely.

The blind become accustomed to their world by their adjustments to it. They think they know their way about in it. And this is what you are doing. *They learned it, not through joyous lessons, but through the stern necessity of limits they believed they could not overcome. And still believing this, they hold these lessons dear and cling to them because they cannot see.* You are using all of your genetic memory in this dream. *They do not understand the lessons keep them blind. This they do not believe. And so they keep the world they learned to "see" in their imagination, believing that their choice is that or nothing. They hate the world they learned through pain. And everything they think is in it serves to remind them that they are incomplete and bitterly deprived.*

Thus they define their life where they live, adjusting to it, as they think they must, of course, and they're *afraid to lose the little that they have. And so it is with all who see the body as all they have and all their brothers have.* Listen. *They try to reach each other, and they fail, and fail again. And they adjust to loneliness, believing that to keep the body is to save the little that they have. Listen, and try to think if you remember what we will speak of now.* The lovely mysticism of the *Course* emerges here. All of our teachings in regard to the possibility of a new reach of consciousness occurred in these next sentences. I'll let you read them to yourself. They are on page 416 and 417 of the Text of the *Course.*

Beyond the body, beyond the sun and stars, past everything you see and yet somehow familiar, is an arc of golden light that stretches as you look into a great and shining circle. And all the circle fills with light before your eyes, and the edges of the circle disappear, and what is in it is no longer contained at all. The light expands and covers everything, extending to infinity forever shining with no break or limit anywhere. Within it everything is joined in perfect continuity. Nor is it possible to imagine that anything could be outside for there is nowhere that this light is not. (Text, 21:1) That is a lovely mystical expression, this transformation that your mind is undergoing.

This Text of *A Course in Miracles.* What lovely teachings! *Every idea has a purpose, and its purpose is always the natural outcome of what it is.* Wow! *Everything that stems from the ego* — the limited mind, you, a human being, *is always the natural outcome of its central belief, and the way to undo its results is merely to recognize that their source is not natural, being out of accord with your true nature. I said before that to will contrary to God is wishful thinking and not real willing.* Wholeness, God, *His Will is one because the extension of His Will cannot be unlike itself. The real conflict you experience, then, is between* your human mind, your no-mind's *idle wishes and the will of God, which you share. Can this be a real conflict?* Can you really be in conflict with yourself?

Yours is the independence of creation, not of autonomy. Do you hear that? *Your whole creative function lies in your complete dependence on God...* or wholeness. You, literally, are God creating. *...whose function He shares with you. By His willingness to share it, He becomes...* Are you ready? *...as dependent on you as you are* *on Him.* What an astonishing notion!! Are you willing to accept that? *Do not ascribe your own arrogance to Him Who wills not to be independent of you.* He doesn't mind sharing Himself with you. You consider that to be blasphemy. That's nonsense. That is just the ego talking. *He has included you in His Autonomy. Can you believe that autonomy is meaningful apart from Him? The belief in your own autonomy* — in the human, in the ego — *is costing you the knowledge of your dependency on God, in which your freedom lies.* So what happens? *The ego* — you, the human being — *sees all dependency as threatening.* Of course. It is the idea of wholeness. It is the idea that he would let go of himself. *...and has twisted even your longing for God into a means of establishing itself. Do not be deceived by its interpretations of your conflict.* All assertions of the mind, all attacks of the human mind, the ego, are attacks on behalf of separation.

Believing it has the power to do this — and you do — *it does nothing else, because its goal of autonomy is nothing else. You are totally confused about reality. But you do not lose sight of your goal. It is much more vigilant* — you are much more vigilant — *because it is perfectly certain of its purpose.* We're speaking now of you as an "I." You know exactly what you want to do. *You are confused because you do not recognize what your real reality is.*

You must recognize that the last thing the ego wishes you to realize is that you are afraid of it. For if the ego could give rise to fear, it would diminish your independence and weaken your power. Yet its one claim to your allegiance is that it can give power to you. Without this belief you would not listen to it at all. How, then, can its existence continue if you realized that, by accepting it, you are belittling yourself and depriving yourself of power? And I assure you that you all do it.

You don't mind that *the ego can and does allow you to regard yourself as supercilious, unbelieving, 'lighthearted," distant, emotionally shallow, callous, uninvolved and even desperate, but not really afraid. Minimizing fear, but not its undoing, is the ego's constant effort...* This is what the human mind is. *...and is indeed a skill at which it is very ingenious. How can it preach separation without upholding it through fear, and would you listen to it if you recognized that this is what it is doing?* (Text 11:5)

Of course not. So all of the psychology of: "Let's establish what we are in our emotions" is nonsense. It is a statement, continuing proclamation of your own separation. This is the assertion that you can't "have" anything. You can only "be" it.

And the only way that you can know that you have everything is by giving it away. Then you are it because you begin to create. This is our whole lesson: Protect everything that you love by giving it away. Do not be possessed by your own limited ideas about yourself. That is the evil — that is being possessed by thought, thought-forms that establish your unreality. The closest that you can come to creation here is giving or forgiveness. And total forgiveness allows you to see that you are the creator of everything that is about you. Isn't that lovely?

Let's talk just a little bit about the great mystery, the *Philosophia Perennis*, the statement that nobody really wants to get involved in — that the basic teachings of all religions are to the transformation of the mind, the admission that perceptual mind cannot know the truth and that by an enlightenment or a resurrection it can come to know the truth. These are the basic teachings of all religions and, most particularly, Christianity. Christianity, finally, as a message from all awakened minds or all initiates —and most particularly, Jesus Christ — since we're calling it Christianity, is a statement that you can come to know God and become God and whole as the Son of God through the transformation of your mind, or the relinquishment of your limited association with yourself. Now, the idea that perception will do this voluntarily, that is, through its own attainments, appears to be valid until you would examine it within any context. Obviously, if separation is self-identity, it will not and cannot willingly relinquish itself to the whole truth that is all around it. This has been expressed in many ways in so-called initiatory processes.

The whole idea of mystical Christianity is the statement of the Pentecost — that there will be a spirit that will come into the limited state of consciousness. The process of the Workbook of the *Course in Miracles* is a statement that there is a method — you become Methodists, don't you — there's a method in which you can bring about this change in your mind. It is very important that you see at this point, and we will teach to it just a moment, that you are very fearful of this occurring because this is very simply a statement of the death of yourself and brings about the assertion: "Know ye not ye must be born again." (John 3:3) And to be born again, of course, you must die. The lovely parable that is in Matthew that nobody really understands is a direct indication of the premature awakening of the energies in physical transformation that the Eastern traditions call Kundalini, or the waking of the centers of your body. And a lot of Christians have turned to physical awakenings, as found in the Eastern traditions, without really examining the incredible wealth of information concerning the mystical experience and subsequent transformation that is in all of Christianity and is axiomatically denied by established Christianity, which would be an indication of the necessity of the establishment to *understand* God rather than the relinquishment of establishment in order to come to *know* God.

Jesus, in describing what the Kingdom of Heaven is in Chapter 22 of Matthew, says this: *The kingdom of heaven is like unto a certain king, which made a marriage for his son, and sent forth his servants to call them that were bidden to the wedding: and they would not come. Again, he sent forth another servant, saying, Tell them which are bidden, Behold, I have prepared my dinner: my oxen and my fatlings are killed, and all things are ready: come unto the marriage. But they made light of it, and went their ways, one to his farm, another to his merchandise.* Isn't that lovely. *And the remnant took his servants, and entreated them spitefully, and slew them. But when the king heard thereof, he was wroth; and he sent forth his armies, and destroyed those murderers, and burned up their cities.*

Then saith he to his servants, The wedding is ready, but they which were bidden were not worthy. Go ye therefore into the highways, and as many as ye shall find, bid to the marriage. So those servants went out into the highways, and gathered together all, as many as they found, both bad and good; and the wedding was furnished with guests. And when the king came in to see the guests, he saw there a man which had not on a wedding garment; and he saith unto him, Friend, how comest thou in hither not having a wedding garment? And he was speechless. Then said the king to the servants, Bind him hand and foot, and take him away, and cast him into outer darkness; there shall be weeping and gnashing of teeth. For many are called, but few are chosen. (Matthew 22:2-14)

The indication *many are called but few are chosen* is the indication of the attempts to join in a wedding feast with God in the upper reaches of your energies — if you want to get a little esoteric with this — without the proper preparation of the relinquishment of your self. In the Eastern traditions this is known very simply as the premature awakening of what they term the Kundalini. Obviously, there will be no awakening until you get past this fear threshold. This is what the initiation process is. Jesus in the *Course* deals with it very, very thoroughly in some of the statements that He makes, particularly in regard to the fourth Obstacle of Peace, the fear of God.

What would you see without the fear of death? See, this is what you're afraid to go through in this transformation. *What would you feel and think if death held no attraction for you? Very simply, you would remember your Father. The Creator of life, the Source of everything that lives, the Father of the universe and of the universe of universes and of everything that lies even beyond them would you remember. And as this memory rises in your mind, peace must still surmount a final obstacle, after which is salvation completed, and the Son of God entirely restored to sanity. For here your world does end.* Are you ready?

The fourth obstacle — this is physical now, in your meditations — *to be surmounted hangs like a heavy veil before the face of Christ. Yet as His face rises beyond it, shining with joy because He is in His Father's Love, peace will lightly brush the veil aside and run to meet Him, and to join with Him at last. For this dark veil, which seems to make the face of Christ Himself like to a leper's, and the bright rays of His Father's Love that light His face with glory appear as streams of blood, fades in the blazing light beyond it when the fear of death is gone.*

This is the darkest veil, upheld by the belief in death and protected by its attraction. The dedication to death and to its sovereignty is but the solemn vow, the promise made in secret to the no-mind never to lift this veil — listen — *not to approach it, nor even to suspect that it is there. This is the secret bargain made with the ego to keep what lies beyond the veil forever blotted out and unremembered. Here is your promise never to allow union to call you out of separation; the great amnesia in which the memory of God seems quite forgotten; the cleavage of your Self from you; — the fear of God, the final step in your dissociation.*

Now, suddenly you are in this meditation and this thing is happening to you, and you have been practicing service to your brother in love, and you have been giving up, and you begin detaching, and you have been doing the *Course*, and you have been being quiet, and now, suddenly it happens.

And the appeal of death is lost forever as love's attraction stirs and calls to you. From beyond each of the obstacles to love, Love Itself has called. And each has been surmounted by the power of attraction of what lies beyond. Your wanting fear seemed to be holding them in place. Yet when you heard the Voice of Love beyond them, you answered and they disappeared. Now you listen to what happens to you in this moment. This is a little Gesthemane here.

And now you stand in terror before what you swore never to look upon. Your eyes look down, remembering your promise to your "friends." These are the consciousnesses around you, the other human beings, your thought forms. *The "loveliness" of sin, the delicate appeal of guilt, the "holy" waxen image of death, and the fear of vengeance of the ego you swore in blood not to desert, all rise and bid you not to raise your eyes. For you realize that if you look on this and let the veil be lifted, they will be gone forever. All of your "friends," your "protectors" and your "home" will vanish. Nothing that you remember now will you remember.* No wonder you are afraid. Perceptual consciousness is afraid to do this, isn't it?

It seems to you the world will utterly abandon you if you but raise your eyes. Yet all that will occur is that you will leave the world forever. This is the reestablishment of your will. Don't be afraid. *Look upon it, open-eyed, and you will nevermore believe that you are at the mercy of things beyond you, forces you cannot control, and thoughts that come to you against your will. It is your will to look on this. No mad desire, no trivial impulse to forget again, no stab of fear nor the cold sweat of seeming death can stand against your will. For what attracts you from beyond the veil is also deep within you, unseparated from it and completely at one with it.*

Now, looking ahead just for a moment in *The Lifting of the Veil*: *No one can look upon the fear of God unterrified, unless he has accepted the Atonement and learned illusions are not real. No one can stand before this obstacle alone, for he could not have reached this far unless his brother walked beside him. And no one would dare to look on it without complete forgiveness of his brother in his heart.*

Now, you must come to this spot in your meditations. This is the teaching of the transformation. You remember this: The sole purpose of any real spiritual teaching; the sole purpose, obviously, of the *Course in Miracles*, is to bring about this transformation of your mind. You begin with the premise that you are very fearful of doing it because this is a place of fear.

Stand you here a while and tremble not. You will be ready. Let us join together in a holy instant, here in this place where the purpose, given in the holy instant, has led you. And let us join in faith that He Who brought us here together will offer you the innocence you need, and that you will accept it for my love and for His. Ready?

Nor is it possible to look upon this too soon. This is the place to which everyone must come when he is ready. And we are going to speed up some time here, dear teacher, and tell you that you can be ready for this transformation of your mind if you choose to be. You can be ready right now. Is this going to involve the abandonment of yourself in your own meditation? Sure.

To look upon the fear of God does need some preparation. Only the sane can look on stark insanity and raving madness with pity and compassion, but not with fear. For only if they share in it does it seem fearful, and you do share in it until you look on your brother with perfect faith and love and tenderness. Before complete forgiveness you still stand unforgiving. You are afraid of God because you fear your brother. Those you do not forgive, you fear. And no one reaches love with fear beside him. (Text 19:4)

The important indication now for you to see in these teachings is the necessity for this transformation, this illumination to be brought about in your own mind. This is the pure teaching of Christianity. All of the secret societies, all of the Masonry, all of the Rosicrucians, all of the Knights Templar, all of the Brothers of the Free Spirit, all of the high Gnostic teachings, all of the directions will be to this admission of your union with God through prayer, through transformation. That is what we have come here to teach because this is what has come about in us. And we present it to you in its truth now.

This is a place of transformation, and you are beginning to feel these stirrings now. Perhaps you will want to contact us. Certainly, if you have been doing the *Course in Miracles* with these other pursuits, somewhere within you, you are feeling the necessity to complete your own transformation process. We hope you'll join us. Thank you, brother.

One of the consciousnesses inquired, "Where in the Christian tradition are the references to the Kundalini awakening or the seven centers of the body?" The whole Apocalypse, the whole revelatory statement of the final book of the New Testament, is a declaration of the Kundalini awakening. It is associated glandularly with the churches as are presented in the esoteric teachings which were well presented by the mystic scribe Edgar Cayce. I don't think there's any question in mystical Christian circles that the Apocalypse is this. The breaking of the seals, the Seven Seals, are all directly connected to the physical awakening, as is the association, for example, of the helix of the genetic code with the *I Ching*. Where does this begin, and where does it end? Nowhere, if you remember that your sole purpose here, now, in this awakening of your mind is to remember who you are.

As this energy comes into you more and more, everything that you do will become a parable and finally will reach a higher and higher state. You will discover that you have indeed been dreaming. And, as you let go of fear and begin to love, your service in love will become more evident. One of the great teachings of all traditions is, to awaken the energy, you must serve. Jesus teaches it as forgiveness — that you must give yourself away to be free, to detach, to go through this fear threshold. Through this surrender and abandonment, your mind will expand to the reality of you.

Remember, this is your transformation, individually. You are the savior of the world. Without you there is no Heaven and no salvation. And I mean you. I am speaking directly now to you in this regard. We love you and we await your return.

About Time

TIME! Let's look at one thing really clearly and emphatically. No matter what you are doing in regard to this awakening, it involves time because you invented it. *Perception is time* – the distance between events. Now, here's the problem: Very simply, Jesus says that you invented time, but you do strange things with it. I'll start out right at the top of this: If space is the distance between events or observed events within the nomenclature of the imaging of the perceptual mind, we must observe *texture* (that would be a good word) in the relationship of our ideas in order to expand our perceptual association to the congruity of image-reality.

The teachings of a meditative notation are to bring you into the NOW. Is there anyone here that doesn't understand, whose perceptual mind will not see, that NOW is the only time there is? That really isn't hard to do. When you project thoughts from your mind into the future, you are still making an admission that you are here and that you are now. You may cover that with the notations of linear time or, as Jesus would say in the *Course*, sequential time – the distance between your associate thoughts in regard to the construction of you, of your mind, within that framework. The question would never be whether you do this or not because existence, obviously, is based on associate thought. You project form from you, which is nothing but thought – thought of a different time – a tree, a house, a bird, a human being, a thought of a different time, and then you hold a distance between your past and future thoughts. This is what perceptual thought is. There isn't going to be any real disagreement with this.

The immediate problem that occurs is once you have the form – and there is no question that you have the form, and you can't get away from having the form – you are faced with the dilemma of the texture or the quality of associate thoughts between the image association of the consciousnesses who have actually established themselves independently of each other, and of how they attempt to bring together the creative notations of the reality of the now. Since this obviously involves perceptual thought, and I am perceptually thinking about it, it would be increasingly obvious that the only manner in which you would change the texture of thinking would be by a transformation of your mind. You are not going to do it any other way. It doesn't make any difference how many thoughts you would be together. Jesus has a couple of sentences in the *Course* that says, "Levels do not communicate." He has made an allowance for levels of consciousness. So what? The only level of consciousness there really could ever be is the one that you are at in this moment.

You literally invent through the manufacturing, through the association of ideas contained within you, time. There isn't any question that you do. Isn't that amazing? You can see very plainly that you can do that. Time is only in your mind, individually, in associate thoughts. What I am teaching is that I can take that image and bring it together in a higher degree of texture association – a wider range of space within the whole framework of space/time thought. Yes! I am telling you that your mind is capable of doing this. How would it not be? It does it all the time, but it only does it for the moment that it brings the sequentiality of its associations of ideas into the single framework.

In the *Course*, Jesus will say if you keep a distance between your past and your future in continual sequential thoughts, you are really no thing. Obviously. You can see very plainly, if you are just thought, and that thought is gone, you just keep replacing it with another thought, and you sequence it within a framework of your associate memories with yourself. This is the *I Ching*. This is what you call the Akashic Record – your genetic association with probability – since you are sitting somewhere within the whole framework of space/time. What a strange thing to do. You actually – you, individually – take these ideas that are in your mind, construct a reality, literally, in association with the form, and give it meaning! My whole teaching from a new range of consciousness, this is Master Jesus again, is that I must tell you that it has no meaning – not because it does not have meaning to you – in fact it establishes your meaning – but because it is not real. Do you see? It simply is gone. It is gone away. No matter how many times you would bring that up within the framework of your previous association, if you remember it and it is gone, you simply live within that framework of association. I am telling you that you can change your past by changing your mind. If you change your past, by remembering, you will change your future. This has to be done within your mind, doesn't it? Everybody got this? You don't have to use this in a religious sense; I would love to take the religious vernacular out of what I teach.

You will not get this from the idea of mind association without involving time. The ludicrousness then of a separate mind within a framework of what appears to be longevity constructing its own death will be funny to you. That would include the earth – that includes a million years. Listen: If we are going to change the fabric of time – actually what we are doing is changing the distance between the beginning and the end of it. We are simply taking all of the thoughts that were in association with all of time and pinching them together. In order to pinch them together in perceptual mind, you have to change the essence or the quality of your thinking. Have you got that? All I really teach is to do that. There will be a point in your mind, where through the accumulation of quantity, which is nothing but full purpose – if you really get purposeful (this is the teaching) – to bring about this transformation, the quantity of time is accumulated to the point where the texture or the quality of the time actually shifts.

Primitive man was much aware of this, just incidentally. Primitive man would set up a Sabbath. He was absolutely aware that one day a week the quality of time was different. Why? Because on that day he would literally do nothing human. These are the teachings that have come down to the Blue Laws, and all the other things that you don't adhere to. He knew that he was functioning within a framework of time and he also knew that on the seventh day God rested. You guys are hearing this a little bit. There would actually be a difference in the quality of the time. The old Quakers who would get together for seven hours in church were aware of this. This has been lost now. We have become more mechanized. But the idea that you could come together in a congruity of associate thought for a seven-hour period in worship was literally bringing together space/time. It is exactly the same thing as the Year of the Jubilee, when the Jewish calendar would say, "Every 100 years we are going to take all the thoughts that we have had, all the properties we've got, all of the so-called farms, all of the grain. We are going to throw it all back into the hopper, and we are going to start all over." This is exactly the same idea as going to church once a week.

What I am directing you to is that if the texture or quality of your reality —literally your individual association with yourself – can be changed, wouldn't it be beneficent to you to change it rather than remain in the conflictual association of sequential time? Of *Course!* This is very difficult to press on a consciousness that is holding onto its identity in its limited association. How can it express itself? Really, creation is only self expression. It is so obvious that if you limit, within your own genetic framework, the definition that you have given to form, you can't create. If Beethoven wrote his first symphony when he was six years old, he obviously did not construct limited associate form to do it. No matter how tempted you are to believe he snuck into his uncle's manuscripts and somehow put the notes together, that is not the case. He changed the texture of the association of the perceptual thoughts. That is what creation is. Of *Course.* That is what masterpiece is. That is what genius is. That is what mind expanded is. That is what you are doing!

Hey, we're into time here! Have you got any more time for this? No, your time is up! Once these thoughts begin to come to you, you can be walking along the street – this is the *Course in Miracles* Workbook. See what you are supposed to do guys, out there, who are supposedly doing this? You literally stop your sequential thinking. You change the quality of time at that moment! Do you know what else will happen as you continue to do it? The perceptions you have outside yourself will change and you will work miracles. Do you hear that? You think it is just contained within your own mind, dummies. It is not! The world is your creation. Come on. If time can be changed, space can be changed. The whole teaching would be: There is no such thing as space, except limited sequential time. When you change your mind, you literally change the events going on around you. Holy mackerel! It is not the observation of the limited bringing together of a miracle that is what a miracle is; the miracle is the changing of the total event in association with itself – with the totalness of it. Got it?

What time do you have? 6:30 I looked at these new little digital computer times. They have even taken space out of a clock. You see a clock that has hands has space in it. » It is like a sundial, it is like a horoscope. They have reduced that into an image of numbers that appear on a little thing. They just keep squeezing it down. Don't let them do it to you, brother. Back to sundials.

We have a lot of excitement about time, don't we? Where does God fit into it? What's God got to do with it? God is nothing but total time. You are the one who is constructing something divine, or separate, or evil. What could be evil except sequential time, which is possibility? The notation of possibility is fearful because it is an indication of something that can happen to you. Come on, guys. See how easy this gets? It is not hard to do this. Don't compare, and it will change. Don't compare at all, and it will change completely. It is a real fundamental teaching.

Is that the same as – do you want to back it off to – *forgiveness*? Sure. You are nothing but a series of ideas of conflictual associations. It has nothing to do with good or bad. It has nothing to do finally with the thought forms that you have endowed with a moment's reality in order to hold onto your identity within the framework of space/time.

Is this you, then, that's doing this? Yes! Why is that so hard? You have looked up at the sky at night, and you saw a trillion, trillion, trillion stars. You go, "Oh, wow, look at me, here I am with 3,000 billion separate forms here, and this is me." Come on. Look what your mind is doing here. Why not just accept that you have constructed the earth? The continual gathering, then, of those limited thoughts will give quality to them and will actually change the texture of your time. There is no other way to do this. You are in time. Jesus says that time and remembering (perception) are the same thing. This is the *Course*, just for a moment it is the same thing. Time, in itself, does nothing.

You give time all the meaning that it has, just as you give memory all of the meaning that it has. It is given by you and your ideas. Now you can begin to see why, while this may be painful to you, we – in association with our own apparent reality, the conglomeration of the microcosm – we are not equal in time. We force equality on ourselves in our perceptual associations. When creative mind really begins to think, it expands vertically outside of the framework of the perceptual mirage or image that is going on in perception. You call this genius. That is really what is happening to your minds here now. That's nice.

Here is what you are faced with. If time is not sequential – and I am directing you to change the associate ideas that you have in the quality, in the dimensions, of your time – each moment, then, must contain all of time, and of course it does. If you will bring those moments together, this is really what the definition of a miracle would be. But nothing prevents you from bringing all of time together, totally, each moment, and transcending your own mind, or changing the whole relationship that you formerly had with yourself. This is called enlightenment. Is it bodily? How would it not be bodily? Is it earthly? How would it not be earthly? Is it Heavenly? How would it not be Heavenly? It is you! It is your mind. What is the difference between solid and liquid and gaseous? All you have to do is reach out with your thoughts and you can penetrate any form that you've established as a distance between you. You see how simple transcendentalism becomes, then? Of course you can do it.

We have a divine brother who is leaving now. He has to go. He is very much aware that he is stepping into what you would call a slower sequential time. There is going to be momentarily, for him, a little more distance between his thoughts, because he is going to have to make allowances for thicker – I'm using these terms kind of interchangeably – or darker textures. There is not enough of what you would call Light shining on them. They are not fast enough. When Jesus says we are speeding up time, this is what He means. Of Course! We are changing the texture. This is a notation that should be made. You can detect a difference in the textures of your thinking when you listen to a higher emanation of energy response in association with itself. This is a definition of a Master or whole-mind teacher. If you do that with *A Course In Miracles*, you would see immediately that the thought forms and patterns that are brought together by Master Jesus in the *Course* are not human thoughts. No matter how much the scribes are determined to pull these incredibly lovely light total concepts into some sort of framework of their limitation, they are not succeeding, and it is becoming ludicrous. Somewhere along the line, somebody – and the groups that are doing it now – is going to have to look at it and say: "Hey, this is true! The reality we have at this moment can be transformed to a different framework of associate space/time."

I'm not going to get into the psychology of the resistance of that, because obviously the limiting factor of what is termed death, sequentiality, what you call aspects and degrees and intervals, and waxing and waning, is a part of perceptual mind. Very simply, perceptual mind, then, within its framework of a limitation, defends itself from Wholeness or Eternity. Of course. That is where the conflict is. That's what a human being constructs as his limited framework. The distance between his thoughts is conflictual, isn't it? Is that real? Hey, that's real! He's got thought forms out there that are literally attacking him because of his previous and future associations.

We're bringing a lot together here. If you can get it outside of your limited, incredibly limited, associations of religion and philosophy and pull it all together in the simple statement that you are speeding up time – bringing together the Alpha and the Omega, the cause and the effect. The idea of evolution, the idea of the moment from slowness to fastness, is the whole idea of your mind. What a glorious notation! If you could take a sentence that Jesus says, that no matter how tempted you are to believe it, finally cause and effect are not apart, that would step you out of time, wouldn't it? Automatically! The closer you bring it together, the more responsibility you take for thought, the closer you bring the effects together with you, and the closer you get to eternity. This is all we really present to you. Your dilemma, and the dilemma of the earth is the admission of this. But, come on, I'm sitting right here in your dream sequencing! The reason we call this a dream, or an illusion, or hallucination is because it literally cannot be real. What you call the ego – don't say that's not what you are, because it is what you are as long as you are associating thoughts in time– the ego cannot be real. It simply isn't. Never mind the idea, "Well, it is real, and then it works to do something." That is nonsense. If you are going to look at changing the quality of the thought form in time, you will see immediately that it is not real and never was real. No matter what you do, you are not going to make it so. But that is not going to prevent you from being real, and associating in any manner in which you wish to associate.

It's funny how the mind holds on to time and makes a prediction about its death. It says, "I'm going to do it." It literally dies at that moment, but it can't see it. If time is really not separate, if there is really no distance between cause and effect, it holds onto the tension between the two and simply invents its own death. This is what I present to you. Death is your invention. How absurd. All you need do is simply say, "I am not going to die." And you won't die. All you need do is say, "I believe you, teacher." Are you ready for that? You don't want to hear that. I'm telling you that you can't die. You cannot finally sequence time. You insist that you can because you are the sequencing of the events, aren't you? Do you attack me when I present this? Of course. You are attacking the notation of no death. But you can't die, you cannot succeed in obliviating yourself, let's not be absurd.

You can make up all the inventions you want about going somewhere later on, coming back here, you can do anything you want with it within your own framework. The only time you could ever wake up and see your wholeness is NOW. The notation that you are asleep can be very valuable to you. Everywhere you look, all you are seeing are your thought forms at some place within the fabric of the distance between the beginning and the end. Do you do that? Sure. And I am telling you that you, individually, and only individually in your whole mind power, can transcend this. The forms that are around you literally have no meaning. This is a course in the transformation of your mind. Stop doing your limited genetic associations of falsity. This is a course at a nice, new level for you. Jesus says that your relationships are killing you. What else would kill you? If you have constructed death, what kills you more readily than the forms you have established to retain your limited identity? Why is that so hard for you? The only way you can come to know that, obviously, is by the relinquishment – we're back into the teaching – or the nondefense of yourself in association with your determination to hold on to the limited state of consciousness. Does anybody out there not hear this? You hear it all right. You don't like it.

All I really want you to do is make an obvious, simple choice between time and dying, and Life and Living forever with Love. Why should you have to lose something? Why do you defend your own demise? Can you hear me, you dummies? I don't mean you are dummies. What I mean is, you are dummies. What I mean is, your eyes are not constructed to see. Any vocabulary that you have in response to this is designed to defend yourself. As Jesus said, you invented speech, or babble, The Tower of Babel, to keep from seeing the very obvious – that you are whole and beautiful. If I offend you, that's okay. I am sitting in the middle of your dream, though. How are you going to get away from me? You can't. This is all over. Isn't that funny. Jesus, in the *Course*, says the most you can say about the past is that it is over and gone. If you will understand that your future is your past, then the future will be gone. If that's gone, you can see immediately that all of this is gone.

The sentence of Jesus, "This old world was over a long time ago" perhaps will begin to mean something to you, you dummies in your own dream. You think I'm attacking you? I'm trying to shake you loose from your own perceptual poop. Excuse me. That's not a very scientific term. But everything that is constructed in form has no meaning. Jesus would say you put a frame around it, you guild it, and you give it credit. This is lovely stuff. And it just rots on you. It just goes away. It stinks finally. And you keep burying it, and worshipping your death associations. Then you stand around the consciousness that you have killed with your own mind, and bemoan the fact that it is dead. Would you care to look at that, funeral-goers? This is in the *Course*, too. You gather around the bier and bitterly complain about the time you have established for your own demise. Is the word *insanity*, perhaps, appropriate at this time? This is very early in the *Course*. How could you not observe the craziness and the nuttiness of the determination of a consciousness to intentionally inflict on himself sickness, pain and death? Salvation, obviously, comes from my new certain mind that this is not real so that I don't have to judge it in its limited associations with itself. Do you hear me? Come on, new minds. Is this a new teaching? Yes!

Is the earth real? Don't be absurd. Look at the relationship of where you are to the universe, for just a minute. Now, be happy that your mind is in this expansion. Jesus says be a happy learner, rather than trying to crunch down and listen to the calls of all of your previous murderous intents. These are the images and thought forms that you have sent out to bring you back the message that what I am teaching you cannot be true! Don't tell me you can't learn this *Course*, Jesus says, don't tell me. You wrote it. But you wrote it in a different sequence of thoughts and have returned with me now for a moment to bring it into the focus of our joint reality – the moment that we shared in true perception.

We are at God's Country Place, just sitting here and talking about being out of time, which is where we really are. We have come just for a moment to remind you that you did awaken and are gone from here, and all of the torture and pain and death that you are feeling has absolutely no reality. I know this is difficult for you. But the necessity is that you accept my certainty that love and goodness and wholeness are real and forever, and they have no association at all with your perceptual mind of sickness, pain and death.

It must be obvious to you why we teach this as forgiveness. Really quickly, you psychologists – the idea that you would hold a separate thought form out from you, and deny that you have created it in your own mind, is what conflict is. Come on. Does anybody want to look at this? Who really wants to hear this? It would be obviously necessary for you, then, to change your mind about the form that you have put out there. The way you do that is by including it in with your own mind. This is a *Course* in inclusion, not subtraction. It appears to be a *Course* in meditation or quieting your mind in order to still it down in its concepts. But remember that mind is active all the time. There is a caprice creating going on in here. By stilling the sequencing of time, the mind expands automatically. This is what we want you to do. The idea of practicing forgiveness will become real strange to you, finally, because you will see immediately that you have constructed sin out there, and you will immediately forgive it and bring it into wholeness. This is what we want you to do with your mind. But the idea that you are going to practice that really doesn't make any sense. Why would it make sense? It will change if you let it. The real problem that you have is that possession of thought form is what holds you in existence. The idea that you must give in order to have is very difficult for you.

All you really are is an expression of your conglomerate associations – your genetic memories. If you hold yourself in a distance between your thoughts, you will be possessed by the thoughts, and will only squeeze out of your perceptions that association within your own mind. The notation of giving, then, becomes imperative, so that you can come to see that having and being are the same thing. They are not separate. You don't really have thoughts, you *are* the thoughts. This is what happens when whole mind comes whole. It begins to extend from itself its expanded identity. Finally it becomes a single, whole identity in the transformation of the mind.

Nothing can be solved by conflict, obviously. Your idea is that conflict can be solved by balance, or by taking your previous forms in a time framework. All you do is extend longevity. Eternity is not a long time, and you have done this for a very long time. The result of balance must be death, because it is the idea of duality or that there really are separate thoughts. Listen to me! Number one: *An idea never leaves its source.* So every thought that you ever had as the source of it, is contained within you. Number two: *There are no such things as separate thoughts.* The only thoughts there could ever be are the thoughts that are emanating from your mind. Take hold of that, so you don't look out and pretend that you don't know something.

Don't give construct to something and then deny that you know it, and let it instruct you from its own limitation. This is what a relationship on earth is. Neither one of us knows what we are; I'll deny you, you deny me, and we'll base our reality in time for just a moment on nothing, and then die and mourn the fact that we don't have a solution to this. How absurd! It is very hard to teach that not knowing is a denial; it is a decision. You literally make a decision not to know. Who are you kidding? I know you better than that. I know you all perfectly. How would I not? If you want to fit us somewhere in time – we have to fit somewhere in time because you are a combination of light refractions or rays harmonizing (in the sense of creating limitedly) in a particular sequencing framework of time; we, then, come together. But we are only thought forms. I must know you completely. Am I meeting you in different phases of the fabric of time? Jesus says that it is impossible to meet a stranger. Not only that, but if you meet him, you must have met him in an earlier and a later framework. You like that. That's reincarnation. I'm telling you that you are *carnated* all the time. You never "re" it. You only change it each moment. You like that? Somebody asked Jesus in the Teacher's Manual, "Is reincarnation valuable?" Anything that would let you know that life is continuous is valuable, and the scribes immediately take hold of it and practice their own death ritual, and then proclaim that the Master says that reincarnation is okay. That's nonsense. I tell you that everything is okay until you change your mind about it, dreamer of the dream. This reality is only your dream. It is not more than that, and you can step out of here at this moment by changing your thought form associations. Moving mountains, like Master Jesus says, is the least you can do. Why would you bother to do that? You are just reconfigurating the illusion within the limited framework. Can you do that? Wow! You are doing it! Every moment. I am teaching you to die now to live. Let go to live. Change the sequence and shorten the time! Can you hear me? Let those who can hear, hear. Do you hear this? Is that opening up in your mind now? Are you bringing together that perceptual disassociation, that distance in your own body/brain? Are you undergoing a change to open up the Holy Spirit?

Listen, here is the difficulty you have, this is why we need places around the world like God's Country Place, a place where you can come and have the serenity of the disassociation from the conflict of the world. Obviously, if I look at the clock now, I see that it is a particular time. That immediately places me in association with getting up this morning, going through the day, and ending this day. The next thing you know, you are planning for your pension and for your vacations. The idea that you can stop doing that is obviously not looked on with favor in a world that bases its reality on the passing of time and your termination. Why? You will stop buying life insurance policies. Finally, you will stop sending your children to school in order to establish some sort of posterity, so that when you are dead, they can go on living. Do you see why whole thought is attacked?

Where do you seek solace for this attack, which is inevitably going to come in the judgment of you in your previous associations? Hopefully, in this maturation of mind, there are other brothers, other teachers, who are speeding up their time. This is what Jesus calls the Circle of Atonement, so that you can come together, so that there is value in your coming together in the exchange of the energy mind associations with us.

So, here is what you do: You begin with the positive admission that there is no way out of the dilemma of sequential time except by the relinquishment of the limited self. This is all fundamental initiation teaching. You make the admission to the necessity for transformation of your mind on an individual basis. Then, let everything that you do, each moment within this apparent sequencing, be directed to this certain assertion that, as Jesus would say in the *Course*, you can shorten time indefinitely. You can literally bring it to a close. Why? While you may not know that you have invented perception, you in fact have. The admission that you have, since obviously you have the knowledge within your framework for a future reference use, why not use your future reference now and come whole in the sharing of our reality?

If there is in fact an evolution of mind and you have made that statement, why not make it a mutation and bring about the end, to the glory and the realization that you never really left Heaven, and that you are really here in glory now with the whole brotherhood? Is that individual? Sure. But we do understand; we know the dilemma of the associate phenomena of the miracle which you are denying. You are seeing miracles now in this new framework of you happening all around you, and you are perforce made to deny them and you are forced back into the limited perception by your previous associations. Don't do it any more. The heck with it. Now you have a legitimate choice whether to proceed along the human route to death or to step back, as Jesus would say, and say, "NO! There is a different way to look at this, and I'm going to find it." Then, more and more, you make that commitment. And each time you do, you come closer to when time ended, because remember, time ended when it began. You are completing a journey that really never occurred.

You are simply awakening. I am awake. I am in your dream. You cannot possibly fit me into the sequencing. If you would accept that, it would be of great benefit to you. No matter what you do – you can deny me, you can attack me, you can admit to me, you can do anything you want, but I will not fit into your category because I proclaim to you there is no such thing as this category. It is like I am coming along and literally shaking you awake. Come on. I am doing it with love and understanding. You are the one that has constructed these things you see – the sickness and the pain. Why not just let it go? What are you afraid of? Love can only be letting go of fear. Is that the same as letting go of self? Hey, self is fear. Change that line to: Love is letting go of self. Wow! Simply give up. Relinquish your defense mechanisms and remember the wholeness and love of Universal Consciousness.

Remember, I just told you, I know you. We all know each other perfectly well. We are reminiscing about this, and have come back for a moment in this fabric of dream to share in the Atonement, to repair the rent of eternity that caused the momentary unreal schism, for which you feel the guilt and responsibility that I share with you for just a moment. This is the Atonement. This is the covenant or the agreement that we shared, the acknowledgment of the horrendous error that never happened.

Wake up and come on home! We will see you, as we see you garbed in Light. Let these changes happen to you. Let the miracle occur. Come on. Do you know we could see you soon in person for just a moment and that our job in the atonement is to come into your minds.

I can come into your mind right now. If there aren't any separate thoughts – a lovely idea. There is no real distance between us in time or space. That is impossible. I am with you always, even unto the end of the world. That is what I do. Why is that so hard for you? You were afraid of that. Boy, is that intimate. Don't get too close to me, like Jesus said. You let me walk alongside of you, but you are not going to really integrate me. Why? You would become me. You simply would immediately spring into your own Christhood. That's what we teach. That is really the declaration I am making to you now.

This has been a talk on time. But we can't talk about time without talking about eternity, because they are opposites, as long as there is an idea of opposites in your mind. Remember, though that they don't communicate at all. Associate thoughts do not communicate with reality because reality is a single thought at the creation of a whole mind – we will call it God for a moment. He made you perfectly within the totalness. It has nothing to do with the sequential notations that you have about yourself.

Wake up, dear brother, wake up. We love you. We will see you soon. Reach up, and come to your Light for just a moment. This is your assignment. Be happy. You are free. Be free. Wow! That's it.

Time is not sequential. That is, time being consciousness of association of thought, or space really, is not sequential. Finally, if there is only a single time, this moment, that would be as close as the idea of time could get to *no time*. These are abstractions, but I'll give you the thoughts anyway. Any reasonable mind can see that eternity, that is *no time*, is the opposite of time. Now, you can then do all sorts of machinations with your mind in relationship ideas of associations between beginnings and ends, and you call that life! And indeed it is life, but it is in conflict finally with, or it is a disassociation from, eternity – or the single certainty of truth and wholeness.

You can get into Socratic discussions about time and no time, and the number one and the impossibility of two, and the certainty of subjective reality. And that's fun, and a lot of you guys like to hear it. We will do that. Let's get into quantum, and we will make statements that everything contains the whole, or everything is going on at one time. Your mind contains all of the aspects and degrees of nonlinear time in a congruity of reality, and your mind is all a part of it. These are all true statements. Here you are sitting, and you are doing *A Course in Miracles*, for example. Jesus teaches no time, and you pluck out of the *Course* statements like, "You can get this over a period of time," or statements like, "This can take a very long time to do" – that is in the Teacher's Manual because we have to give it to you. We cannot take from you the mechanism of decision within a perceptual framework. And that, dear brother, is what linear or progressive time is.

Now let's get to what you don't want to talk about, great philosophers. What you don't want to do is make application of your pseudo-philosophies into the psychology of the forgiveness of your past frames of reference. What does Jesus say? *Time is a sleight of hand*. The free-willists do not like the idea that everything has been determined. We will give them total freedom within the determinist framework of the inevitability that all time is past. But we will not allow them to have the will to annihilate, because the will to annihilate or to obliviate is impossible.

You are nothing but a conglomeration of grievances. You have brought with you into this framework an idea of lack or need or defense or attack. You might just as well stop, philosophers, with what you are doing right now and take a look at the associations that you have brought with you in this particular karma frame of reference – the images that you have projected from yourself. You must, if you are going to do this *Course* in initiation, if you are going to come to me, if you are going to make declarations of your need for transformation, you are going to have to go to the fundamental issues of the refusal of you to accept the inevitable statement that you are inflicting pain on yourself. Until you get that, you don't have anything. This is what Master Jesus says. This is really all the *Course* teaches.

I know you don't want to hear it, but we might as well start with this premise. There is no sense in telling me that you are practicing forgiveness, that is absurd. Practicing forgiveness is an attack on reality. Everybody smiles, and says, "Yes, well, I'm certainly working on giving up my grievances." What absurdity. You are nothing but a grievance. Somewhere within your framework you really believe, in this dream, that you have constructed and placed these images outside of you in this little wherever you think you are – dismal alcove, Jesus calls it. You are letting these dream thoughts that you send out come back and attack you! If that's not hallucinating, what is it? But that being said, until you are willing to address it in relationship with yourself, there is no sense in coming to me with all the philosophies. There is a lovely so-called transpersonal psychologist named Ken Wilber. Maybe you know of him. He wrote some lovely notations of the merger and advancing of consciousness in the evolutionary process to the certainty of truth. He presents it beautifully until he reaches a point of his own psychology, and then he makes inane statements like, "I wish my guru would go up onto a mountain top so I wouldn't have to judge him, so that I could put him separate from my own reality." He makes no real attempt to judge himself in relationship with the illusion. My direction to you is this: You have all of the power in your mind. The only time the transformation can occur is now. If you will give up your past previous associations of yourself in this sequential time, you will undergo a change in the quality of the time. This is really what forgiveness is.

There are elements contained in this teaching that smack of detachment to the point of surrender. Obviously you guys on this so-called serious spiritual path have the notion that you are going to understand God. You are very determined that, within this framework of your grievance and limitation, you will bring to whole truth your ideas about what God ought to be. But if we use the word *surrender*, you don't like it. "I know, but, let's all get together and pull together and we can solve these problems." How do you solve the problem of death? Your mind has already constructed the problem of termination – this is the whole notation that you are sequencing time, isn't it? And I say Don't Do That!

How can we teach that, then, in the psychology? I'm going to tell you how. Are you ready? Here's what I teach: DIE NOW! We have got them now, haven't we? Everyone who comes here, comes here for no reason but to put off the inevitable. How absurd. Is there another choice between fending off or protecting myself from disease, sickness and death and disharmony and jealousy and hatred and greed? Is there any other choice? Yes! There is a choice not to participate in it at all. There is a choice to simply look at it and say, "The heck with this. I can't do it. There's got to be another power. There has to be something else in my mind other than my human relationships, and my perceptual falsity. There has to be." And, of *Course*, there is. But you can't know that until you let go of your own concepts. Is this forgiveness? Yes, naturally. It's resist not evil. It's turn the other cheek. It's walk the extra mile. It's serve your brother. Why? You are only serving yourself. Why? You are only forgiving yourself. How easy, yet how difficult. You guys out there, you don't want to hear this, but I'm telling you, you have to hear it. How long before you hear it? You always heard it. When will that be? It always was. Then you say, "I'm not going to listen to you anymore," and you shut the book.

When will you finally make a decision, or when *did* you make the decision to take this initiatory step? When the pain got too intense. When you finally woke up one morning and you looked, and you said, "Hey, what is going on here? My 14 year old just got run over by a truck. I'm in a condition of fear that my pension has been lost. I worked for 50 years. There is no justice here. There is no one I can rent my rage on any longer." Maybe then you will take a deep breath and read what Master Jesus says in the *Course. You are doing this to yourself. You are in conflict with reality. You are asleep. This isn't so.* Does this take a certain temerity on your part? Do you have to test your spirit against the determination of the pseudo-consciousnesses to stay here and die? Of course! This is what you don't want to do. Remember they are only your previous judgments in association with yourself. They have no reality.

Somehow I moved from the beginning of this talk, which was a talk on time and space, into a talk on grievance. But remember this, Time is Grievance. Time is the notation that you can work out a solution to a problem that is nonexistent. If the problem does exist, there is no eternity because you would have two things: time and eternity. That is not possible. Only a split mind would think that it could be separate from the whole. How does it identify itself? By its previous memory associations within the whole fabric of time. In reality, the closest that you can get to eternity is this moment. This will be an indication then, of the possibility of separation – the acknowledgment of that position of separation and the return in time to the impossibility of it. This is the schism. How long did it take? How long do you want it to have taken? A thousand years, a million years, just a moment?

Let's go to the premise: Your perceptual mind has invented time. In fact, perceptual mind is an invention of time and space. Beyond you, beyond this little association of memories that have no meaning in your sleeping mode, there is a whole, bright, true, loving reality. If you look at what we are presenting to you now, you will be able to see that I am contained within your framework of perception. If that is true, the admission that I am instructing you from outside of time – the admission that in fact I have come at your direction to instruct you outside of time – would be very beneficial to you. Are you ready to do that? You don't like to do that. You attack me for presenting you with your power. I give you all power of mind, and you attack me in order to not to have to assume responsibility for the projections of your hatred and greed which are outside of you. You say to me, "Well, I'm going to work that out in time." Dear brother, you will never work it out! There is no future. Your futures are always based on your previous frames of reference in association with sequential time. You literally are covering your now. You cover your eternity.

Those of you who feel the glorious stirrings now of singularity that are coming into the mechanisms of decision that are contained in your perceptual body/brain will begin to really like what I'm saying. Why? Because the miracle is starting to occur to you, and the previous images or forms that you established and identified outside of you and then brought together in the falsity of sequential time improve or become brighter in relationship with themselves, and you undergo the metamorphosis to New Mind that transcends the nothingness of the association of the distance between cause and effect. Does anybody hear me? This is nothing but a metamorphosis, an awakening. I'm going to give you, for a moment, the idea of evolution with a statement that the cognition that *I am aware that I am aware*, which is a conflict of the ego, is a necessary step in the evolution of the consciousness in its return from potential to reality. But what possible excuse could you afford me, if you are in that statement of acknowledgment, and have reached any sort of definitive conclusion that you are the cause, through your perception, of the pain of your brother and the pain of yourself and all the terrible things that are happening in your nightmare, that you simply would not step back and say, *'I am not going to do this anymore?"* The strange idea that something can die, that you will go through a process of aging and death, and that sometime in the future you will be able to do this, is exactly what is holding you in your death process. What you are saying to me, literally, is, "I would rather stay in time and become diseased, age and die, than listen to what you are telling me."

The scribes, the consciousnesses that are practicing their perceptual observations of *A Course in Miracles,* are denying the fundamental principle of the *Course.* They are very fearful of the fundamental teachings of the *Course* that consciousness is singular and whole, and that they are that consciousness, and that the admission of the falsity of their associations, the bringing together of the evil and the good, is what the transformation is. Is their alter defiled? Sure, it is defiled by the guilt of their conceptual associations. My proclamation to you is that sin and sickness and death are not real, and your associations with love and truthfulness and kindness within your sequential time framework is what death is. If you will look at the absurdity of sequential time, you can see very plainly that life, as you define it – as though life had to be defined – is based on your ultimate termination. That cannot be life! Life based on death?! If the qualification for life is not being dead, and that seems reasonable to you, you might as well stop reading.

I say to you, unqualifyingly, that consciousness is singular, that truth is whole, that there is no death. There is no such thing as termination.

How many are ready to hear the simple statement that there is no sickness and death, that they are whole, that they are the only living Son of God (as Jesus would say in the *Course*). That doesn't have to mean anything. All that has to mean is that you are living and that you are whole and singular mind and there is no conflict going on outside of you. The notation of future conflict – the need to store, the need to hold on, the need to possess – is only an indication of the limitation of your mind, that's all.

We started out this wonderful talk on the perceptions of time, and the fabric of time, and the quality of time, and we end up saying, "Why don't you forgive your brother? Why don't you try to experience the pain that you are causing to him?" Then you will see that the inane statements you make to me like, "Well I know I'm the cause of this, and I'm going to work it out," are nonsense. When you begin to feel your brother's pain, you will stop doing it, brother. And I assure you that if the process of knowing is giving, if the process of being is giving, when you give pain you must be holding onto it. Come on. These are lovely statements of relinquishment. I think it is time you did it. We are with you here. I am with you here in this dream, for just a moment, as you instructed me, to the awakening, to the glory of your realization of remembering that this is not real. Come on home! We have a base in the Pleiades, we will pick you up there. We closed off this section a long time ago. You like that story? It was a screw up, but it has been taken care of. Is a screw up the same as a mistake? Yes. Do you want to admit to the mistake? Why not? If the mistake has caused you all the problems, why don't you simply admit to it and spring into Heaven? Why hang on to them? The ship is leaving any minute. Are you at the rendezvous point? The covenant – you have this deep in your cellular memories – is the certainty that what I am saying is true. Get excited about it, brother! This is your way out, and you can remember it. We love you.

Let's look at this through the teachings of Master Jesus and the *Course in Miracles* for just a moment. We are proclaiming to you that time is not sequential, that every thought that has ever been in all memory is contained in you. If you want to call memory – consciousness – your genetic code, that's perfectly all right with me. If you can gather together all the notations of relationalship thought, and you want to call that an evolutionary process – you want to show me how the zygote evolves through the phases to a metamorphosis of a human being – I'll take all of that. Do that with me. What I want to show you is that finally, finally, the universe is only mind, and mind in perception must be the mechanism of decision. By bringing together the variant mechanisms that you have made application of to hold yourself in the limited framework of consciousness, you can indeed transform. This is early in the *Course* where Master Jesus is talking about guilt. This is Chapter 13. What He says is this: Guilt has nothing at all to do with right or wrong or sin or sickness. Guilt is simply the organization of your own thought system. You are going to be responsible for the associate thoughts. There is a sentence in Chapter 13 where the Master says that it may seem strange to you that you have no need to order your thoughts in any direction. In fact, if you do, you will hold yourself separate from the truth. Listen to this: Here is an admission that it is possible for perception, for a moment, to be true, you transcendalists out there. The moment of truth that you have come into is a perceptual truth, but what is involved?

Finding The Present: To perceive truly is to be aware of all reality through the awareness of your own. Isn't that something?!?! *But for this no illusions can rise to meet your sight, for reality leaves no room for any error. This means that you perceive a brother –* you see the things outside of you, you see your associations – *only as you see him now.* Are you ready to really look at this? I will show you what forgiveness really is in your mind. You see your brother only as you see him now. Why? *His past has no reality in the present, so you cannot see it.* This is literally the way I look at you, if you care to look at what a whole mind is. No matter what you would present me with in a perceptual evaluation of yourself and your need to associate with me, I assure you that it means absolutely nothing to me or to any whole mind. The idea that you are going to formulate yourself from our previous associations and present to me a program of relationship doesn't mean anything. It doesn't mean anything to any advanced teacher. He is simply going to look right through you and say what? You are the only living Son of God! *His past has no reality in the present, so you cannot see it.* Now, this is if you have true perception. *Your past reactions to him are also not there, and if it is to them that you react, you see but an image of him that you make and cherish instead of him.* That has to do with whether you love him or hate him. You can cherish hate just as much as love, and you do. You actually construct this image based on your previous reactions to him, and this is nonsense, and perceptual mind does it. It bases its reality on its past, doesn't it? *In your questioning of illusions, ask yourself if it is really sane to perceive what was as now. If you remember the past as you look upon your brother, you will be unable to perceive the reality that is now.* Later on, in Chapter 17, Jesus will say that when you look at him, you are literally seeing no thing! He is an image of your past associations, or of your future associations, which is a prognostication of devastation since it is based on a previous frame of reference – that's the apocalypse, right?

You consider it "natural" – this is the condition of the human mind – *to use your past experience as the reference point from which to judge the present. Yet this is unnatural because it is delusional. When you have learned to look on everyone with no reference at all to the past, either his or yours as you perceived it, you will be able to learn from what you see now. For the past can cast no shadow to darken the present, unless you are afraid of light.* This is exactly what you are afraid of! You are afraid of the true you, so you hold yourself in the bondage. You are possessed by your previous thought relationships. Oh, my goodness! *And only if you are would you choose to bring darkness with you, and by holding it in your mind, see it as a dark cloud that shrouds your brothers and conceals their reality from your sight.*

This darkness is in you. The Christ as revealed to you now has no past, for He is changeless, and in His changelessness lies your release. For if He is as He was created, there is no guilt in Him. No cloud of guilt has risen to obscure Him, and He stands revealed in everyone you meet because you see Him through Himself. What a lovely sentence! You see Him through Himself. *To be born again is to let the past go, and look without condemnation upon the present. The cloud that obscures God's Son to you IS the past, and if you would have it past and gone, you must not see it now. If you see it now in your illusions, it has not gone from you, although it is not there.* This is the whole basis of forgiveness. Here are the sentences that we are going to read about time. Listen:

Time – which is your invention, is completely abstract, it's a condition of the mind – *can release as well as imprison, depending on whose interpretation of it you use. Past, present and future are not continuous, unless you force continuity on them. You can perceive them as continuous, and make them so for you.* And you do. *But do not be deceived, and then believe that this is how it is. For to believe reality is what you would have it be according to your use for it is delusional. You would destroy time's continuity* – now wait, we gave time continuity, and I'll come back to that – *by breaking it into past, present and future for your own purposes. You would anticipate the future on the basis of your past experience, and plan for it accordingly. Yet by doing so you are aligning past and future, and not allowing the miracle* of whole-mindedness *which could intervene between them, to free you to be born again.*

Notice that we use the word *continuity*. The direction, then, is to bring all of your thoughts together in one statement of forgiveness, to what? Remember the now, and to make yourself whole through that remembering!

The miracle enables you to see your brother without his past, and so perceive him as born again. His errors are all past, and by perceiving him without them you are releasing him. And since his past is yours, you share in his release. Do you hear that? His past is only yours! Why? He is only a memory that you have. For goodness sake! If you are holding a grievance against him, with all of this so-called reincarnation, I would suggest that you release him, and get away from your modality of attack and defense.

Judgment and condemnation are behind you, and unless you bring them with you, you will see that you are free of them. Look lovingly upon the present, for it holds the only things that are forever true. All healing lies within it because its continuity is real. No conflict! *It extends to all aspects of the Sonship at the same time, and thus enables them to reach each other.* There is no distance between your thoughts and the end of the universe. Isn't that lovely? Ready? *The present is before time was, and will be when time is no more. In it are all things that are eternal, and they are one. Their continuity is timeless and their communication is unbroken, for they are not separated by the past. Only the past can separate, and it is nowhere.* Wow! Isn't that lovely? Statement from where? Out of time! If you would like to stop for a moment and think about it, and look at what I just read you, go ahead. The assertions of a whole mind, out of body, in the declarations of what you just read – that is an extraordinary thing!

Why don't you begin with the concept that what you just read, and what I am presenting to you, is real? At least seriously entertain the possibility that sickness and death and sequential time are not real. As you look out at the night sky and see 100,000 trillion stars with 5,000 million billion so-called individual inhabitants, wouldn't it be time for you to at least tentatively accept responsibility for the earth? For goodness sake, why would that be such a big deal for you? You are running along this string of time. As you return from the potential back to the source, time becomes faster. I am encouraging you to shorten time by igniting your memory relationships within the potential of your reality. Can you do that right now and step out of time? Dear brother, you are out of time in reality. The part of you that is performing this ritual of return has no reality to me at all. We stopped by to do a little cultivating in this section of the galaxy. We are repairmen, for goodness sake. What is the Christ if He's not a repairman? That's another talk.

We are given particular assignments. We assume memory garbs, and we simply come in to reconnect the disassociation – the break in the communication that occurred within the fabric of time. Isn't that fun?! Come with me now, out of time, let's jump back out for a little while, and then decide on another mission, and you can come back. But allow me my mission. Since I have a perception of you, you must be included – are included, and were included – in this time fabric, with my salvation which is accomplished and evident to me. Wow! Come and be with me, dear loved ones. I have created you in the perfection of the certainty that my Father created me in wholeness, love and beauty. There is no fault in us. Together we stand in awe.

It is inevitable, if you are going to look at how your mind sequences time, that you are going to have to look at your own demise or death. This is the objection that I present you with. If what I am teaching you is true, and I am sure it is, you obviously have constructed your own destruction or annihilation within your genetic memory of time. It is impossible that this not be so. You make an admission of it, as though somehow time is going to run its course within you, and you are going to disappear. What a strange idea! (Time on my hands, till the end of time.)

You are so preoccupied with time, as though you can really use it up! The idea of using up time is the idea of aging. And the idea of sickness or a little death is the whole idea that you can actually use up time. So you have a time clock built in you in a genetic association and you literally grow old and you die, and I make this proclamation to you: *that's impossible.* If you will stop associating with your linear time sequences, you will not get old. Those of you who have come around us now and are feeling the energy of unity and continuity are springing up to life and have brightness around you and are becoming spirited. In this healing process, how young you look because you see that aging is an absurd notation.

You look in the mirror, consciousnesses identified with the body, and we will paint lipstick on you and put fashion on a skeleton and then you watch it age around you. Obviously that is not occurring! In no sense are you really aging. How could you? You insist that you are, but that is only because you have identified yourself in that structure of the body. But there is only a single consciousness contained in every fabric of you, in every microcosm, in every cell, that must be this light of reality. And it is. And through taking it all – this is the way Jesus teaches it in the *Course* – to taking every thought that you ever could have, which is all the thoughts that there are, since an idea cannot leave its source and go anywhere, you simply bring it all together in the single memory of the wholeness of you.

My declaration to you is that there is a process, and there has always been with man – the secret wisdom of illumination – that you can do this. I declare to you that it is an individual process. You can't do it in accord with the projections that are outside of you in the denial of this. If you can hear us, let us know. I know you are out there. How much pain are you going to continue to inflict on yourself in your determination not to see how simple salvation really is? As much as you need to, I guess. But whenever you say, "I'm going to keep on doing this," it is just an indication that you are not in the pain. I hate to tell you this, but you have given the pain to your brother, because all around you is pain. If you can somehow console yourself with the terrible things of hell – and this is where you are, in hell – you go ahead and do it, my brother. Obviously, then, you have not accepted responsibility for what is occurring. Those of you who have gone out in high service in time and retained an identity of satisfaction in the deliverance of your brother through the attitudes of service and giving realize this: You remain the constructor of this. Until you come to know that only service to God or Truth has value, and not service to your self imaging, will you get this. I know that is a big step, but come and take it now with us in this incredible statement that The Time Is Now! We will be in Heaven together. We'll see you soon.

That being said, let's have a quiet time together. Lay down your past associations. Still your minds. Now if you feel the thrill of anticipation of what is occurring to you, and you can feel it in these words, just keep being free-flowing with your mind. Don't hold on. Your mind will seek real high levels. We will teach you a very active meditation. Utilize all of your thoughts, but don't hold on to any of them. Keep letting them go. You will come right to the Light. The salvation of the world depends on *you*, not on the effects that you have constructed outside of yourself to retain death-sequencing in your mind. Come home. We hope you will join us now in this *Course* in individual transformation. We are not an establishment here. We are a guide to your reality. Seek and ye shall find. Knock and it will be opened unto you, dear brother. We hope you will come and spend some time with us. You can hear this. You let us know. We have been looking for you for a very long time. Now we have found you and we are going to let you come home. Come on home.

Jesus Christ,
The Miracle Worker

The confession of personal saviorship involves the intimacy of this karma memory contact that you have had throughout the ages with the spirit, or as the Christ, in association with your own karma memories. As this unfolds now, in this period in your own memory patterns, it is very obvious to you that contained in you is all the memory of this Christhood. So the statements made by Master Jesus in the *Course in Miracles*, which indicate dramatically and directly that you are the savior of the world, will be entertained more directly by you in the romance of your own cyclical journey through time. And you will remember when you came into the village late at night and stayed in this little thatch-roofed hut before the oil lamps to confess the certainty of this mysterious communication of the Christ, of the energy, of the new you, of the emergence of the new man, the drama being played on this little planet, this little place, this dream.

How real it then becomes to you and now, as you sit wherever you are with yourself, you begin what? To re-enact once again the part of your Christhood as you did before. This time with more certainty. This time with more alacrity. This time with more determination. This time with more definitive results apparent, because you are closer to the certainty that the things being projected from you are actually a part of your wholeness and through this self-expression, then, you begin to create. Certainly in this regard, the auspices of Master Jesus

Christ, the great man become God, as expressed in the new era in the *Course in Miracles,* would be an extremely valuable tool – and was a valuable tool for you, wasn't it? How very personal then is your association with this man-God since you are man-God in association directly with Him and, in fact, are Him manifest in this timeframe – it is not different than that. That is the teaching of the scripture of the *Course in Miracles.*

What I am going to do, since I am revealing to that Truth, will be to draw you to what Master Jesus says personally in His intervention statements through the channel of the *Course* in regard to your saviorship, and in particular association with Him and what He is. I am going to do it very briefly or very certainly now with the real, real dramatic statement that occurs in one of the early chapters of the *Course* that is actually, if you would care to look at it, an absolute statement of all that Christianity is. Here, suddenly, sitting right in front of you, in the English language is something that you can understand within this framework of time. It will be a statement by an historic figure who you have identified in your perceptions – Jesus Christ, crucified, teaching for only three years and then gone and 2000 years later will make the statement that I'm going to read you for about the next five minutes, that directly proclaims first His saviorship and then yours in the immediate association that you have in your body/mind with Him. That's exceptional.

You listen to this now: *The Gift of Freedom.* The first paragraph contains a Socratic declaration. Listen: *If God's Will for you is complete peace and joy, unless you experience only this you must be refusing to acknowledge His Will.* Now there is a negative statement that cuts right to the core of the whole teachings of all saviorship of Christ, of my certainty of your maturation of mind. If you are not experiencing peace and happiness and joy it must be that you are refusing to acknowledge the dharma, the total will of the energy of Truth and Love. It cannot *not* be so. *His Will does not vacillate, being changeless forever. When you are not at peace it can only be because you do not believe you are in Him.* What a lovely sentence. *You do not believe that you are in Him.* Yet since He is singular, if you are not in Him, you are nowhere. So it must be that if you are separate from Him you are in a condition of nowhereness.

Yet He is All in all. His peace is complete and you must be included in it. His laws – now, these are the singularity laws – *govern you because they govern everything. You cannot exempt yourself from His laws, although you can disobey them.* How about that? You cannot disobey His laws in reality, but certainly in your own perceptual mind – not in Truth. *Yet if you do, and only if you do, you will feel lonely and helpless, because you are denying yourself everything.* Certainly you can see that if you would deny yourself God or deny yourself a single thing you would subsequently being denying yourself immediately of everything, because you would then have to assume the responsibility for the assemblage of the thought outside of the wholeness which is God. Now these are Jesus' words and these are His statements. This is early in the *Course*, and now He is going to declare Himself. Are you ready for this?

I am come as a light into a world that does deny itself everything. It does this simply by dissociating itself from everything. It is therefore an illusion of isolation, maintained by fear of the same loneliness that is its illusion. Can you understand that? What a lovely phrase. Now these from the mouth of Jesus Christ: *I said that I am with you always, even unto the end of the world. That is why I am the light of the world. If I am with you in the loneliness of the world, the loneliness is gone.* You cannot dissociate yourself from yourself. *You cannot maintain the illusion of loneliness if you are not alone. My purpose, then, is still to overcome the world. I do not attack it, but my light must dispel it because of what it is. Light does not attack darkness, but it does shine it away.* And shows that it was never there. *If my light goes with you everywhere, you shine it away with me. The light becomes ours, and you cannot abide in darkness any more than darkness can abide wherever you go.* You listen: *The remembrance of me is the remembrance of yourself, and of Him Who sent me to you.* What a declaration, dear brothers, of the singular association of our own masterful minds, this declaration of the trinity.

Listen: *You were in darkness until God's Will was done completely by any part of the Sonship. When this was done, it was perfectly accomplished by all.* It is impossible that this not be so. How else could it be perfectly accomplished? *My mission was simply to unite the will of the Sonship with the Will of the Father by being aware of the Father's Will myself."* This is exactly what your assignment is, dear teachers of God. *This is the awareness I came to give you –*And you listen *–and your problem in accepting it is the problem of this world.* I am giving you the awareness of the certainty of your own Sonship, of your own Godhood. *The world must therefore despise and reject me, because this world is the belief that love is impossible.* Of course. If love is possible there could not be a world, or sickness, or pain and death. *If you will accept the fact that I am with you, you are denying the world and accepting God.* You are denying the world and accepting God. *My will is His, and your decision to hear me is the decision to hear His Voice and abide in His Will. As God sent me to you so will I send you to others. And I will go to them with you, so we can teach them peace and union.*

You can call that scripture if you want to. Those are declarations of a wholly awakened mind, out of body, speaking to you from another plane or level of consciousness, directly to the association that we have here in this dream. Now this is what I am going to be addressing: The idea of the absolute connection in time at this moment with your saviorship and the necessity for you, through your atonement, through your at-one-ment, to save the world for indeed the world is your dream.

Do you not think that the world needs peace as much as you do? Do you not want to give it to the world as much as you want to receive it? For unless you do, you will not receive it. This is the whole notion that as the savior of the world – the world being your mind – your ideas must be extended from you in the certainty of your perception of yourself – the truth of you in association with this divine will of God, for you to perfect the world in your own mind. *If you want to have it of me, you must give it.* The only proof of having everything, if you care to look at it with me, would be by giving it away. That is the proof that you have it. That is the action of creating. *Healing does not come from anyone else. You must accept guidance from within. The guidance must be what you want, or it will be meaningless to you.* No matter what I tell you in this regard, if you don't want it, if you don't want the peace of God, if you can't see that the things that you have constructed in your mind are withering and dying and hopeless, you will not want the things we are offering you and this is the whole basis of the teaching. *This is why healing is a collaborative venture. I can tell you what to do, but you must collaborate by believing that I know what you should do. Only then will your mind choose to follow me. Without this choice you could not be healed because you would have decided against healing* – which is what the earth is – *and this rejection of my decision for you makes healing impossible*. This is the direct statement that if one mind is healed all mind is healed. This is also the direct statement that if you are unhealed, if you consider yourself to be separate, if you resist the power of this certainty, you are the single mind in resistance to it. You literally become what? The anti-Christ. Of course.

Healing reflects our joint will. This is obvious when you consider what healing – bringing together – *is for. Healing is the way in which the separation is overcome. Separation is overcome by union. It cannot be overcome by separating. The decision to unite must be unequivocal, or the mind itself is divided and not whole.*" This is obviously the way the perceptual mind is, the way the human mind is, isn't it? Listen. *Your mind is the means by which you determine your own condition, because mind is the mechanism of decision*. Mind is the mechanism of decision! *It is the power by which you separate or join, and experience pain or joy accordingly. My decision cannot overcome yours, because yours is just as powerful as mine. If it were not so the Sons of God would be unequal*. That's absurd because God creates singularly, doesn't He? *All things are possible through our joint decision, but mine alone cannot help you. Your will is as free as mine, and God Himself would not go against it* – and cannot and does not know of it. *I cannot will what God does not will. I can offer my strength to make you invincible, but I cannot oppose your decision without competing with it and thereby violating God's Will for you*. That is a statement of free will. Look at that very carefully. That is not a statement that you can choose to die or be in pain or construct a world outside of God. You can assert this power to do it but you can not make it real.

Nothing God created can oppose your decision, as nothing God created can oppose His Will. God gave your will its power, which I can only acknowledge in honor of His. If you want to be like me, I will help you, knowing that we are alike. If you want to be different – this is a statement of time – *I will wait until you change your mind. I can teach you, but only you can choose to listen to my teaching. How else can it be, if God's Kingdom is freedom? Freedom cannot be learned by tyranny of any kind, and the perfect equality of all God's Sons cannot be recognized through the dominion of one mind over another. God's Sons are equal in will, all being the Will of their Father. This is the only lesson that I came to teach.* This lesson, now, being taught by Jesus through these words, through me, through you, are the statements that our minds are singular and we are whole, that we are indivisible as created by God.

If your will were not mine it would not be our Father's. This would mean you have imprisoned yours, and have not let it be free. Of yourself you can do nothing, because of yourself you are nothing. Of yourself you can do nothing because of yourself you are nothing! *I am nothing without the Father and you are nothing without me, because by denying the Father you deny yourself. I will always remember you, and in my remembrance of you lies your remembrance of yourself. In our remembrance of each other lies our remembrance of God. And in this remembrance lies your freedom because your freedom is in Him. Join, then, with me in praise of Him and you whom He created. This is our gift of gratitude to Him, which we will share with all His creations, to whom He gives equally whatever is acceptable to Him. Because it is acceptable to Him it is the gift of freedom, which is His Will for all of His Sons. By offering freedom you will be free.* By offering freedom you will be free!

Freedom is the only gift you can offer to God's Sons, being an acknowledgment of what they are and what He is. Listen! *Freedom is creation, because it is Love.* It has no barriers. It has nothing conflictual about it. You listen to me now in your perceptions, teachers. *Whom you seek to imprison you do not love. Therefore, when you seek to imprison anyone, including yourself, you do not love him and you cannot identify him. When you imprison yourself you are losing sight of your true identification with me and with the Father. Your identification is with the Father and with the Son. It cannot be with one and not the other. If you are part of one you must be a part of the other, because they are one.* Listen: *The Holy Trinity is holy because It is One. If you exclude yourself from this union, you are perceiving the Holy Trinity as separated. You must be included in It, because It is everything. Unless you take your place in It and fulfill your function as part of It, the Holy Trinity is as bereft as you are. No part of It can be imprisoned if Its truth is to be known.* (Text, 8:4) This is exactly the same statement that you have created the world in your own mind, and it is equally valuable if you realize the statements that will follow in the *Course* that there is literally no Heaven without you, that everything is contained in the power of your mind. We are reading the words of the Master Jesus Christ from the *Course in Miracles* which is teaching you of the certainty, that by bringing into association all of your past frames of references in memories of your so-called persecution, that the passion of the resurrection and the transformation of your body/mind can be accomplished – and indeed was accomplished.

We are talking about our brother Jesus Christ of Nazareth, the figure, the perceptual identification. Now we might as well be talking about Nicole Francis, or my brother Carlos Martinez, or my brother anyone, my brother Susan. What would be the difference? What is the difference then in the identification in perceptual consciousness if the relationship of reality is finally man-godly. That is, if the sense of separation which is identified as personality, finally must come into a whole association with its own identity in order to glimpse reality without the sequential obligations of time, without the necessity to continue to what? Dissociate from the fabric of consciousness which is the whole notation of space/time. We are talking about, in this case, since our perceptions are so concrete, a voice out of this range, or out of your range of perceptual consciousness, that is identifying itself as Jesus Christ of Nazareth. How is that different than the fellow across the street who is identifying himself by plowing his field? It is not different at all, except in your mind which is being held in a perceptual connotation of sequential time, isn't it?

What occurs when you sequence consciousness or moment-by-moment reality, you dissociate from the congruity of your own mind, and this is all we really want to present to you. We don't do anything else but this. I was reading from Chapter 8 where Jesus Christ of Nazareth –yes, that's the historic one – who went on just a moment ago and is going on right now, is sitting with us in that idea right now and expressing to us a whole truth. It will not be different than the expression of your whole truth, will it? Because all you are going to do is gather together your previous dissociations in time and bring them into whole declaration of your mind. And I will bet you that if I open the text the next thing that Jesus will talk about will be dissociation, or a break in communication.

Let's look. *The Undivided Will of the Sonship* which means precisely that. *Can you be separated from your identification and be at peace?* How could you be? You are in conflict with yourself and reality. *Dissociation is not a solution; it is a delusion. The delusional believe that truth will assail them, and they do not recognize it because they prefer the delusion. Judging truth as something they do not want, they perceive their illusions which block knowledge.* That is all there is to it.

The undivided will of the Sonship is the perfect creator, being wholly in the likeness of God, Whose Will it is. Now we have it, don't we? Listen: *You cannot be exempt from it if you are to understand what it is and what you are. By the belief that your will is separate from mine, you are exempting yourself from the Will of God which is yourself.* ...from the Will of God which is yourself! *Yet to heal is still to make whole. Therefore, to heal is to unite with those who are like you, because perceiving this likeness is to recognize the Father.* This is exactly what you do in the admission of the falsity of your grievance against the illusions that you have placed out there in your space/time sequence. Are you ready? *If your perfection is in Him and only in Him, how can you know it without recognizing Him?* This is the declaration in perception that you must recognize your own creations of your own mind. Ready? *The recognition of God is the recognition of yourself.* (Text, 8:5)

This is from the *Course in Miracles* and this is a statement by a perceptual consciousness identified as Jesus Christ. If this is the case, somewhere within us we make the admission of the possibility of a consciousness in a higher frequency of organized thought. You might want to say "later on in time" or "closer to the end of this." But in reality, since time is not sequential, the Master Jesus Christ is with us all the time and more than that, is nothing but *you* coming to your own truth. He cannot be more or less than that. Why? Because all the observations of the associations of thoughts are literally not true. Chaos is not true until it becomes whole. The manner in which you organize the chaos has exactly nothing to do with what we are teaching, because when it comes to fullness you will be the Christ and must be. Remaining within the vernacular of your historic karma association – if I may use that term – we will give now, and one of our dear brothers out of time, at the completion of this insertion of energy which we call *A Course In Miracles*, was directed from the chaos to give a definition of our dear Master Jesus Christ. He is smiling here. He is a young awakened mind. Of course, asking for a definition of Christ, he will speak to you in the third person. This is in the Teacher's Manual. He is going to speak to you as if Jesus was third person because you are holding Him in an historic frame of reference. You will notice that as you advance in your own spiritual acumen you may begin to speak of yourself in the third person, too. That's perfectly all right.

The question, sitting right here now among us is Jesus Christ. Let's attempt a definition of Jesus Christ based on the things I am telling you. *There is no need for help to enter Heaven for you have never left.* (TM, C5) See how this beautiful young mind doesn't want to give you the idea that you can validate yourself separate from reality and pretend to use the Christ to get there. Let's chunk through that right now and begin with the certainty that truth is true and nothing else is true and in fact you have never left Heaven. *There is no need for help to enter Heaven for you have never left. But there is need for help beyond yourself as you are circumscribed by false beliefs of your Identity.* Now sit with this a minute. All around you are these thoughts, these genetic memories that are in your self identity, aren't they? And they keep turning on themselves, and time seems to pass. The effort of this message which indeed did succeed is to simply bring you into the realization of your whole mind – to return you from the split mind of time to the reality of yourself. Listen. *Helpers are given you in many forms, although upon the altar they are one.* That is, since everything is only your thought about it, the manner in which you look at it in your self association will be the degree to which it brings about your enlightenment. The truth of the matter is that if you were to glance at anything totally wholly, it wouldn't matter what it is, you would automatically bring your mind together, wouldn't you? That object then would be your savior, I suppose. Why not? It's your whole mind anyway.

Beyond each one of these apparent thoughts or thought-forms *there is the Thought of God, and this will never change. But they have names which differ for a time, for time needs symbols, being itself unreal.* Oh! Oh, I see! Time needs symbols. Why? Because it is unreal itself and so are symbols. Really all we are going to do, then, is gather together all of the thought-forms that have ever been in time, which are contained in us as a memory, and see them wholly unobstructed by the light of our own consciousness. Boy, is that nice. *God does not help because He knows no need.* You might as well hear that right now. *But He creates all Helpers of His Son while he believes his fantasies are true.* Of course. Since the power of God is your mind or God creating, all the help that you could ever need in regard to this must be given to yourself by you. You can deny it if you want to, or you can begin to listen to what we are saying here. That will be your decision. *Thank God for them for they will lead you home.* And did lead you home, didn't they? Now are you ready?

The name of Jesus is the name of one who was a man but saw the face of Christ in all his brothers and remembered God. So he became identified with Christ, man no longer, but at one with God. "A man no longer" means that He no longer was held in the limitation of His perceptual thoughts. That is really all it means, isn't it? That He came together and saw the face of Christ. Are you ready? *The man was an illusion.* Just as you think of yourself as reality. Is that a tough sentence for you, theologians? Of course! The Master Jesus Christ as He identified Himself as a man was obviously illusion. He was in sequential time association and that is not what reality is. *The man was an illusion, for he seemed to be a separate being, walking by himself, within a body that appeared to hold his self from Self, as all illusions do.* This defines a human being, doesn't it? *Yet who can save unless he sees illusions and then identifies them as what they are?* This is the statement of the necessity for a savior to have undergone the atonement.

If you would listen to what I am saying to you, and listen to this voice that is speaking to you, it would begin to become obvious to you that somewhere within this voice constitution there is a different identification of reality – a statement that brings together associate thoughts of separation and presents them to you in a true fashion. This will be true when I read the *Course* to you which are Jesus' words or when I read the words of anyone in my self association of my own reality within the space/time framework. Did that define me? Perhaps. But it will be a false definition. What I am saying is that the thought organization that comes together in enlightenment or true perception will emanate from all consciousnesses who have reached the maturation point of their own admission of whole-mindedness. It cannot *not* be so. *Yet who can save unless he sees illusions and then identifies them as what they are? Jesus remains a Savior because he saw the false without accepting it as true. And Christ needs his form that He might appear to men and save them from their illusions.* And he will do it literally. You have a tendency to take some illusions and separate them from your apparent perceptual reality and give concrete evidence of other illusions. Remember, dear teachers, this is a dream. When you awaken from one perceptual dream, you are simply in another perceptual dream. You are but reliving events in separation, perhaps you might express them as identifications of your passion that historically was realized by Jesus Christ. You have played all these various parts of dissociation and now you are going to assume the role of your own saviorship in association with these apparent characters that re-enact for you the drama of your own death/ life sequencing.

In his complete identification with the Christ – the perfect Son of God, His one creation and His happiness, forever like Himself and one with Him – Jesus became what all of you must be. Not what all of you must *become*, teacher, you listen to this, what all of you must *be. There is no need for help to enter heaven for you have never left.* Now we can look at the idea that the obstruction to what we are teaching you here is contained in your own mind. And that you are literally defending yourself from your own Christhood. Boy, what a statement! We are going to do it with the identification of Jesus Christ. *Jesus became what all of you must be. He led the way for you to follow him. He leads you back to God because he saw the road before him, and he followed it. He made a clear distinction, still obscure to you, between the false and the true. He offered you a final demonstration that it is impossible to kill God's Son; nor can his life in any way be changed by sin and evil, malice, fear or death.* The life of Jesus Christ reformed, reconstituted, resurrected, is exactly the same as it was in your historic frame of reference 2000 years ago, and He sits next to you now with that declaration. Wow! What an auspicious time to be alive! You get kind of suspicious of this. You say, "Well, how could this really be the time?" And I say to you, what other time would there be but now? Isn't this coming into your mind now? Aren't you hearing this now? Aren't you listening to these statements?

And therefore all your sins have been forgiven because they carried no effects at all. This is the same idea as the atonement, where all the ideas you had of falsity have absolutely no effect at all because they were never real from the beginning. The recognition of that in one single mind would have to be the recognition of it in all minds because, indeed, mind is singular. *And so they were but dreams. Arise with him who showed you this because you owe him this who shared your dreams that they might be dispelled. And shares them still, to be at one with you.* This is the burden of light perception that a whole mind that identifies itself as a savior takes on and tolerates the sickness, pain and death of the earth for just a moment, so that you can come to know the truth. And this is the part that you are asked to play, isn't it? You are asked to do this.

Is he the Christ? O yes, along with you. His little life on earth was not enough to teach the mighty lesson that he learned for all of you. Isn't that lovely? *He will remain with you to lead you from the hell you made to God. And when you join your will with his, your sight will be his vision, for the eyes of Christ are shared.* I'm going to do that once more for you: *And when you join your will with his, your sight will be his vision* – there will be no difference between Jesus Christ of Nazareth and you. The vision of truth that shines from you, then, will save the world. *Walking with him is just as natural as walking with the brother whom you knew since you were born, for such indeed he is.* Isn't that lovely? *Some bitter idols have been made of him who would be only brother to the world. Forgive him your illusions, and behold how dear a brother he would be to you. For he will set your mind at rest at last and carry it with you unto your God.*

Is he God's only Helper? No, indeed. For Christ takes many forms with different names until their oneness can be recognized. But Jesus is for you the bearer of Christ's single message of the Love of God. You need no other. It is possible to read his words and benefit from them without accepting him into your life. Of course. *Yet he would help you yet a little more if you will share your pains and joys with him, and leave them both to find the peace of God.* Listen! *Yet still it is his lesson most of all that he would have you learn, and it is this:*

There is no death because the Son of God is like his Father. Nothing you can do can change Eternal Love. Forget your dreams of sin and guilt, and come with me instead to share the resurrection of God's Son. And bring with you all those whom He has sent to you to care for as I care for you. (TM, C5)

These, then, are the statements of your whole mind and the statements of my mind and the statements of the mind of Jesus Christ of Nazareth – the statements of your coming to your Christhood by the inclusion in your mind of the previously disassociated thoughts, the chaos, that just for a moment entered your mind – and it was just a moment, dear brother. This place is not so. These thoughts that you are jockeying around in your mind are not real. Yet you can use them to maturate, to transcend, into this new reality that has always been all about you. You never left Heaven. Isn't that what we said at the beginning of this? It's all about you yet you sleep, contained within this chaotic association of the limitations of your perceptual mind. These are our declarations. These are the declarations of all awakened minds. These are the statements of the non-embodied consciousness of Jesus Christ who continues within this accelerated time framework. What a lovely message where Jesus says we have altered time – the sequence of the fabric of apparent time in order that you may see your own reality. This message is for you, individually, not in consort with the perceptions that you have brought with you in order to deny your own reality. Can you hear this? We hope so! And we hope that you will join us in this circle of atonement. We'll see you soon.

Just for a minute, here's what we're faced with. We're sitting here with the brothers at the kitchen of God's Country Place and we have made an admission here and now that's not really acceptable in theology. The statement is that the scripture emanating from Jesus Christ, as He teaches this in the *Course in Miracles,* is what you would call theology – the statement of truth from the horse's mouth. Jesus smiles. The whole statement of what He is – this is pretty devastating to perceptual mind that has required an establishment of association of thoughts in order to give identity to the Christ. This is why the *Course in Miracles* is not acceptable. But remember, it's no more or less acceptable than any idea of totalitarian, an absolute assertion of uncompromising truth, would be. Yet here we are sitting with the scripture! I don't know where you are in your own framework of time with the admission of the truth of these statements. I think perhaps it would be important from an associate form-thought idea that you begin to entertain the notion that either everything we are saying here is true, or none of it is true, so we can keep you from this false self-identification of your demand to associate these declarations of wholeness with your previous historic falsity. If you begin with the certainty that all of your thoughts are false, and not real, and that there is no sickness, pain and death it would be very beneficial to you. Indeed this is scripture! Indeed this is new Christianity! Indeed this is a statement of uncompromising love which was declared by Jesus Christ 2000 years ago.

The Think System

Listen to what I'm saying just for a minute because it comes to my mind very strongly, sitting here. The idea of specificness versus what we would call extension of singularity, or degrees of truth or spiritualness – one of the great moral allegories in American theater is *The Music Man*. Contained in *The Music Man* is every single element in regard to spiritual awakening and definitions of God in limited context that there is. It starts out immediately with man in defiance of truth, singing a song, "You Have Got to Know the Territory," which is a way of saying, you must think specifically in a relationship of cause and effect in order to communicate. The icon of that is the anvil salesman, who is absolutely concrete. What is he doing? He's seeking out what? The magician. He is searching for the magician. Why? Because the magician is what? Selling an idea. A magician doesn't have to know the territory. Does God have to know the territory? That's absurd. He doesn't have to know the territory. So what does the anvil man say? He said, "He sells band instruments and uniforms and instruction booklets." And the other guy says, "What's wrong with that?" And the anvil salesman says, "He doesn't know a concerted thing. He can't read a note, and he doesn't know a flugel horn from a Jew's harp." Of course not! Why? He has an idea.

Now, when you attempt to convey an idea, you must present duality with a specific problem. So what does the Music Man say to Buddy? He says: "I don't know if I am going to stay here. I must give them a problem, make them recognize..." What? "They have a dilemma." Which he does precisely with the song, "Pool." He gives them an intense problem and shows them that through his idea he can solve the problem. Isn't that nice?

In the allegory of *The Music Man*, here he is, in fundamental extension of love and charity and goodness, why? Because it brings together unity in regard to the community. But what is finally missing? What one element is missing in this? Love. Of course! The element is that love is not in there. And that includes love of himself. What occurs then in the symbol of Marion the Librarian, who what? Perceives the good that he is doing in his relationship in the community. Subsequently – first intellectually and with apparent discernment – overlooks his shortcomings, doesn't she? This is love now, a beautiful example of it. She justifies her reactions to him in an intellectual manner. When finally her ideas about God, which is really what they are, become so intense that denials that are brought directly to her attention by the anvil salesman – by the specific idea that you must look at the parts of this man rather than looking at his wholeness – she finally succumbs totally to the idea of communication with him and loves him totally. What does he do? Responds immediately and loves her. What happens? The Think System, or the *idea*, then triumphs. Obviously! How could it not triumph? Do you see that?

That is a very beautiful example of how man, even unbeknownst to himself, will construct allegories of truth. He inevitably does it. What we are really trying to say here – and this is difficult to get; this is what Jesus teaches in *Course in Miracles* – actually mind, idea, is totally abstract. The moment that it becomes specific, it dies, because it has established a form of reality in judgment outside of itself. This is precisely what Jesus tries to teach in *Course in Miracles*. Now, literally what you have is this: You actually have the choice of being the anvil salesman, which means you literally reduce all life to a single object that you can identify, which is death, concreteness, or you turn totally to an idea of wholeness or truth or love, which is God.

Now, what we are attempting to do with you here is to cause to come about in you, literally, physiologically, mentally, emotionally, morally, in any regard, through action, through passiveness, a recognition momentarily of the containment of Truth or God, versus death. That is all we do. We may do it in a lot of fashions. We can say to you, for example, "If there is a God or truth, there literally cannot be such a thing as death. Period." Now, you will not find that idea here on earth because it is not here. The construction of the earth in your mental process is based on duality or fractured-ism or specific-ism or death. As soon as you limit anything in any regard, you literally die. What we are really trying to get you to do is to think abstractly. And that's difficult, because all of your ideas of selfness are based on false discernment in regard to the memory patterns contained in you in relationship to a false identity. Do you see that?

I can say things on the highest level to you. If you have any form of fear in you, it is literally impossible for you to love. The way that Marion came to know him was simply to look right through all of his fears, all of the possibilities of him what? Not being exactly what she had always waited for. In all of the songs that she sings, she is waiting for what? God. But she doesn't find him where? Outside of herself. She finds him where? In recognition of herself in relationship to the wholeness of the community in her love for him. That's very nice.

You remember this, it is impossible for you to have a form of emotion that is eventually not objective. When you are angry, you must be angry with something, someone, some circumstance, some idea. You may not be able to identify it, but you are. Because anger, death, grief must be what? Specific! They must have an object. The strange idea contained in Christianity as it is taught today, that man as manifest in Jesus is required to go through a physical death process, or be persecuted or tormented, in order to resurrect or discover the truth, is absurd. Death can never lead to life! If there is such a thing as death, there could never be eternity, there could never be life. It literally could not be. You watch the services that go on this Easter in the relationship of man's absolute determination to acknowledge death rather than God. He absolutely will do it. He cannot *not* do it. It is the manner in which he is constructed.

I'm going to read you just a minute from Course in Miracles while it's on my mind because I want you to get this. Oh, I could mention this, but this may not help you. Listen. *Complete abstraction is the natural condition of the mind. But part of it now is unnatural. It does not look on everything as one. It sees instead but fragments of the whole, for only thus could it invent the partial world you see. The purpose of all seeing is to show you what you wish to see. All hearing but brings to your mind the sounds it wants to hear.*

Thus were specifics made. And now it is specifics we must use in practicing. You see that? Listen. *One brother is all brothers. Every mind contains all mind, for every mind is one. Such is the truth. Yet do these thoughts make clear the meaning of creation? Do these words bring perfect clarity with them to you? What can they seem to you but empty sounds; pretty, perhaps, correct in sentiment, yet fundamentally not understood nor understandable. The mind that taught itself to think specifically can no longer grasp abstraction in the sense that it is all-encompassing. We need to see a little, that we can learn a lot.* (Lesson 161) Wow. That is high truth. That is what we are teaching.

If you will come on a day-by-day and moment-by-moment basis to see this, it will help you in relationship with yourself. As you come more and more into your own focus of truth, keep in mind every moment, as much as you can, that you literally cannot die. This will help you. Inevitably you are translating in a false pattern of who you are from yesterday to tomorrow. You cannot do it. You literally think that you can get up and walk out of here and go somewhere and do something. You all do. You can't. You are dealing with yourself directly in your own limitations, and because of that, are in direct association with your own death. You have to be.

Course in Miracles, Lesson 163: *Death is a thought that takes on many forms, often unrecognized. It may appear as sadness, fear, anxiety or doubt; as anger, faithlessness and lack of trust; concern for bodies, envy, and all forms in which the wish to be as you are not may come to tempt you. All such thoughts are but reflections of the worshipping of death as savior and as a giver of release.*

Embodiment of fear, the host of sin, god of the guilty, and the lord of all illusions and deceptions, does the thought of death seem mighty. For it seems to hold all living things within its withered hands; all hopes and wishes in its blighting grasp; all goals perceived but in it sightless eyes. Wow! *The frail, the helpless and the sick bow down before its image, thinking it alone is real, inevitable, worthy of their trust. For it alone will surely come.*

All things but death are seen to be unsure, too quickly lost, however hard to gain, uncertain in their outcome, apt to fail the hopes they once engendered, and to leave the taste of dust and ashes in their wake, in place of aspirations and of dreams. But death is counted on. For it will come with certain footsteps when the time has come for its arrival. It will never fail to take all life as hostage to itself.

Would you bow down to idols such as this? Here is the strength and might of God Himself perceived within an idol made of dust. Here is the opposite of God proclaimed as lord of all creation, stronger than God's Will for life, the endlessness of love and Heaven's perfect, changeless constancy. Here is the Will of Father and of the Son defeated finally, and laid to rest beneath the headstone death has placed upon the body of the holy Son of God.

Unholy in defeat, he has become what death would have him be. His epitaph, which death itself has written, gives no name to him, for he has passed to dust. It says but this: "Here lies a witness God is dead." And this it writes again and still again, while all the while its worshipers agree, and kneeling down with foreheads to the ground, they whisper fearfully that it is so.

Listen. *It is impossible to worship or acknowledge death in any form, and still select a few you would not cherish and would yet avoid, while still believing in the rest. For death is total. Either all things die, or else they live and cannot die. No compromise is possible. For here again we see an obvious position, which we must accept if we be sane; what contradicts one thought entirely cannot be true, unless its opposite is proven false.*

The idea of the death of God is so preposterous that even the insane have difficulty in believing it. For it implies that God was once alive and somehow perished; killed, apparently, by those who did not want him to survive. Their stronger will could triumph over His, and so eternal life gave way to death. And with the Father died the Son as well.

Death's worshipers may be afraid. And yet, can thoughts like these be fearful? If they saw that it is only this which they believe, they would be instantly released. And you will show them this today. There is no death, and we renounce it now in every form, for their salvation and our own as well. God made not death. Whatever form it takes must therefore be an illusion. This the stand we take today. And it is given us to look past death, and see the life beyond. Wow!

That seems simple, intellectually. It seems simple, the idea, and a lot of you will look and say, "Oh, I understand very well that I can't die." The manner in which you express that is a pretty good indication that you are going to. Do you know why? You are caught in the incredible dilemma of cause and effect. You actually believe that the things that you did yesterday are going to change what happens tomorrow. I assure you, you do. What are you doing? You are ordering your thoughts, you dummies! As soon as you do that, you're going to have to accept responsibility for what you're doing. If you accept responsibility for what you are doing, you're going to have to be what? Specific! You're going to have to learn the damn territory! You are going to go and try to get cash for the dry goods. You are going to have to decide what you want to be okay, and what you don't want to be okay – specifically. As long as you do that, you will die. Sorry. Why? Because you have limited your own idea about yourself.

What do we teach here? Love! What do we teach? Brotherhood! What do we teach? Forgiveness! You look right at somebody. Are you finally an idea of what I think you are? Are there forms about you that I should look at? Do you sometimes get angry? Are you sometimes greedful? Do you sometimes love? Are you sometime lustful? Do you sometimes get fat or thin or ugly? Do you hate sometimes? Do you love sometimes? Who am I really judging? Myself, of course! What have I done? Constructed an idea of who you are within the framework of my limited consciousness. Good grief!

Do we teach the Think System here? Hell, yeah, we teach the Think System. You don't have to know the notes. Do you think that Beethoven wrote the Fifth Symphony by getting together a bunch of notes? No! People will take the symphony and divide it up and make parts out of it. That's not what it is. He used the Think System! Mozart directly says, "I use the Think System." They said, "When are you going to write this? When are you going to write it?" He says, "I've already written it. I've already thought about it," is what he says. And it is complete in him.

So we teach what? We have to come into the illusion and teach you specifically not to be specific. So I stand before you as what you might term an advanced teacher of God. At the very highest level I will say to you, "Don't believe anything I tell you." You can only misconstruct me in your mind if you endow me with any qualities in regard to my relationship with you *unless* you consider me to be the risen Christ. Then you will be, of course, right. I look at you as nothing but the Christ. This is *Course in Miracles* as taught at its highest level. It is impossible for you to even have an idea or conception of truth or unity or Godliness without you literally being that thing.

As Jesus would teach it in the Course, you decide that it's there and then deny it. It's like walking around and saying, "I don't believe in God." That's absurd. God does not, obviously, require your belief in Him. Your brother's Godliness does not require that you believe that he is Godly, darn it. He *is,* whether you think so or not. The dilemma is always yours in the denial of Him. *Love the Lord thy God with all thy might and power, and thy neighbor as thyself.* Brother, that is the only basic teaching. The absurdity of present Christianity, that somehow you can love Jesus and hate your brother and attack your brother, is insane. Of course.

The high truth involved in *Course in Miracles* and what I teach you is precisely this, and this word is used several times in the Course: Coming to be able to extend total love in recognition of who you are is a transformative quality. It occurred, for example, with the magician, the Music Man, when he is absolutely presented with love. He can't get away from it. He says to the little boy, "I'm going to be honest with you." He is going to really try and be honest here at this moment. The little boy says, "Are you a liar?" He says, "Yeah." And then he tries to justify himself. He says, "Well, you have got your band." And the little boy says, "What band?" He says, "I always think there's a band." Then he says, "Well, I got my foot caught in the door, and I can't get away." Why? His foot is caught in love. So that's really what we teach – forgiveness.

Inevitably, what is taught in the illusion will be taken by the individual identity and he will attempt and must attempt to establish it within the limited framework of his own individual consciousness. And he will give qualities to God. He cannot *not.* Actually what we teach is acceptance, non-judgment, the realization that through surrender or acceptance there will occur in you a process of recognition of your true heritage. That is what we teach.

The idea of icons, the idea of symbols in the illusion representing the Truth, are true because it is only through the word that the idea can be firmly established. That can be expressed in a lot of ways. If I look at this candle, you and I may together, if we wish, in communication, share the total recognition that this candle is the light of the world. I assure you that it is. Each one of you has within this mush of unreality a light, a spark. In your re-establishment to the Great Rays – this is Jesus' expression in the *Course in Miracles* – you facilitate in your microcosm the recognition of the mutuality of your identity with that of the entire universe. How do you do that? Through the subtraction of your karma, or your memory, or your dimness in regard to what you had constructed yourself to be.

The highest manner in which that can be conveyed is the admonishment, "As above; so below." As long as you have in your mind the idea of potential, you will think that something can be accomplished in the future or next week, and you have limited your idea about yourself. That is literally impossible.

God, as represented for example in The Music Man, is finally action. The whole universe is nothing but a constant state of maximum total identity. There is nothing passive about consciousness because consciousness finally is eternal creativity. It is the dilemma of the anvil. It is the dilemma of something static. It is the incredible idea that something can contain a potential not yet released that holds you in space/time. Do you see? Thinking that something can be static or brought about in the future is precisely the same idea as death. In reality the most single active thought you can have is of death. The idea of death is totally active! Of course! What else would it be? You cannot think of potentiality without activating it. The universe is your idea in action. You! Literally you!

Now, the problem you have in your dualistic thinking is you are willing to grant me that you can have a thought and that somehow you are pulling off a reservoir of thoughts and that you are going to take a little piece of that thought and activate it. Now you are caught. Why? Because you've got a God outside of you. You inevitably have constructed God as a potential. Not true. Here's the highest thought I can give you: Until you activate it, it literally is no-thing. Now, here is the problem: Since there is no such thing as no-thing, actually your idea of activating it is dualistic. I can't teach you this, but I assure you that it is true. God's Will will be done literally because it always has been done and is being done on a continuing basis. Get a hold of that, if you can. If you pull that down a little bit, darn you, you are making your tomorrow. Quit doing it. Don't make your tomorrow. The script that you wrote for yourself is really junky. No matter how you may try and polish it up and tell me how much you love and what you think you are, there's nothing. All of your memories are what we call post-schism. They are since you have separated yourself from the single truth.

If you want to read these chapters in *Course in Miracles*, that was Workbook lesson 163. Lesson 164 talks about the Ancient Melody that is in you, that you can hear now, that we play together in the realization of our eternity. That is what you're coming to know. And that is very joyous. We end up teaching what? Direct quotes: The salvation of the world as you conceive it depends on you. You literally have constructed and consider to be elements in duality that are your creations. You do this with your family, with your job and your ideas about yourself. All we ask is you do this: Accept total responsibility for the whole world. To be a Christ you must be willing to take on the burdens joyfully. Because why? You recognize that there aren't any. You are very willing, as you sit there – and I watch you do it – accept responsibility for a lot of the things that are occurring on earth, but ultimately, somewhere along the line, you are going to say to me, "I can't be responsible for that." I tell you as I stand here to awaken you from your dream, that you are responsible for the world. Until you came here, it wasn't here, until you constructed it in fractured-ism, until you looked through the mirror darkly, it literally was not here and could never be here.

We are teaching you to think abstractly. Now, that is going to stir a great deal of memories in your individual karma. Why not? How many experiences have you had within your individual relationship of consciousness with yourself? You listen carefully to what I am going to say: You have had and are having all that has ever occurred since the schism originated. Can you understand that? Listen to me. The crucifixion of the Lord Jesus Christ is going on right now. Who are you? Are you the man on the cross? Yep. Are you the Roman soldier? Yep. Got a feel for that? Are you Peter in denial? Yep. Are you Thomas, looking at the palms? Yep. Are you Judas, who betrayed him? Of course, you dummy. Who did you think it was?

Why do you think you are here if you're not in a continual denial or crucifixion or acknowledging death when all He ever said to you was, "Look, there isn't any death, you dummies!" In *Course in Miracles* he says, "I gave you a very graphic description of it." Literally, what He did was reorganize particular combinations of energy cells to duplicate himself. That's a pretty high form of what you would call magic, if you want to call it that. When concreteness suddenly appears in a closed room, which is a pretty good analogy, all it really does is present you with the ultimate miracle, which is a way of saying that nothing is finally miraculous, because the term miracle, by definition, implies that something could be ill, sick, evil and separated; and then overcome, as man says, by a miracle. That's absurd.

A Course in Miracles is a course, as is described by Jesus, in coming to know who you are. It is a course in atonement. And what happens? As you recognize yourself, what do you do? You forgive yourself, so you don't find anybody else guilty. See how simple? Then you subtract the idea of cause and effect. You see that you are absolutely sinless and divine. You transcend and you are in Heaven, and the earth is gone. See how easy that was?

You know the nicest thing about what we teach? You can't solve the problem here, outside of you. At least you are at that nice idea that you can only solve it within yourself. You have all got a lot of Music Man in you or you wouldn't be here. You have got a lot of Anvil Man. You have got a lot of Marion the Librarian. There's a lot of gullibility, as occurs in the Mayor. He is willing to accept something totally one minute, and deny it the next. They will all be represented there for

136

you. Can you see that? Do you see the beautiful art form that the school board is brought together in? They're in total chaos intellectually. As soon as they blend together in a single melody, the Rays comes together in love, and from then on, they are inseparable. See how easy that was? Just an idea, that's all. Idea about you.

Nothing is ever specific. No actions or admonishments that I ever give you will lead you to the truth, literally. There is no path that you are on. What you seek, you are determined not to find. That's nice to know. There's a lot of thorns out there, and there's a lot of crosses being borne. And there's a lot of ideas about the moaning and the chains and the death process. "Let's learn the territory. We can solve the problem here." No, you can't. Have your dream. W.C. Handy came to town. John Philips Sousa. The whole band together, in unity playing together.

We understand that you are blowing a lot of clinkers now, as they would say. You haven't quite got it. You are playing a little counter melody there, and it's very pretty, but finally it has to blend in with the whole. Requiem masses are always a joy. That's very nice.

You remember what we're saying now. As in the allegory of *The Music Man*, you do not have to know the territory. Here is Lesson 166 from the *Course in Miracles*. Listen.

All things are given you. God's trust in you is limitless. He knows His Son. He gives without exception, holding nothing back that can contribute to your happiness. And yet, unless your will is one with His, His gifts are not received. But what would make you think there is another will than His?

Here is the paradox that underlies the making of the world. This world is not the will of God, and so it is not real. Yet those who think it real must still believe there is another will, and one that leads to opposite effects from those He wills. Impossible indeed; but every mind that looks upon the world and judges it as certain, solid, trustworthy and true believes in two creators; or in one, himself alone. But never in one God.

The gifts of God are not acceptable to anyone who holds such strange beliefs. He must believe that to accept God's gifts, however evident they may become, however urgently he may be called to claim them as his own, is to be pressed to treachery against himself. He must deny their presence, contradict the truth, and suffer to preserve the world he made.

Here is the only home he thinks he knows. Here is the only safety he believes that he can find. Without the world he made is he an outcast; homeless and afraid. He does not realize that it is here he is afraid indeed, and homeless too, an outcast, wandering so far from home, so long away he does not realize he has forgotten where he came from, where he goes and even who he really is.

Yet in his lonely, senseless wanderings, God's gifts go with him, all unknown to him. He cannot lose them. But he will not look at what is given him. He wanders on, aware of the futility he sees about him everywhere, perceiving how his little lot but dwindles, as he goes ahead to nowhere. Still he wanders on in misery and poverty, alone though God is with him, and a treasure his so great that everything the world contains is valueless before its magnitude.

Listen because now you are being described here, aren't you?

He seems a sorry figure; weary, worn, and with threadbare clothing, and feet that bleed a little from the rocky road he walks. No one but has identified with him, for everyone who comes here has pursued the path he follows, and has felt defeat and hopelessness as he is feeling them. Yet is he really tragic when you see that he is following the way he chose and need but realize Who walks with him and open up his treasures to be free?

This is your chosen self, the one you make as a replacement for reality. This is the self you savagely defend against all reason, every evidence, and all the witnesses with proof to show you this is not you. You heed them not. You go on your appointed way, with eyes cast down lest you might catch a glimpse of truth and be released from self-deception and set free.

You cower fearfully lest you should feel Christ's touch upon your shoulder, and perceive His gentle hand directing you to look upon your gifts. How could you then proclaim your poverty in exile? He would make you laugh at this perception of yourself. Where is self-pity then? And what becomes of all the tragedy you sought to make for him, whom God intended only joy?

Your ancient fear has come upon you now, and justice has caught up with you at last. Christ's hand has touched your shoulder, and you feel that you are not alone. You even think the miserable self you thought was you may not be your Identity. Perhaps God's word is truer than your own. Perhaps His gifts to you are real. Perhaps He has not wholly been outwitted by your plan to keep His Son in deep oblivion, and go the way you choose without your Self.

God's will does not oppose. Do you hear that? It merely is. It is not God you have imprisoned in your plan to lose your Self. He does not know about a plan so alien to His Will. There was a need He did not understand, to which He gave an Answer. That is all. And you who have this Answer given you have need no more of anything but This.

Now do we live, for now we cannot die. The wish for death is answered, and the sight that looked upon it now has been replaced by vision which perceives that you are not what you pretended to be. One walks with you Who gently answers all your fears with this one merciful reply, "It is not so." He points to all the gifts you have each time the thought of poverty oppresses you, and speaks of His Companionship when you perceive yourself as lonely and afraid.

Yet He reminds you still of one thing more you have forgotten, for His touch on you has made you like Himself. Hear that? The gifts you have are not for you alone. What He has come to offer you, you now must learn to give. This is the lesson that His giving holds, for He has saved you from the solitude you sought to make in which to hide from God. He has reminded you of all the gifts that God has given you. He speaks as well of what becomes your will when you accept these gifts, and recognize they are your own.

The gifts are yours, entrusted to your care, to give to all who chose the lonely road you have escaped. They do not understand they but pursue their wishes. It is you who teach them now. For you have learned of Christ there is another way for them to walk. Teach them by showing them the happiness that comes to those who feel the touch of Christ, and recognize God's gifts. Let sorrow not tempt you to be unfaithful to your trust.

Your sighs will now betray the hopes of those who look to you for their release. Your tears are theirs. If you are sick, you but withhold their healing. What you fear but teaches them their fears are justified. Your hand becomes the giver of Christ's touch; your change of mind becomes the proof that who accepts God's gifts can never suffer anything. You are entrusted with the world's release from pain.

Betray it not. Become the living proof of what Christ's touch can offer everyone. God has entrusted all His gifts to you. Be witness in your happiness to how transformed the mind becomes which chooses to accept His gifts, and feel the touch of Christ. Such is your mission now. For God entrusts the giving of His gifts to all who have received them. He has shared His joy with you. And now you go to share it with the world.

And so the Music Man becomes a true Son of God and recognizes what he had always known in truth – that he never really had to know the territory because the whole world is his territory, and in his changing his mind he extends from him in love and joy, all of the reality of his Sonship and his union with the Father. Thank you very much.

Free to Create:
Choose Not To Die

Freedom here is actually a bondage to a conservation of self. It's a notation of freedom to perform particular repository "rites" – it's not a bad word. There is a constant need to express freedom in relationship to bondage of the self and its apparent environ.

These words that I wrote this morning are pertaining to the method or the idea that we have a method of meditation or contact with ostensibly super consciousness, that affords us a freedom different from the freedom that is expressed by perception. Once more we'll read it: "Our high meditation, our indication of union with God or with wholeness, does not bring freedom to perform but rather freedom from performance. Not freedom to persist but freedom to absolutely relinquish. That's real freedom, isn't it? Freedom to be free, not freedom to have free or to act free. The freedom of no necessity, not a new kind of obligation. To a perceptual consciousness there is something terrifying about the idea of the notation of absolute freedom. The concept of necessity, the concept of bondage, the concept of survival is the premise on which perceptual consciousness is based." N'est-ce pas? Isn't that so? Of course.

So if a super consciousness, say, in the method of my awakened mind or in the method of the teachings of the character, Jesus Christ in the *Course in Miracles* presents or has presented or did present you with the relief or release from your notation of time, which is what death is, you will inevitably view that as frightening. You are literally afraid to live – to be eternal, and that's very interesting. But until you look at the possibility which is ingrained, which is inherent, which is *a priori* of the idea of a wholeness; until you apply the mechanism of the mind or the thought to the notation of eternity, you will forever turn on the limited concepts and bind yourself to the notation of death, isn't that so? And of course that's exactly what you do. All of the processes or apparent methods of religion, folding back, are designed to make the notation that contained within you is a faculty of remembering or bringing together all of the atoning – Jesus would say, the word *at-one-ment* – all of the genetic memories or patterns that constitute your symbiotic relationships. Isn't that amazing? You see yourself as a body yet every part of that body, as defined by wholeness, must contain the whole everything.

It's a little early in the morning here at God's Country Place. It is only 5:30. We are up early around this place. This morning we are speaking of freedom for those of you who are arriving now from your Land of Nod or should I say, other Land of Nod since what better defines perceptual reality than the notation that this is the Land of Nod. And we are nodding off here for a moment.

There is a descriptive passage in the text of the Course with the indication that it may occur to you that when you awoke this morning, you awoke to a dream. The idea of certainty that you are in fact dreaming. Perhaps "dream" is not the best definition, but since perceptual mind requires definition, you have within you a conscious acquiescence to the notation that when you dream, you awaken and it is not real, so that using that factoring, I can present you with the certainty that when you awaken from this dream, you will see immediately that it is not real. That's the object of the transformative process and that is the only object of the transformative process.

Our notation is that this is a dream. Okay. Now, the admission that it is a dream is beneficent in this regard: No matter how we may eventually view it or assuage the idea, the earth is the place of pain and fear and eventual death. Now, to deny that is absurd and there are almost no consciousnesses within the framework that are going to maintain within their own limited shell of reality that they have carved out a place in this place of chaos where they manage to sustain themselves for a period of what is termed time and then die a rotten death of some sort. So what we are dealing with here, is finally as Master Jesus would express it, no limited consciousness can tolerate the pain of separate existence indefinitely. Somewhere there is a confrontation with himself in relationship to what he sees about him. Now the idea that that is occurring all the time is taken for granted in his relationships. He's born in pain, he's taught the progress of aging – which when you stop to think about it is abominable – the idea that he will age and eventually be terminated is taken for granted in the relationship he has with himself. It is astonishing. He never really questions the idea that there might be something wholly beautiful and wholly true and wholly non-conflictual and without opposition. Yet everything that he points to, everything that he makes acquiescence to in his apparent relationship with the people around him, are a tacit admission of a wholeness of truth and beauty, yet he issues a disclaimer within his own memory that he in fact could obtain that. And when presented with the certainty that he is that, he emphatically denies it in defense of himself. How did he get this way? What difference does it make how he got this way if the notation is he is in fact in conflict. Better he address his relationship with himself in regard to the pain that he apparently feels and the obvious memory of wholeness and beauty and God that he has in him. Is that the process I am presenting to you? Yes.

Now just for a moment, within the philosophy, we inevitably must deal – and I am not going to deal with it in detail – momentarily with the idea that if there is something whole and true and beautiful and perfectly disordered in the sense that no order would be required, there could not be something false or painful or conflictual. Now that's a statement of reasonable fact but it's a statement that that cannot be tolerated by frictional mind because the basis of the reality of perceptual mind is conflictual. And the admission of a whole truth – an absolute non-dictatorial, what you would call fascism of reality, where there is no conflict because there is no judgment – obviously is not a conceptual idea but rather the relinquishment of the conception in order that the consciousness see that he is whole. That's the transformative process that all history has expressed. This is what Christianity is.

Christianity is a statement that limited man, man as defined, earthly man, can through a transformative process, through a resurrection, through an enlightenment, through an atonement, through *A Course In Miracles*, come to know the reality of his association with beauty and truth that is Universal consciousness. That is precisely what Jesus Christ teaches in the process of relinquishment of self. He teaches nothing but this. He makes no claim to doctrine. Incidentally there is no doctrine in *A Course In Miracles*. The problem with teaching the concepts of the Course is that, and as Master Jesus would indicate, it is important that you get out of the concepts as rapidly as possible, since obviously they are in direct conflict with the established Christian church – not because they are particularly derogatory to the establishment of Christianity, but because they are absolutely derogatory to any association in perceptual reality which constitutes establishments of the earth itself.

The whole teaching is you are not of this world. The whole teaching is you are not from here. The whole teaching is you can escape this through surrender of yourself. See how simple it is? Is this an individual teaching of your own atonement? Sure. Obviously the problem that you would have with it is the process of relinquishment of the limited you in association with your sociological obligation which will bring about an avant garde feeling of detachment resulting in an Eros expression of freedom. You literally don't want to participate in the chaos and death that constitute the world and for that you will be derided and castigated. You are expected to perform the ritual of aging.

One of our associates saw one of his Nazarene friends recently. They said, "how is your health?" and he said, "well I haven't been to the doctor in twelve years, I feel fine, I am all right." The consciousness said, "well quickly go and get a complete physical so you can find out what's wrong with you in preparation for the time when you need do something about it." His reaction was exactly the opposite of how our reaction would be in our teaching that pain and death are impossible. He is in a condition, in association with a body, of maintenance. You are in a condition, through your enlightenment, of the relinquishment of the body. This is the whole teaching of *A Course In Miracles*. You go out and you teach this. I am not a body I am free. I am still as God created me. How many times do you have to say that in a day to come to know that that is true? I don't know. How many minutes are there in a day? How many hours? If the statement is true, how determined are you to awaken from this dream, as we've expressed it? How determined are you to see that there is another way out of this besides your continuing deterioration to obliviation? That's what we are presenting to you now. That you can in fact find it.

No course in atonement could be at all without the assertion of the power of the perceptual mind. This has nothing to do with the indication that the perception itself is false. The idea of resting power is the idea of the fall, or the determination of the consciousness to hold itself separate from the single reality, which is innocent power or guiltless power or whole power. So the apparent methodology is to give the consciousness the absolute power of his perception which is inevitable since he is all power, which cannot detract from the certainty that mind is the mechanism of decision by which the conclusion is reached through the assertion of the individual consciousness power. This is pure – what is termed from the philosophical standpoint – existentialism. It is the statement, before the progression to singularity of *Cogito Ergo Sum* or "I think, therefore I am." We start with this premise. No one is going to deny or could ever deny that you are consciousness. The question is not that, but rather the question that *you* interpose in the statement "ergo" or "therefore", which is the manufacturing of time, is what am I? This is the lovely Lesson 139 from the Workbook of the Course. Finally wholeness involves or must involve at least reasonable assertion, and Jesus says it this way: The only thing anything alive could ever know, ever, forever, is what it is. But here you are with *Cogito Ergo* "therefore" I am. *Cogito Ergo Sum* – I think, therefore I am. You've got a lot of air between "I think" and "I am"!

That is what perceptual consciousness is, and here's the tanglement that an existentialist like Hegel will run into with a purist like Kierkegaard. They are both proclaiming existentialism, but remember that we are teaching to the nature, since the mind is limited in its concept of itself, to the transcendence of the limited state. Now we are into Neoplatonism. Now we are into the ideas beautifully expressed by the transcendentalists - Ralph Waldo Emerson, classically. This is transcendentalism, this is the expansion of the whole mind to the realization of its particular whole existence. This is called transcendental existentialism, for want of a better expression. If there are any of you philosophers that would like to hook on this in some sort of Socratic venture, I'd be happy to oblige you. What we are really teaching is whole mind.

Now we must add a notation here – and this is where the difficulty arises. The so-called greater mysteries, which you would call the *Philosophia Perennis* and Huxley beautifully expresses it, is a statement that since there is a God, we must know about it and the evolvement of the mind is to that single reality. This has to, then, involve the Christian or the Christ statement of the transformation of the mind: *Know ye not ye must be born again.* (John 3:3) Now this is the mystical experience, or to raise it up a step as you're going to teach it as a later day teacher or Master, it's a statement of the acceleration of the evolutionary process of man to the realization of his Gnostic consciousness. Somewhere within your framework, you like this idea, you like the idea of power. What you can't tolerate is the idea of unopposed power. That disturbs you because that would be an admission of perfection. So in the teachings of Christianity, we say your brother is your Christ and is all about you, but you in your perceptual judgment have projected from him a statement of yourself in association with the illusion or with the dream.

I ought to open the text and read you a little Chapter 21. After the Easter Chapter which is 20, Master Jesus provides us with Chapter 21 which is going to say what? That you are a condition of subjective reality going through a metamorphic process of the realization that there is nothing outside of yourself. Wow!

Chapter 21: Reason and Perception. Projection makes perception. This is the whole idea that there are separate thoughts. This is the whole idea there is something outside of yourself that is acting upon you. No wonder you are fearful. No wonder you get old. No wonder you die. Here is all this incredible power of consciousness being denied by you and creating conflictual symbiotic associations of yourself. That's absurd. No wonder you die and get old. How could you help it? I am here to tell you you can't die. You want to attack me? Come on. I think it's time that we took on this deathful place. Why don't we begin to let the dead bury the dead? Why don't we begin the process of giving, of the relinquishment of the potential of false self? How can you come to know then your creative potential? Through giving all that there is within your own mind. You will automatically go through the transcendent state. That's the mechanism. That's the device.

The world you see is what you give it, nothing more than that. But though it is no more than that, it is not less. Wow what a statement! Obviously if it is what you give it, it cannot be more or less. You will inevitably give qualities of good and bad or hot and cold or right or wrong or whatever you do with your own machinations of manufactured mind but inevitably it is not more or less than what? What you make it. Not more, not less. *Therefore, to you it is important. It is the witness to your state of mind, the outside picture of an inward condition.* Oh Wow! *As a man thinketh, so does he perceive. Therefore, seek not to change the world, but choose to change your mind about the world. Perception is a result and not a cause.* This is the key teaching to the subtraction of objective reality, to the progress from Newtonian physics to quantum. The great leap to the singular assertion that everything is contained within each thing, and it is in your mind.

And that is why order of difficulties in miracles is meaningless. Everything looked upon with vision is healed and holy. Nothing perceived without it means anything. And where there is no meaning there is chaos. And this is what is in your dream because you attempt, through your objective perceptions, to hold together, within a time framework, through sequentiality of thoughts, a limited idea that you have about yourself. No wonder you're chaotic. You are in a constant attempt to establish within a chaotic framework, some sort of reality. It doesn't work.

Damnation is your judgment on yourself, and this you will project upon the world. See it as damned, and all you see is what you did to hurt the Son of God. If you behold disaster and catastrophe, you tried to crucify him. If you see holiness and hope, you joined the Will of God to set him free. There is no choice that lies between these two decisions. You think there is but there isn't. The whole statement of the unequivocalness and the uncompromisingness of wholeness when confronting falsity is a very valid and necessary tool in the mechanism of teaching. Why? Because any compromise is death. Truth is true and nothing else is true. *And you will see the witness to the choice you made, and learn from this to recognize which one you choose.* And there's value in that because I am presenting you with the inevitable alternative of certain sickness and death or eternal life and happiness outside of time. Okay? Wow!

Never forget the world the sightless "see" must be imagined... This is you contained within your own cocoon, within your own kingdom. *...for what it really looks like is unknown to them. They must infer what could be seen from evidence forever indirect...* This is the *reflection* of light contained in the Great Rays and this is very mystical and Jesus will talk about it at some point or I will. For in this fracturedism of light are associated thoughts in that light is really consciousness or an aspect of it. *...and reconstruct their inferences as they stumble and fall because of what they did not recognize, or walk unharmed through open doorways that they thought were closed. And so it is with you.* You listen. *You do not see. Your cues for inference are wrong, and so you stumble and fall down upon the stones you did not recognize, but fail to be aware you can go through the doors you thought were closed, but which stand open before unseeing eyes, waiting to welcome you.* This is the whole notation that your perceptual reality, your scientific method of observation, is so obscure and so limited within your body framework, in the projection of these memories that constitute your genetic make up, that you literally aren't seeing anything. You are blind. And who is so blind as those who are determined not to see, or are determined to establish some sort of spiritual path that are going to lead them to another degree of blindness. Wow!

How foolish it is to attempt to judge what could be seen instead. It is not necessary to imagine what the world must look like. You don't have to do that. *It must be seen before you recognize it for what it is.* That's the transformation. *You can be shown which doors are open, and you can see where safety lies; and which way leads to darkness, which to light.* Listen! *Judgment will always give you false direction...* Always. *...but vision shows you where to go. Why should you guess?* All judgment is false, and always in association with limitation. *There is no need to learn through pain.* Laugh, everybody! We have a proclamation here from the great Master, Jesus Christ, that there is no need to learn through pain. He was a perfect example of the crucifixion, of the non-necessity of sacrifice, or so we say. You may, we'll grant, feel a little conflict in your assertion of this. There is no need to, because the moment that you would make a positive, unequivocating statement, you would spring into bright light and disappear from the chaos of earth. Hey! Wow! How about that!

And gentle lessons are acquired joyously, and are remembered gladly. What gives you happiness you want to learn and not forget. This is what we are trying to do with you. *It is not this you would deny. Your question is whether the means by which this course...* by what I am saying to you, *...is learned will bring to you the joy it promises. If you believed it would, the learning of it would be no problem. You are not a happy learner yet because you still remain uncertain that vision gives you more than judgment does, and you have learned that both you cannot have.* Wow! That's an advanced statement. I am presenting you the uncompromising assertion you can't have earth and Heaven, because any definition is what hell is. And earth is a definition of associated pain and death. Holy Mackerel! Isn't that something!

The blind become accustomed to their world by their adjustments to it. They think they know their way about in it. They learned it, not through joyous lessons, but through the stern necessity of limits they believed could not be overcome. And still believing this, they hold these lessons dear, and cling to them because they cannot see. This is a description of karma and why the mind keeps turning on itself. *They do not understand that the lessons keep them blind. This they do not believe. And so they keep the world they learned to "see" in their imagination, believing that their choice is that or nothing.* They have forgotten what? That this is a dream that they, and this is going to be presented to you now, that you are actually the dreamer of this dream, the instigator of objective reality. *And so they keep the world they learned to "see" in their imagination, believing that their choice is that or nothing. They hate the world they learned through pain. And everything they think is in it serves to remind them that they are incomplete and bitterly deprived.* A place of lack.

Thus they define their life where they live... are you ready for this? *...adjusting to it as they think they must, afraid to lose the little that they have. And so it is with all who see the body as all they have and all their brothers have. They try to reach each other, and they fail, and they fail again. And they adjust to loneliness, believing that to keep the body is to save the little that they have. Listen, and try to think if you remember what we will speak of now.*

Here is a very famous line in the Course about the ancient melody. It has very strong transformative ideas contained within it.

Listen, –perhaps you catch a hint of an ancient state not quite forgotten; dim, perhaps, and yet not altogether unfamiliar, like a song whose name is long forgotten, and the circumstances in which you heard completely unremembered. Not the whole song has stayed with you, but just a little wisp of melody, attached not to a person or a place or anything particular. But you remember, from just this little part, how lovely was the song, how wonderful was the setting where you heard it, and how you loved those who were there and listened with you.

The notes are nothing. Yet you have kept them with you, not for themselves, but as a soft reminder of what would make you weep if you remembered how dear it was to you. You could remember, yet you are afraid, believing you would lose the world you learned since then. And yet you know that nothing in the world you learned is half so dear as this. Listen, and see if you remember an ancient song you knew so long ago and held more dear than any melody you taught yourself to cherish since.

Beyond the body, beyond the sun and stars, past everything you see and yet somehow familiar, is an arc of golden light that stretches as you look into a great and shining circle. And all the circle fills with light before your eyes. The edges of the circle disappear, and what is in it is no longer contained at all. The light expands and covers everything, extending to infinity forever shining with no break or limit anywhere. Within it everything is joined in perfect continuity. Nor is it possible to imagine that anything could be outside, for there is nowhere that this light is not.

This is the vision of the Son of God, whom you know well. Here is the sight of him who knows his Father. Here is the memory of what you are; a part of this, with all of it within, and joined to all as surely as all is joined in you. Accept the vision that can show you this, and not the body. You know the ancient song, and know it well. Nothing will ever be as dear to you as is this ancient hymn of love the Son of God sings to his Father still.

And now the blind can see, for that same song they sing in honor of their Creator gives praise to them as well. The blindness that they made will not withstand the memory of this song. And they will look upon the vision of the Son Of God, remembering who he is they sing of. What is a miracle but this remembering? And who is there in whom this memory lies not? The light in one awakens it in all. And when you see it in your brother, you are remembering it for everyone.

What a beautiful incredible statement of the certainty of the glory and honor and wholeness of the human mind. Wow! What a declaration of the necessity to remember before time was and after time wasn't. To transcend that moment of madness that cast you into this dreaming of pain and death which you now have chosen to awaken from. How very lovely to be with you, brothers, now in this declaration of faith. To stand apart from the world, from death, and proclaim salvation and wholeness through the transformation of your mind.

If what I am saying to you is true, that you are going through this incredible metamorphosis, this process that we read in Chapter 21, you are right square in the middle of the transformative process yourself. Anyone who really is going to present the Course or the words of super consciousness, Jesus Christ, to this chaos, begins and ends finally with the premise that knowledge is transformative, and that it is gained by this process that you are undergoing. This is where the Course begins and where it ends. We understand that we are dealing with the idea of choice and very early we say we have no alternative to the impossible situation of perceptual reality. But that being said, let's be about it. Let's not get tangled up in obscure concepts of relationalship catechisms of what constitutes Christianity or certainly not in some sort of Eastern modality which proclaims the impossibility of a perceptual God, which apparently some Eastern teachers are doing.

We make an immediate adjunct statement that God is not perceptual, that wholeness can not be known by limitation, and proceed from there to the Christian statement that it is gained by the transformation of you, by what we would term whole body enlightenment. Is this still a secret? Is this initiatory process one that still must be kept hidden as it was in the societies of the association of mystical Christianity with the death process of the established Church? Are you going to be burned at the stake for the presentations of wholeness? I don't think so. We have 600,000 copies of the absolute statement of love and truth – sitting on coffee tables and being sold at rummage sales around the world. These words are the true words of the wholeness of your mind. We seem to be doing pretty well with that.

Now the advanced teachings, of course, are that you through your positive initiative of relinquishment of the limitation of your self conceptions can go through a glorious revelation of the transformation of your mind and this is physical. To deny that it involves the whole you, is to present the absurdity that part of you is going to transform and that the remainder of you is somehow going to remain in some sort of chaotic association. That isn't true. If you want the apparently ignomatic statements of the Course, that God only has one son and it's you, I'll give you that. If you want the statements of the certainty of a single death, single wholeness that are contained in the statement that you are the only savior of the world, you can have those.

I am saying to you that the necessity is the process of your own awakening. Now you don't mind that notation, what you object to is the inevitable method that I'll present you with by which you can come to know your wholeness. And that, obviously, is the relinquishment of your limited self, the giving up of the previous false value system of apparent reality that keeps you in sequential time. We'll be reading and talking about it more. Suffice now to say that we teach here transformation and nothing else. We teach from the certainty that if one perception is false, all perception must therefore be false. And that if there is a God, and if there is a Heaven, then the earth is not real, and cannot be, and that evil and sin cannot exist. Are these the statements of the *Course in Miracles* that are so assiduously avoided? Of course. There is no life outside of Heaven. Therefore, this cannot be real.

Now, since we are teaching the transformative process, in the remaining few moments on this side of the tape we'll put on a transformative meditation that may serve as a guide for you in your own individual pursuit of reality. Use this Light. It is available to you in unlimited supply. It will bring you grace and happiness. That's it. Open the door. Step right out. Be grateful. The greatest feat has occurred: The great transcendence. The awakening. And it's you! It's you not someone else, not some concepts you have of someone outside yourself, just you. You were the dreamer. You are the awakened one and were. This is past now, and over and gone long ago. You are free and whole. In perfect ecstasy. Thank You, God.

I don't know how long this tape will last, but we will try to continue this one with the idea of subjective reality. We got into it here. We are on the porch at God's Country Place and we are talking about the seizure of the opportunity for transformation that is occurring in the individual consciousnesses within the parameter of this energy. And we'll talk about that.

Jesus has a sentence, and I'll use the *Course in Miracles*, although obviously, this is coming from a very wide parameter of perceptual reality emanating from this mechanism of realization. Is that a good definition of me? That all adjustments are of the ego. See, look at that, I put a definitive phrase in the middle of a sentence, and came back around. This is the way the Course is written. It keeps coming back around.

All adjustments are of the ego, inevitably because the persona, Marty John, Ana, Joy, Christian are adjustments to individual mind responsibility. The whole notion of responsibility or the sequencing of the relational thought is an adjustment, and this was the talk that we gave yesterday on the tape, wasn't it? About your determination to seek happiness, peace and joy in finding who you are. If you start with the premise that you don't know who you are, obviously, everything that you do is going to be an adjustment of sorts to find out who you are. Isn't it? So, we come out here unto the porch. This is a particular mind set that people who first come to God's Country Place bring with them. Obviously everything is an adjustment. They'll come from a warm climate into our cold climate and they are cold and they say, "I'm cold" and I'll say that's okay. At what point do we say, I'm not a body, I am free, I am as God created me? I don't know.

We do not teach the discipline of non-adjustment, but rather the certainty that if the mind will be allowed to accelerate, first, through the detachment of associate thought, and then through the ensuing energy that permeates the consciousness as it brings itself together in the atonement process, that what the weather conditions are, where it sits or where it is will have no relationship to what it is thinking or doing at all. Will it? Why would it? I can't see any reason why it would. The whole effort that we are trying to bring about here – there, I'm going to have a drink of this, it's Folger's, and I am going to leave the tape on. Did you know that I drink Folger's Instant Coffee? Maybe General Foods will send us a case. Now when I say that, that will go out abroad and as this matures, in the perceptual evaluation of what constitutes a whole mind based on the things that I am saying, they will do an association of the source, and think that one of the methods to bring about this new mind is to drink instant Folger's, or to get up at five in the morning, or to pretend that you are not cold when you are, or to be celibate, or not to be, or to part your hair in the middle rather than on the side. You'll never stop. Finally these are just forms of adjustments to traditions and this is how tradition is established to bring about associate so-called symbols, icons or examples of the thinking of your mind.

There is a lovely sentence where Master Jesus says nothing represents anything. I don't know. Since the example mind is representational in its adjustments to its previous accords, the idea that nothing represents anything is an astonishing thing. The dualistic mind is literally idolatrous. That is, it creates idols or forms or thought forms in associations with the congruity of its own efforts to establish itself and remain within the framework of the temporal modality. It doesn't make any sense, but the mind does that.

Jesus says never pay attention to the form. This is all lovely stuff that you will find in the *Course In Miracles*. Did I use the Course in my awakening? I am the Course in my awakening. *A Course in Miracles* is not a set of three books that give you a particular direction as to how you can find peace and happiness within the throes of death. *A Course In Miracles* is a complete exposé through the revelation to the insinuation of Whole Truth into death and chaos or separate mind of the single manner, **single manner**, in which a consciousness evolves from his limited perceptual mind to whole mind, which is the natural condition of all consciousness in the universe. That's what it is. The idea that it is a required course, and this occurs very early, of course it is required! If any course is required, the course in enlightenment or the return or the remembering or the religion of your individual mind could be the only requirement. That's not to say that it is a real requirement and here's your dilemma. All awakened minds that stay here momentarily, say as I am doing with you now, are very very particularly certain of the unreality of this place.

The very difference between what I am teaching and what you will teach is first, my certainty of the unreality of this and second, that being the case, the teachings that you have no choice but to awaken and remember your wholeness and your love. Very early in the Course we say to you, Jesus says, we are dealing with the impossible idea that you have a choice between dying – being in time – and being eternal – being what consciousness is. If you would stop to look at it, you might see why Jesus keeps saying you are hallucinating, why he keeps saying this is an insane place. Now to take that just a step further, obviously, socratically and philosophically, if there is good and love and truth and we've said this many many times, there could not be evil and death. Any theological problems or philosophy or finally psychology problems that you may have will be an attempt to equate what you observe here with the *a priori* certainty in your mind that you are whole. That could be the only problem that you'd ever have. That being said, the most efficacious, the most rapid, way to shorten time to come to that certainty would be to commit yourself to the example of no choice – and I teach no choice. Jesus calls it Holy Spirit, and if you take Holy Spirit and define it as one-eyedness or singular determination, the opening of the third eye, perhaps, esoterically, if you wanted to get into the physical ramifications.

That determination in objective reality is what will bring the goal of salvation to you. And certainly this pertains to limited goals that are set by the power of your mind in your executive capacities. If there is one thing that we would say of a so-called born leader, it is that he sets a high goal and by whatever jurisdiction, by whatever means, brings it about. He will make application to that goal. He is able to delegate limited obligations and see the single obligation that he wants to perform. This is not different than the practice of the religious discipline of coming to know God. It is the same idea. If you will set your example, if you will set your goal as eternity or stepping out of time, you will discover rapidly how very naive the truth is. Your declaration of your determination not to die, regardless of how you may feel about it, is the precise certainty that you never will. I know this seems a trifle simplistic, but anyone who has ever come to me, if

I look at them as I am looking at you now, I'm going to say, "there is no death." The consciousness begins to walk around and say, "hey, there's no death. I don't have to get old and wrinkled. I don't have to get cancer. I don't have to see all my loved ones die. I don't have to be finally concerned about providing for my welfare and have a place where I can go and get old-timers disease and rot. I don't have to be concerned about that, there is no death. Certainly if there is no death I couldn't be sick and there will be no aging."

And this is precisely what I tell you is true. And if you hang around here, what happens to you? You don't die, ever. If you will believe – this is back to the original statement of all whole teachers – if you will believe what I tell you, you will remember – you will begin to remember and finally remember absolutely that if there was a path, it's over and that basing your reality on your previous associations with yourself in which you always died is absurd. You always died before, didn't you?

Well, now, I'm here in the middle of your dream, and you're dreaming me. But at what point in your perceptual mind are you willing to listen? Where are you in the gathering of your own associate thoughts, karma is the Eastern term, with the capacity to see the Christ who is obviously all about you? Am I, in that sense, a representation of that? Yes! Since perceptual mind is representational, you are using me as a representation of what you think the possibility of a Christ might be. And that's okay. Is that a form of idolatry? Sure. You will discover if you are with me, that my absolute justice and honesty consist of constancy. All the consciousnesses who have come to me in love have discovered the hard work and difficulty of dealing with a constant mind. I said this to you yesterday, that while I appear not to discipline, nothing could ever be more disciplined or difficult or simple, finally, than the no-alternative presentation that emanates from light to darkness Okay?

I think there is an idea that people who seek illumination or samadhi or enlightenment, that as that progresses on the path they become more blissful and more happy. Those of you who have entertained that idea have come to discover that the process of enlightenment involves the facing, each moment, the conflict between time and eternity. That's the Workbook of the Course, and that's what we teach.

We are rambling a little bit here, let's see if we can get some sort of focus on this. We are speaking of Holy Spirit or one mindedness or seeking a goal. We mentioned that the power of the mind to bring about the conclusion of the conceptual thought is inevitable because finally, subjectively, there is no distance between the cause and the effect. Obviously, perceptual mind doesn't see this and sets very limited goals within time frameworks, doesn't it?

Let's look at the term, "executive mind." A mind of leadership in the world can see a major goal that it wants to bring about. It may for a moment flux in its perceptual need of the necessity to bring that about. But it remains determined, for example, to register within a corporate structure, a particular gain. That may include all the mechanisms of production, distribution, advertising. He is not really concerned about that. He's already done that in his mind. He's concerned only about the finality of the goal that he seeks. Is this an example of George Washington or Abraham Lincoln or Adolf Hitler? Yes. So finally we are teaching power of the mind.

The kind of consciousnesses who are coming here – Master Ana and I were laughing about preparing this kind of pseudo-questionnaire about what the qualifications for entrance into the Masters Academy would be. In the preparation of this questionnaire we discovered that the similarity of our minds and our mind sets and how they work in relationship to our experience in the world is astonishing to people who come here. We discovered that many of us have and do suffer from what we would term "mind speed" where our cause and effects aren't really very far apart. And we go through an adolescence where we see, for example, that the goal of life on earth is finally only death. And this is what, as we mentioned, causes the depression of the adolescent. He then is taught to set limited goals and to achieve them through what? Education, the assumption of sociological responsibility, the advent of children, the passage of time.

But contained within our kind of minds is the frustration of non-satisfaction at the achievement of a goal. Because our consciousnesses have set within our own karma framework the ultimacy of enlightenment, we, very early on, discovered that the success of opening night is dashed by the necessity of a two year run. We don't want to do that. We are a renegade in that nature.

Before my awakening I had many many incidencies of what apparently were very successful episodes in my life, and they were always accompanied by forms of depression, inevitably. And my depressions would occur right in the middle of my so-called highest moments of success. And I know that there are a lot of consciousnesses out there who haven't necessarily reached anything that could be termed a bottom in what we call bottom or certainty of the unreality of this and the impossibility of being what we would term successful. Finally, all of our hopes are going to be dashed in the passage of time to death.

But the closer that comes in your mind, and this is our whole teaching idea, the more you will seek for another route, for a way out of this, if there is one. At what point do you really address in your own mind, and hide behind this frustration you feel when you lock the door and sit down in anguish, and don your sackcloth and your ashes ,and rent your garments, and wail at the wailing wall – and then make yourself presentable and go on out in this chaos? Don't kid me brothers, I know you. When you're out there and everything looks good – come on – the later day teachings will acknowledge this. Not only will they acknowledge it, but they will present you with the optimism, with the opportunity for you now to look at how you are different than your apparent counterparts in this space/time. It will allow you to address the notation that in the evolutionary process, as Master Jesus would say, we are not all equal in time. And the frustrations that you feel with the limited establishment goal can be very very beneficent in your continuing pursuit for something outside this framework of limitation. Isn't that so? Now, does that involve the pain and frustration that you may feel in the death and loneliness of it? Certainly, it does. Sure. That cannot be measured. There is no measurement about who, and any judgment about it will be false, obviously because all judgment is false. But more than that, there is no measurement about who, in their own time framework, is going to begin to hear this message that I'm presenting to you. That may not concern you.

Our concern – now, listen to me – is we are embarking on a very advanced program, taking the basis of the subjective reality presented in *A Course In Miracles* and presenting at a new range of consciousness, the certainty of the individual mind transformation, the final revealing of the initiation process of the individual – not as a group, now, not as any sort of establishment, not even finally perhaps as defined as Christianity. I don't know what you define it as. Who cares? It's the awakening of your individual whole mind to eternal peace and happiness. Now will there be miracles that occur along this route? Oh wow! Why wouldn't there be? If all of the world is only your concepts, as you change your mind about it everything around you must change. Hey, that'll make you feel good. And inevitably it does. These are these moments of happiness that you begin to experience. Now, it's the changing of your mind. I know you all very well. Somewhere within your genetic make up, obviously, you know me very well. There are no strangers. How could there be? This is only your own concept.

Am I a little further along in time than you are? I suppose, if you are looking for a definition within the framework of time to what a so-called Christ or savior is. He is a mind, if you are going to stay in duality for a moment, that has matured a moment earlier in time and presents you with the certainty of your own inevitable future. Okay. What's wrong with that? You hide behind the mask of limitation and proclaim the impossibility of your own Christhood. You give it some sort of idolatry and place it in some sort of moral framework where you can proclaim yourself to be imperfect. That's nonsense. Perception is imperfect, brother. Lay down your crudgeon of defense and stand and look at yourself in relationship to a thousand billion trillion stars. Perhaps at that point you can accept the simple responsibility for your own mind and that's really the requirement. Now, the process of doing that, as we began this tape with, is the process of acceptance of yourself in association with your own mind.

We are going to go to the psychology just for a minute. If all of the evidence for reality is manufactured by your own mind somewhere within the framework of time, and you are resisting them or conflicting with them or sorting them out, the obvious process to enlightenment or whole mind will be the relinquishment of your previous concepts. Come on, now. This is really fundamental. You can teach that as giving up grievances, if you wish. You can teach that as not letting the sun set on some sort of sorrow that you have with your brother and certainly you can teach it within the framework of forgiveness. Will this lead you to the certainty that you are only forgiving your own thoughts?

Of course! That will make you feel real good if you'll do it. I don't have the time nor patience for consciousnesses that are "practicing" forgiveness. That's nonsense. If you can't come to know, before you come to me, that all pain is self-inflicted, there is no sense in you coming to me. Very early on in my endeavor to find some sort of peace and happiness here, I discovered that I was doing it to myself. And that was a big step for me, and that can be a big step for you, so make it, for goodness sake. Then come to me with the certainty that you are doing this but to yourself, and I can show you the relief through the relinquishment of the necessity for you to perform in fear of the responsibilities that you previously engendered within your own time framework. That's how easy it is and how difficult it is. Why? Because it's a single occurrence. It's only going to happen once. And it did only happen once.

Where is the world when you are not here? Nowhere. The world is your construct. Anything outside of Heaven is not real, therefore this is not real, and you are dreaming. The sole responsibility, then, of the initiate is to awaken to his own certainty – to his own whole mind. Now, how is that done? Well, you don't like this process. Blessed are the meek. Resist not evil. Blessed is he who searches after truth and righteousness and is reviled in my name. All the other things that go with what? The process of giving and serving. There is an element involved in the action where the consciousness is in insidious deception that occurs in conceptual mind, and that's why one of our high teachings of relinquishment is in the process of giving, and includes sentences like: You can't possibly know you have anything until you give it away. Obviously the responsibility for the limited self includes the mechanisms of existence. For goodness sake! And the value system that is established in the consciousness in its pursuit of death.

Do you awaken only through forgiving? Of course. How else could you? There is no conflict but in your own mind. Now, is this, within the framework of the Course, unconditional love? Yes! But unconditional love is not a statement of unconditionalness, it's a statement of all condition. A better term would be full conditional love, wouldn't it? It is not the seeing of something sinful and evil outside myself, and the efforts that I have within my own poop to form some sort of forgiveness. That's nonsense. Forgiveness is accomplished in the idea of duality by bringing the dual thought, the thought of sin and immorality into the whole framework of your mind. This is the method of the Workbook of *A Course in Miracles*. There are no degrees to this, obviously, and this is what will begin to cause what? Your recognition that many of the physical manifestations that you have experienced in this lifetime, this carnation, are dealing, have dealt and will deal directly with the need for you to pursue this initiation that's going on in you. Is that a secret? The energy centers of your body, the awakening that's occurring now? This is a whole awakening and this is what we teach. This can give you a lot of peace of mind. You are going to feel very happy about it.

We are teaching happiness and love here, but we are demanding that you not associate it with pain and death. And this is where we are in conflict, and only here. And any whole mind that presents you with total love and happiness, you will resist because the nature of your existence is based on death. You always slay the ones you love because you love them to slay them. What an astonishing thing! If I come into your dream and say to you: Dear teacher, there is no reason for you to lose your children, there is no reason to carry these resentments that you have about what people are doing to you. It is impossible to be unjustly treated. You may not like that at the beginning. But the peace that will come to you as you gain the power of admission is extraordinary. Why? You'll begin to examine your own thoughts. You are not going to let somebody judge what you are in your shared limited association. This is a very valuable psychology, isn't it?

Very early we teach that all judgment is false. So any manner in which a consciousness that's outside of you, whether you can admit that you constructed him or not – he doesn't know who you are. How could he? You don't know who you are. That admission is what speeds up the process to whole mindedness. It's fun. Why? Because as this occurs, the miracle, the healing miracle, literally begins to happen. And it is time for you to look at that. And those who are listening to this tape, it is time to look at the miracle of the transformation of your mind – the inevitability of the mutation, the evolutionary process that's involved in the human mind awakening to its absolute capacity.

Only forgive. Don't hold grievances. Only love unconditionally.

Boy, it's a difficult assignment. We are teaching at the no alternative point for those of you who are really ready to look at this. Finally, if this is a required course, why not be about it? What's the big deal? Why not be mistaken? Why not join the rest of the universe instead of staying in what Jesus calls, "this dismal alcove" of death? Come on, you know in your mind that you have a function to fulfill here, and that's to awaken and whatever process you have to use to do it, be about it. You really don't want to die. Look at it. Look at the offering that is occurring here for you now.

I have a function God would have me fill. *It is your Father's holy Will that you complete Himself.* What a sentence! This is Lesson 192 in the Workbook of *A Course in Miracles* by Jesus Christ. And we are going to read it because I feel like talking about forgiveness for a minute. *It is your Father's holy Will that you complete Himself...* Isn't that a lovely sentence! *...and that your Self shall be His sacred Son, forever pure as He, of Love created and in love preserved, extending love, creating in its Name, forever one with God and with your Self.* Wow! Talk about singular wholeness of mind statement! Isn't that lovely! *Yet what can such a function mean within a world of envy, hatred and attack?* As you look around you, look at how your mind is, in its determination to judge, to be jealous, to hold a grievance and to attack somebody – either directly or by the fake praise that you give him in association with your own false self. Look at human beings.

Therefore, you have a function in the world in its own terms. For who can understand a language far beyond his simple grasp? Okay? Ready? *Forgiveness represents your function here.* To give represents your function here. To forgive is to have relinquished the previous grievances that you held before. It means I have given before. I have given everything before and am not holding that grievance as I view the image of my brother apparently outside of me. *Forgiveness represents your function here. It is not God's creation, for it is the means by which untruth can be undone.* In other words, there is really no sin there is really nothing to forgive, is there? That grievance is just being held by you in your mind. This will make it easier for you. *It is not God's creation, for it is the means by which untruth can be undone. And who would pardon Heaven?* There is a

162

lovely sentence in the Course where it says: Will you forgive God? Will you forgive your brother for this apparent grievance that you are suffering from? *Yet on earth, you need the means to let illusions go. Creation merely waits for your return to be acknowledged, not to be complete.* The universe is going on despite you being asleep with your head under the covers. Everything is going on exactly the way it was before you fell asleep. Early in the Course, Jesus says that you fell asleep, that Adam fell asleep, that you journeyed East of Eden to the Land of Nod, and nowhere does it say that you are awake. You are in your dream, brother.

Creation cannot even be conceived of in the world. It has no meaning here. Are you ready? *Forgiveness is the closest it can come to earth. For being Heaven-born, it has no form at all.* You know how good you feel when for just a moment you have the release, the purgation of forgiving? How you'll cry with happiness at the idea that the bondage that held you with your dear friend that you really love and how relieved you were when you made the one phone call that was necessary. You extend that to the world and you'll begin to feel really good because the process of the miracle will be the discovery that all of the pain in the illusion of death and all of the grievance that you held was only in your own mind. This is a very simple lesson but it needs to be practiced and in the practice is the idea of forgiveness. *Being Heaven-born, it has no form at all.* In other words, it really doesn't make any difference what you forgive, if the requirement is total forgiveness. This makes it very simple. Why? Because the requirement then is to no judgment. How simple it becomes then, if you will not assume the responsibility of the necessity for your own existence through judgment, which is false. You will relinquish yourself and come to know that there is a single whole purpose of creation in the whole universe. Holy Mackerel!

God created One Who has the power to translate in form the wholly formless. What He makes are dreams, but of a kind so close to waking that the light of day already shines in them, and eyes already opening behold the joyful sights their offerings contain. This is kind of a nice definition of the awakening process, of the initiation of the enlightenment that is going on in your mind, isn't it?

Forgiveness gently looks upon all things unknown in Heaven, sees them disappear, and leaves the world a clean and unmarked slate on which the Word of God can now replace the senseless symbols written there before. The memories that you have previously held are relinquished and your slate is clean. This is a form of meditation. *Forgiveness is the means by which the fear of death is overcome, because it holds no fierce attraction now and guilt is gone. Forgiveness lets the body be perceived as what it is; a simple teaching aid, to be laid by when learning is complete, but hardly changing him who learns at all.* Isn't that nice!

The mind without the body cannot make mistakes. It cannot think that it will die or be the prey of merciless attack. Anger becomes impossible, and where is terror then? What fears could still assail those who have lost the source of all attack, the core of anguish and the seat of fear? Only forgiveness can relieve the mind of thinking that the body is its home. Only forgiveness can restore the peace that God intended for His holy Son. Only forgiveness can persuade the Son to look again upon his holiness.

With anger gone, you will indeed perceive that, for Christ's vision and the gift of sight, no sacrifice was asked, and only pain was lifted from a sick and tortured mind. Is this unwelcome? Is it to be feared? Or is it to be hoped for, met with thanks and joyously accepted? We are one, and therefore give up nothing. But we have indeed been given everything by God.

Yet do we need forgiveness to perceive that this is so. Without its kindly light we grope in darkness, using reason but to justify our rage and our attack. Our understanding is so limited that what we think we understand is but confusion born of error. We are lost in mists of shifting dreams and fearful thoughts, our eyes shut tight against the light; our minds engaged in worshipping what is not there.

Who can be born again in Christ but him who has forgiven everyone he sees or thinks of or imagines? Who could be set free while he imprisons anyone? A jailer is not free, for he is bound together with his prisoner. He must be sure that he does not escape, and so he spends his time in keeping watch on him. The bars that limit him become the world in which his jailer lives, along with him. And it is on his freedom that the way to liberty depends for both of them. Wow!

Therefore, hold no one prisoner. Don't judge him, brother. *Release instead of bind, for thus are you made free.* Listen. *The way is simple. Every time you feel a stab of anger, realize you hold a sword above your head. And it will fall or be averted as you choose to be condemned or free. Thus does each one who seems to tempt you to be angry represent your savior from the prison house of death. And so you owe him thanks instead of pain.*

Be merciful today. The Son of God deserves your mercy. It is he who asks that you accept the way to freedom now. Deny him not. His Father's love for him belongs to you. Your function here on earth is only to forgive him, that you may accept him back as your Identity. Hear that? You created him. You have made the image of him in your own mind. Your condemnation of him is what? Your condemnation of yourself. *And you are what he is. Forgive him now his sins, and you will see that you are one with him.*

What a lovely lesson and how very easy it appears to be. Yet when you attempt to do it here on earth you are going to be judged as weak, aren't you? What do you care? You hold the secret to eternal life. We are teaching relinquishment here, not attack and defense. We are teaching a new covenant, not the old covenant of reciprocity, of an eye for an eye. No, we are teaching give up and see the glory of your whole mind reflected in the face of the brother that you have come to love.

We are at God's Country Place, here in Reedsburg, Wisconsin, teaching love and understanding through the high initiatory process of relinquishment that brings about the enlightenment of the whole mind and body. And what a glorious undertaking it is. We hope you'll join us soon. Thank You.

Perhaps till the end of this tape you'll join us in this moment of meditation. Be free now. Let go. Only love. That is what you are. You are God creating. I love you. Be free. I want the peace of God. I have nothing to fear. I am safe in the Heaven I have never left. Thank You, Father.

All things are given you. God's trust in you is limitless. He knows His Son. He gives without exception, holding nothing back that can contribute to your happiness. And yet, unless your will is one with His, His gifts are not received. But what would make you think there is another will than His?

- A Course In Miracles Workbook: Lesson 166 -

Give To Live

Now we begin once again with ramblings in the kitchen of God's Country Place. I call it rambling in the Light. It's important that you understand that everything that I say is coming from a particular frame of reference – and sometimes I forget how very fundamental the directions of an awakened mind are. How very fundamental, for example, the teachings of Jesus Christ in the *Course in Miracles* are. They are much, much too fundamental to be accepted or even admitted to by split minds. The process of enlightenment, that is, the process of coming to whole mind and recognizing yourself as universal consciousness is a process of *giving*.

I want to key in on that word for a minute because the nature of the *Course In Miracles* is a process of *for-giving* which is an indication that this is all over and you have, in fact, given before of yourself. If salvation, then, is the process of giving, we'll use sentences like, "The only way to know you have something is by giving it away." That doesn't seem practical at all to a consciousness who is in a condition of reciprocity or exchange, does it? If I tell a consciousness coming here to give everything away and come to me, he is immediately in resistance of it because of his defense mechanism of having ideas in order to protect his identity. While he is willing to give me, in concepts, the notation that, for example, charity or Christian love is the sharing of God, my declaration that the only way you can know God is to give love completely, is very difficult for him because it involves a relinquishment of himself.

I'll stay in Christianity for just a moment. The clash that occurs with First Covenant consciousness – that is, an eye-for-an-eye or reciprocity or the establishment of laws on earth and *thou shalt not kill* – all of those admonishments always occur with the process of giving rather than receiving – or giving with the idea of receiving which is an indication of what? Lack, or need for substance or need to exist. Listen, you will see how fundamental this is. If what I am saying to you, then, from another level is true, it would be impossible for you to know that you have everything until you gave everything away. And this is met with a tremendous amount of resistance in this Hades, this shade, this dream of reality, this dream of pain and death which, of course, makes you continue to demand recognition within the framework of yourself.

The notations of experience of enlightenment through service will come to you at a very high range, and those of you who come to me have obviously attempted to practice charity. This is a very simple process. You have felt the pain of your brother. You have attempted to give aid to your brother and share with him the abundance that you feel in your own heart. Yet you discover that no matter how much aid you provide him with, he continues to become sick and to die. Now, at that point you have begun to examine the whole structure. You say, no matter what I do, I can't relieve my pain or most particularly the pain of my brother, because while I have been successful in providing abundance for my associates, I see that my brother still suffers. I want you to see how fundamental this is. I will, therefore, send all these packages of goods – I am Joseph in Egypt; I hate to use that reference – I am going to gather up all these packages and goods and give them to my brother and thereby assuage the guilt feelings that I have in association with my abundance and his lack. And it would appear at this point that I am doing a very charitable thing, and indeed I am. Now, to those of you who have been charitable and still are feeling the excruciating pain of your brother and your inability to deal with the apparent chaos and death, these are the consciousnesses that will begin to hear what I teach.

Here is the declaration: If indeed there are such things as sickness and pain that you see about you, they can never be healed. I say that to you in the highest sense of truth. This has nothing to do with your attempts to do it. Of course you will attempt to do it. The whole progress that occurs in the mind is your attempt to give yourself and hold onto yourself at the same time – to have ideas of associations of what you are and to base your identity on giving. Now, you will run into sentences in Christian tradition like – and they're debated forever – "Good works avail you nothing." That's an indication that no matter what you give away, as long as you take credit for it you can't know that you are divine because you will retain the idea of reciprocity and I'm well aware of that. I am going to turn that around just a little bit for you. I am going to say, "Good works will avail you everything," if they are completely good. That is, if you do only good works you'll have no problem. The problem you have is your attempt to sort out what constitutes works and what constitutes being or selfness. I maintain that works and being are not separate because the cause of your thought will be the effect of what you are regardless of what you say. Did I jump in too deep for you there? I guess I did. I didn't mean to go that deep with it.

Now, if you're going to teach the finality of your certainty, of say *A Course In Miracles*, which nobody really wants to practice. Let's try it. The reason that you forgive is that you can only give to yourself. Quite literally, the constructions that you have outside of you are your own pain. This is the little step for you now. You cannot know that they are yours until you give them everything. Jesus calls this brotherhood and love. You literally can't know who they are until you give them everything that you are. There is going to be no such thing in your teachings as reciprocity. Now, the consciousness that has practiced reciprocity and gathered abundance about him in his own relationships will resist you at very high level because his definition of love is one of exchange. Your definition of love is one of giving. He cannot understand the uncompromising attitude of an awakened mind with the certainty that you can only give to be. Quite literally the closest that perceptual mind can get to creating is giving through self-expression.

The higher the range of the giving, the more self-expression goes on because the consciousness, in his giving, no longer correlates himself with a limited identity and expresses a thought form outside of himself in relationship with the whole truth. In a very real way, then, this process of giving is one of coming to know your Self. The basis of the teaching, obviously then, is to take no credit for your giving but only to love and serve. When we have attempted to do this, there is a great deal of resistance here because the associations of success and happiness are based on having rather than being. I'm very much aware of that.

What you finally do with that in your own mind I don't know, but I guarantee you that once you begin to experience the joy of giving, it will become very intense in you, and you will literally want to give everything that you have away in order to be free. It's going to become very obvious to you.

The process of coming to know yourself has to do with giving yourself away. There is no alternative to that because you cannot know that you have everything until you give it away, because *having* and *being* are the same. As long as you are possessed by your own thoughts, you cannot know that. I don't know who takes Master Jesus' sentences in the text seriously where he says, "Protect everything you value by the act of giving it away." Notice He says *act*. It's an act to shorn yourself of these so-called necessities. You say, "Well, Master, it sounds like you're teaching frugality here, that you are teaching poor in spirit, that you are teaching blessed are the meek." Well, I am. I am. You don't like that, out there. I don't care. As long as you have what Jesus calls grandiosity – ideas that you are accomplishing something – you are not going to get this, teacher. This is a process of love and forgiveness and giving. You want to examine the uncompromising statement that you will be possessed by your own thoughts and condemned to stay in time and die as long as you have ideas about yourself. Come on! This is my teaching. This is my declaration to you. Try not to attack me when I give this to you, though. There is no need for you to attack love. Master Jesus says why do you attack love and beauty and truth when it's presented to you? We are really – will you take that off, Ana? We're sitting here in the kitchen of God's Country Place and there is a kettle on the stove and it is boiling – much like what is happening to you now. You are beginning to feel the fervent response of your mind in regard to this plaintive message, aren't you?

It doesn't seem possible that you could actually undergo the experience of relinquishment and feel the joy of creation because the residual of the earth shows no evidence of it. The evidence of total giving is not here, because the evidence of total giving is salvation in Heaven. You might look at that very plaintively, that as long as the exchange is occurring, there is no reality here. This is my declaration to you. In that sense, this is a process of bringing your mind together, bringing your perceptual mind together through an evolution, through a metamorphosis. This is the indication of transformation. That's really what is happening to you. Be of good cheer! It appears, because you are in the nature of expecting a response between your cause and effects, that when you give something in what you think of as love, that the response is not as immediate. The higher the range of your total giving, the less response you get. And that is absolutely true. Remember that you are accustomed to getting in return, something for the act of your thoughts about giving.

Let's go to what the *Course in Miracles* really teaches. As long as you are in expectation of return for love, the miracle cannot occur. You are limiting it simply by the framework of the expectation of the result for the act-thought that's going out from you. The whole idea of the miracle, then, is to simply extend your love through the non-identity of yourself and your limited associations. We are teaching directly now, teachers, from the workbook of the *Course in Miracles*. The certainty that you do not know who you are and the application of your determination to hold onto something, even though you don't know what you are or how you got here, are what are condemning you to time and death. See how easy it is? That's very simple, then, for you to do that.

We're at God's Country Place talking about the uncompromising certainty that life, universal consciousness, is singular and whole and beautiful and has nothing to do with your determination to hold onto your limited self. Let's deal with that just for a moment because it just came up in our discussion here at the table. In our original teachings we used to try to present you with the statements: *relinquish yourself, blessed are the meek* and *blessed are the poor in spirit* in the Beatitudes, with very important statements, literal statements like: *it is impossible for you to be unjustly treated.* This is the statement that the protection of your limited association about yourself is a denial of God – that there really is no pain and grief outside of your thought about it. That practice used to be one of being humble, but in this universal consciousness of split mind on earth, the idea of humility and giving and sharing is not very popular.

Now, if we come at it from the other direction, we attempt to give you, within your own mind, all of the power that there is in the universe. This is called giving you a choice. This is a teaching device now. This has nothing to do with truth, brothers. Very early in the text of the *Course in Miracles*, Master Jesus says we are dealing literally with an impossible situation, which is what perception is. That is, the idea that you can choose reality, and of course you can't. The mechanism of choice, however, is necessary since you have invented it in your time associations. So, of course, we're going to use it. My teaching has nothing to do with choice. My teaching has to do with using choice to see that you have no choice.

Now, as we indicated, the sooner you realize that you really have no choice except to be whole and in heaven and be singular, until you come to know that, you will continue to practice the notation of choice. And you say, "Well, teacher, it sounds like you're teaching "give up". I see in here notations of turning your will and your life and everything that you have over to the care of a power that is not definable." Of course that is my teaching. What did you think? Did you think that I was going to tell you that perceptual mind could arrive at the conclusion of wholeness? Come on. Perceptual mind is the antithesis of wholeness. It is exactly the opposite. The world is exactly the opposite and you cannot come to know that except by going through a process of relinquishment or giving. And finally, you simply commend your spirit into the hands of God.

All of the pain and sorrow that you feel forever and always has been the idea of self-identity in the association with the true identity of your Self, that is, in God. All of the Gethsemanes, all of the dark nights of the soul, are only your attempts to combat yourself in relationship with your own mind. They are nothing but that.

Now, is this a gradual process? You'll hear these terms expressed. What you are saying then is that I must experience a bottom. Have you ever heard that expression, out there? Finally, I am teaching you the futility of existence on earth. But remember, you are not a measurer of the process of your own give-up-ness. At what point do you recoup and regroup in your determination to continue to express your own self-will rather than simply doing this?

These are the teachings, obviously, of the recovery program of Alcoholics Anonymous or, in fact, of the recovery program of all initiation consciousnesses coming from split mind to whole mind. Those of you who read this, we have given talks on the addictive programs in association with the *Course* or wholeness. It's the same teaching. But remember that the teachings of the 12 Steps have really nothing to do with the idea of addiction particular to alcoholism. They are teachings of the relinquishment of limited mind to come to whole mind. It is a process of spiritual enlightenment. Nothing but that. Now, those of you who have had the experience of overcoming the addiction through the release of your mind are well along the way to the idea that through the process of giving up there is, indeed, a power that is self-evident to you behind that veil of deception and resentment you have put up to keep you from seeing your own Godliness and your own reality.

Now in that sense, the relinquishment of ideas about yourself is only the relinquishment of what? Resentments. Jesus calls them grievances. Very simply, if you are a conglomerate of grievances or ideas of combat in association with yourself, you bring them from your past – from your past frame of reference, and base your reality on the grievance or the possibility that you can be harmed. Now here's where the valuable psychology is that you can only cause pain to yourself. All pain is self-inflicted. You do this but to yourself, regardless how tempted you are to believe there is something out there causing you a problem. See how you do this? See how you can practice this? These are true statements.

How does this work? This works simply because you are making an admission that you are the cause of it. Now you are bringing the solution to your apparent problem to where it can be resolved. Obviously, if the problem is outside of you, if you have a grievance against your brother, you hold him responsible for your actions. You respond to him by attacking or defending yourself from him. Do you see how fundamental this is? Remember, I said at the beginning of the talk how very basic this is? I'm looking you right in the eye now, I am looking at your other eye here – at your Holy Spirit eye – and I am proclaiming to you to not be defensive in your own mind-relationships and you will feel the miracle of the transformation that will occur in you. What an incredible, beautiful thing that is! You see? But you see how basic we are? I am telling you to give up your grievances. Because the rest of the world bases its perceptual reality on attack and defense doesn't mean that you should, because until you overcome it, they can't. Would you care to hear that as the final part of this talk this morning?

The basis of the teachings of subjective reality indicate to you that this is your world. No matter how tempted you are to think that there's something outside of your dream about it, there isn't. You are the cause of this. This will give you a real good feeling if you are ready to look at it. The first feeling you will have when you look at this is kind of fearful. You will go, "Holy mackerel! You mean this is between me and the rest of the universe?" Yes! It has nothing to do with the images that you have constructed to hold mutual grievances outside of you – that is, to commiserate with your own death process. No! No! Now, you will like that. Why? Because it's individual transformation, and indeed the transformation is individual and singular.

Now we are into teaching initiation. We want to show you that you can actually go through a process in your own mind where you change the world. This is the declaration of Master Jesus that you are the savior of the world. But why should that be such a big deal if you constructed the world? If you will look at what you've constructed, and I'm talking about the whole world, and are determined to change your mind about it, it will be changed. Remember that the world was constructed outside of the framework of reality. And your relinquishment of it, then, is a necessary part.

A nice way to teach it is to include all of your thoughts in with your conceptual evaluation, rather than exclude. This is forgiveness at its highest level. You literally examine your own guilt and death processes in association with yourself. You don't bury anything. This is not different than the 12 Step program with the indications of the fourth and fifth step that command you to seek forgiveness through the acknowledgment of guilt. I have no problem with that. If you want to seek forgiveness through the acknowledgment of guilt, you acknowledge that you are guilty and I will forgive you. The process is one of you accepting my forgiveness. That's how simple this is.

This will be fun for you as the brothers come together and you practice this changing of your mind. We want to assure you that it involves more than just your perceptions and conceptions of yourself. It must involve all of you. And that's fearful to you. You would much rather take, for example, your ideas of the mind and separate them from the emotions of your heart, but I promise you that an emotion is an idea. I assure you that you can only *be* and cannot *have* ideas and indeed cannot have emotions. You cannot *have* love. You love your brother through service and giving to him, don't you. Finally, the bridge to total love is one of communication. If I am not threatened by my previous thoughts about you, I extend to you the certainty that I have created you in my own whole mind. This association, or a break in communication, is all that the schism ever was. It has nothing to do with the fractured parts that you attempt to bring together in associations of your own limited reality.

I love you! I will do anything in the universe for you because you are in my mind as whole things and you have instructed me within this framework of time to come to you from supertime – this is a course in speeding up time – and remind you that indeed we are reminiscing about this and that you and I never left Heaven.

Here is the crux of the whole teaching: the relinquishment of self-identity. When I speak to you as what we must term a whole mind, what I'm saying is this: no matter what you present me with – this would be true of all *healed* teachers, Jesus calls them – I will indicate to you that there is a single problem and a single solution. When you bring me particular problems within the brotherhood and I express them as singular, you have a tendency to interpret them dualistically in the framework of the problems that you are experiencing within your own time framework. The solution obviously is the total forgiveness of the grievance that you hold against your brother. But remember that judgment is a grievance, isn't it? Judgment is the idea that there could possibly be associate relationships of pain or lack within the framework of reality, and there can't be. Quite literally then, if you come to a whole mind he attempts to teach you "don't judge." Now, I may present that to you in humorous ways. I may say to you, "If you judge me, you're wrong, and everything that I say is wrong, and I have no value in what I am saying." I am very certain that that's true. Why? Because I'm teaching give no value to your perceptions here. I am teaching you to relinquish your notations about me and only love. This is the whole sense of the *Course* teachings, isn't it? All whole minds will do this. Why? They are very certain that within any mechanism of teaching there can only be one problem and one solution.

No matter what you as an ego or personality brought to me, I know you are not so – this is my highest teaching – because the earth is not so. You can present me with all the dilemmas of your associate thoughts and they will have no effect on me. That may be excruciating to you, but the more that you can see the consistency, which is as close to honesty as you can get of a whole mind teacher, the more – if you are determined to find it – you will seek him out. And this is what we are attempting to bring about. Then, by that association you undergo this transformation of your mind. This is a very high teaching. That is what's occurring around the world. Why? Because this is a required course. This is a course in enlightenment. I look at the definitions that consciousnesses apply to what the *Course in Miracles* is, like "a set of books." That's nonsense. *A Course in Miracles* is a simple course of the maturation of your mind of the certainty of singular wholeness. If you begin to look at it that way you will feel the excitement of the way out of chaos and death that are here by the declaration that I give you now. There is no death!

There has to be an alternative to the construct of your mind. And through the relinquishment of that content, you can come to know the truth – through love and forgiveness and giving, through detachment, through non-possession. The more you do it, the freer you will be. The less you possess, the freer you will be. You won't care about the possessions of your other brothers because you see that possession is binding them to death, holding them in time by their associations in their minds. Wow! You can hardly wait to give it away. You will go through periods in this maturation where you will be in direct conflict with the world simply because you don't want to possess. You will be attacked for not possessing, but it won't bother you really, why? Because you will begin to experience the freedom of *being* rather than having to hold on and literally construct sickness and death in order to verify yourself. *Swear not to die, you Holy Son of God.* We keep coming back to that, don't we? You have invented death as a protective mechanism to keep your own identity, and death is only grievance or thinking that something can harm you outside yourself. If you think it will and can, it will and can.

This is about love and giving. But finally my teaching is, there's no reason for this world because there is no reason for pain and sickness and death. But the idea that there is no reason for this world eliminates the necessity for you to be here. This is the paradox, this is the cusp, this is the dilemma of trying to teach at this level.

In a very real way though, I give you choice. I assert that you have no choice and are only whole and beautiful and true and loving. When expressed in psychology this becomes "unmotivated action." Master Jesus says, you never do things for the reasons that you say you do. This is literally true, and if you will give up reasons for doing things, you will come into a whole new sense of your own reality. Then the miracle, the miracle of lesson, of the Chapter 28, of Lesson 170, will come home because if you don't motivate your mind, your whole mind will assert automatically, because you are indeed whole-mindedness.

I know I came back into "don't plan for the future" and "don't lay up stores." Don't plan to die. You don't like this. Give up your possessions and you can't die. As long as you possess you must die, because possession or having is what death is. Are you listening to this? All of the teachings of the New Covenant of Jesus indicate only, don't plan, don't lay up stores, let God be what He is, don't judge Him. Isn't it nice? You're not attacking me too violently when I teach this anymore, are you? Remember that 2000 years ago when Master Jesus walked into the temple and taught this, He was immediately crucified. Today the teaching, as Jesus says in the *Course*, is you crucify the Christ everyday by denying the certainty of your own reality through the exclamation of the possibility of this grievance of pain and death that we speak of. That's what perceptual mind is. When you go to teach this, you are going to end up with some pretty hard statements, aren't you? Statements like, "You are either for me or you're against me." You don't like that. You are going to end up with statements like, "You are either Christ or Anti-Christ." You are going to end up with statements like, "The world of perception is attack on God." That's all right, because finally we want consciousnesses looking at themselves and the individual association with themselves, and in that sense, it doesn't have to do with how many images or groups they gather about themselves to verify this excursion that they pretend to be on.

Wake up! Feel this lovely flow of truth that is engulfing you now, and come to know who you really are. We hope we'll see you soon. Brothers are moving around the world now, teaching this high message. Those who are ready to hear them, or are at least determined to listen, are calling. And their calls will be answered. Perhaps the magnitude of this teaching is dawning on you – that through the process of relinquishment of opinion and judgment, you formulate around you an energy of non-defensiveness, of freedom. For you stay in this perceptual bondage just for another moment and then the earth is gone. It is a hatching out. You become free. And you literally step out of time into eternity. And this is what I am presenting to you, that this can come about in you, and that it will make you very happy. And all of the pain and frustration that you are feeling because of your associations with sickness and death and hatred and love and truth and beauty, will disappear and you will become only love. These determinations of yours to formulate notations of time and death and attack, with wholeness and love will begin to be very absurd to you. You are looking directly now at why is it that the things that you love leave you? Why is it that if there is truth and happiness, no matter what you do, you can't find it here? Why is all the intensity of your necessity to express yourself in truth and beauty dashed by the necessity of cancer and heart attacks, pain and sickness? Come on, brother!

Our whole notation is that this is not so. This is indeed a dream, a dream of death and chaos, and all around you is the beauty and light of whole consciousness and love. This is all I really present to you. And you will hear it because you did hear it. This was over a long time ago. You are coming to see that now. We hope that you will contact us. It's just beginning, and you are a vital part of it, aren't you? In fact, it can't be done without you, can it? Without you there is no Heaven. Isn't that amazing? Without you there is no earth. Take your choice.

Let's have just a moment of quiet together here. You can see the Light. You are not a body, you are free. You are still as God created you. Be free.

I want to make one more observation. We are aware you are reading this in your own particular environs and experiences whether in a group or individually. It is very important that you hear this. Don't belittle your own enlightenment process. Our whole teaching is that this is a metamorphosis occurring in you individually. It has nothing to do with the consciousnesses around you or, in fact, even the expression of the associate ideas of what's happening. So if you feel this intense pressure to contact us, you do that. You know where this came from, and if you have this necessity now to seek and find, that's what we are here for. We serve that purpose and none other. Don't believe that because we are saying this, we are some sort of establishment, because we are not. We are teaching to your whole mind within your dream framework, individually. But we are teaching at the light source so that you can see the truth of you. We are not an establishment. We are making a statement of the whole single truth that is you. So welcome home! We hope we will see you physically and that you can come in this declaration of your new-found mind.

Give it away. Don't be possessed anymore. You are free. Some of you are feeling this directly. It is very lovely, very beautiful. Stay with us now. We're with you forever and ever.

We are sitting here at God's Country Place. We are at the kitchen table once again, and we are talking about the association of so-called normal or perceptual mind with the *disease* of spiritualness, and how finally the idea of whole mind and the idea of the relinquishment of associate ideas in regard to personalities are considered to be mental diseases by perceptual consciousness. It is very evident to you in the new way in which you are thinking and doing, that you are different than the constituted reality of earth, and perhaps you always have been. Many of you who are reading this now have always been different, yet you have been forced to acclimatize – acclimate – yourself to the notations of perceptual reality in regard to the things that you did, the goals that you set, the modality of your thinking in cultural relationships. All of these things have environmentally been forced on you from the hereditary or genetic or karma standpoint – you always felt different.

We have come to tell you that the different is good. We have come, finally, to tell you that total different is total good because the real condition – as close as you can get to it in perception – of heaven, of wholeness, of goodness, has absolutely nothing to do with constructs of the mind of the earth. That is a statement of fact. It begins perhaps early in pre-adolescence. The consciousness observes that, to some degree, people do not say what they mean and there are a lot of young clairvoyants who have suffered the apparent stigma of listening to an adult while the adult's mind was saying something else. Have you ever heard of that? Did you know that? And that's a fairly common thing many of us early on experienced. So we were taught hypocrisy, and it was at a higher level even than, "Do what I say, not what I do." It was more, "But Dad, you're thinking differently." The whole world thinks differently than it acts or the whole world finally is basing its reality on the consciousness that it is denying. And this will come later on to you and this causes great frustration.

You have become what? A search for perfection. All indications that will occur in adolescent schizophrenia, for example, are statements of a need to be a whole consciousness. When puberty is reached, when the energy passions mature to creative necessity, there will be statements of a need to be whole which manifests itself, obviously, in the need to create or re-create or to have issue. But at a higher level, it is a statement of the need for the consciousness to identify itself, to know who it is, to find some reality. This has to be accompanied by perceptual split mind because this is a split mind place, and unless the consciousness can adjust to the idea of the tragedy of the association of pain and death with love and security, he will kill himself perhaps, or he will begin to sedate himself, which is more common. Or finally he will find a compromise that fits into a form that, while it is not true, and he knows it, it has to be acceptable to him in the relationship of the limited goals that have been set for him.

Many of you have gone through these periods in your life, then adjusted to them and gone on, perhaps to school and gone on and found avocations and occupations that gave you at least some sense of satisfaction, only to discover that in terms of what you really were in the reality of the universe – in your need to know – they literally didn't fit the bill. Now you are ready. Now you are really looking, aren't you? Yet everywhere you look all you can see is a temporary satisfaction derived by a conflictual consciousness in association with the things around him. Wow! Now we are into the teaching. There is no answer here. Conflictual mind cannot find answer because the derivative of the solution is the cause of the problem, and quite literally he is his own problem. You have discovered that now, and this is what we teach.

The problem that apparently exists in your associations is nothing but mind possession. Jesus in the *Course in Miracles* uses this term quite often. He says, in the old biblical expression, that the consciousness is possessed, and we mean that literally. The consciousness has ideas in association with his limited framework of time, doesn't he? He is actually possessed by things. Jesus calls them perceptions or idols. You find in your text, "Do you think you know what an idol is?" Take a look at what idols really are. Idols are associate ideas about yourself in relationship to the objects that are around you. Idols are the need to hold on and to identify yourself in this persona, in this limited association that you find yourself. You will always judge them falsely because all judgment is false. And this is why you can't find the Christ.

I'll say this once more. When Jesus says, "Let's face it, if you could find the Christ you would kill him," He means quite literally that perceptual mind defends itself from reality, from wholeness. So the process of coming to know what we teach – that is, the mechanism of coming to know – has to be relinquishment. This is the basis of the *Course in Miracles*, that your mind, your perceptual mind, is the obstacle to the reality that is all about you. Only through the relinquishment of your possessions can you come to know that. Now those of you who have decided to take this tack on the Kings Highway are beginning to have the feeling that you want to divest yourself of things. This is a nice indication. You wake up one morning, you have gone through a change of mind, and you literally start to give your things away. You don't want to be connected with security. You seek out insecurity in order to allow the miracle to occur.

This is the teaching of the Workbook of the *Course*. The whole idea of ordering your mind or looking to the future or gathering evidence of survival in time are the exact notations that are causing your death and aging. What we are dealing with for the moment is that the consciousness literally undergoes this, and society, which is structured on longevity and subsequent death, cannot understand the foolish tactics of a spiritual mind that is trying to get rid of itself. It often is judged and appears, within the framework of the balance of perceptual mind, to be insanity, doesn't it? Is this the awakening of the energy forces? Is this the evidence of paranoia and schizophrenia that may come about? Sure, sure.

The fundamental teaching that we present to you is that you are undergoing a transformative change in your body/mind of all of your systems in regard to your relationship, including your glandular associations, your circulatory functions – what you are in truth. With that admission, all the apparent aberrations that will occur in this process will be looked on as beneficent because they become a continuing means to identify the change that is going on in you. Isn't this nice? If you have been doing the *Course in Miracles* or reading this, you begin to seek out consciousnesses who are experiencing the phenomena of the enlightenment without giving credit to it within the limited framework. Many of them would walk on water, or they would levitate, or they would see bright lights, or they would feed the multitudes and perhaps even raise the dead. They go through all these things and they are in a perceptual state where they have to finally acknowledge – and this is the difficult step, but you better make it – that you are different. You finally cannot come to hear this without the whole statement that your whole mind will be different, at least for a moment, than the perceptual establishment that appears to be outside of you. You can't get it without going through it. And that's okay.

If we're going to take the sentences, let's take them whole from the *Course: You are the only living Son of God.* That is a statement of whole mindedness, that God created you singularly and wholly. Is that true of the things you see around you? Is that true of what appears to

182

be happening on earth? Does the body really construct itself in divine associations? Of course not. Therefore the necessity for you to appear to be different is going to be very obvious to you. Why? Because you are different! It may start out with you marching to a little different drum, then the melody begins to play for you and you begin to hear other things. Then you reach a point where we say: "Can you hear this?" where the mind has expanded sufficiently, where it has relinquished its previous karma associate ideas to the point where it puts them together in a new framework and *now* it begins to hear this. This is the brotherhood. This is what we will be gathering together, loosely, not in a doctrinal organization, around the world and it is occurring now. That framework of thought is literally transcendent and is in a constant state of occurring. How lovely then, to realize that the necessity that you are feeling now to divest yourself of your goods, of your worldly possessions, is all a part of this determination being exercised by you in your whole mind in this space/time framework to return to reality, to wake up. You have been asleep, haven't you? And now you are going to wake up.

So the need to give yourself away is very valuable. In fact, the fundamental teaching has to be that the closest you can get to creating in perceptual consciousness is to give. And when you give yourself completely, you will no longer be held in the bondage of the memory patterns that constitute your apparent genetic reality. Holy mackerel, come on home guys!

Strangely enough, the idea of necessity, the idea of lack, the idea of scarcity, is exactly why you don't give things away. Yet obviously, until you give them away you can't know that you don't need them. You are nothing but a series of sequential possessions of an unreal consequence because the beginning has not reality. But the teaching has to be that you give, or forgive, in order to know that. You cannot know that there is nothing outside of your mind. Then the sentences – listen to how dramatically different this will sound to you: *You can only forgive yourself. You can only give to yourself. God creates, you are a creator in correspondence with the certainty of that reality.* Obviously you can't know it unless you give it away. But the defense mechanisms (obviously defensiveness is fear) that you have in the admonition that you must give in order to know you are real are very strong. This is nothing but the New Covenant of Christianity. This is nothing but the notation of mercy, of love and giving in order to become whole, in order to communicate, in order to see that you are single consciousnesses. *Protect everything you value by the act of giving it away.* The universe is only thought. You begin with the notation that everything is ideas and that the ideas are yours and this includes God. You have this marvelous idea of perfection. Then you see that no matter where you look there isn't any because you are possessed by needs. Then you give the needs away and come to *be* rather than *have.* Then you see that being and having are the same thing. Then your whole mind suddenly explodes on you and you are in the glory of the recognition of love without the necessity to defend yourself in any regard. You have been found not guilty of ordering your thoughts. You have made the admission of single source. Wow! That's astonishing. You discover that strength is in absolute dependence on the single truth rather than the establishment of some sort of kingdom outside of reality. How foolish to do that and die in the attempt. So, don't be possessed. Does possession include opinion? Hey, possession is opinion! Thought forms are opinions about your relationships. Don't judge and you will spring into Heaven.

Let's take a look at the inevitable outcome of this kind of thinking, of the idea that you must give everything away in order to discover what you are. All establishments, that is all perceptual associations on the earth, or the earth itself, are statements of the denial of whole mindedness. Jesus' Christian admonitions that your kingdom is not of this world, that you literally have to give up your established mind in order to come to the truth, are all very much a part of this. But look at the intensity with which the consciousness will defend his mind establishments.

Many of you who are doing the *Course in Miracles* are looking at the chapters that deal with special relationships and go a step further and begin to speak of holy relationships. What we have been talking about in regard to sequential time or perceptual mind is what special relationships are. All limited mind functions are nothing but special relationships. You might want to look at the certainty that they only communicate with themselves since they are projections of a limited mind. Obviously you don't believe this. All of the establishments that you have on earth are objective establishments making allowance for thought forms in their own constructs in association with themselves. You actually give them an identity and pretend that they didn't emanate from your own mind, don't you? That constitutes a special relationship. Actually, if you walk into a room and identify somebody by a name, you have given him a special association in the drama of your mind, haven't you? You attempt, then, to communicate with him by presenting to him your ideas in association with his. *They have no reality at all.* Not only do you only present him with things that you may particularly want him to hear, but you hold within you and defend other notations that you feel will offend him, perhaps, or cause him to judge you falsely. There is a lovely sentence in the *Course* where Jesus says you end up with what is considered to be a so-called perfect relationship on earth, a perceptual relationship that the consciousnesses have literally contributed nothing to. It becomes nothing but form and it appears to be very stable and it has absolutely no reality at all.

In the process of giving yourself – there's another sentence in the *Course* you may as well hear: *While we are all equal and certainly emanate from God, we are not equal in time.* Some of you are beginning to experience, as you go through this metamorphosis, that the conditions around you do not keep up with the variances of the occurrences in your mind. And this can be very painful because it is a re-structuring going on at a different condition of consciousness or level of consciousness.

Here is the positive manner in which the miracle will occur. The only possibility of a failure in any sort of relationship you have on earth will be the failure of your own mind in your contribution to the relationship. *The only thing that could ever be missing in a relationship is what you don't bring to it.* And that's very difficult for you because you have been counseled on opinions and judgments in regard to associate reality for a very long time. If you give everything that you are and have to every relationship – that's not a relationship, that's love! That's creating! That's extending from you – you will not long remain in any form of establishment of your mind on earth. That is the truth of it. Again and again you have brought with you perceptual thought forms in this framework of time, either to attack you, or with which you are determined to associate and seek surcease of sorrow in the conflict of your own mind. This is very lovingly expressed in several pages in *A Course In Miracles*. Inevitably they lead to death because they are defense mechanisms. It is important for you to remember that you are only memory. All perceptual mind is only memory. This was over a long time ago, dear brothers. You are simply in a framework of sequential memory. It is impossible for you to meet a stranger, since you are constructing the consciousnesses in your own mind. Yet, since you have a drama of conflict, of hate and terror and fear with a lot of the array associations in your energy patterns, you establish very quickly in your new karma memories as you carnate – as you come into a recognition of yourself – your loves and hates, and base your reality on it. How absurd! You see now the necessity of forgiveness and practice of forgiveness? I am very much aware that you seem to be constituted in primordial hatred for particular types of cultures or associations. I am aware of that. But remember this, as long as you defend yourself, you become a part of the pattern of hate/love, of fear and death. So the practice has to be one of relinquishment or forgiving of your opinions in regard to it.

Can that be done by asserting the power of mind or by the relinquishment of the power, by going to humility? Well, it will work both ways. But remember this, the conflict is only in your own mind. If you will start with that premise, you won't need to define a holy relationship because you will discover through the absolute giving away of yourself, of your possessions, in what formerly held you in bondage, that you have become whole and free. Free in mind. Free to be, not free to do. Free to live, not free to die. These will be the natural occurrences as you come more and more into this new framework of reality, through this transformation that's going on in you now. So, be of good cheer. You are not going to fail.

I might tell you this: all judgments of yourself in regard to the progress you're making in this are false. It is impossible that you don't get it. It is impossible that you *didn't* get it. You are only love, and as you come to know that, you will become a happy learner. It will make you feel real good to make a commitment to this, teacher of God. And the higher the range of your commitment – the more you commit – the happier you will be. Did you know that?

There are some old biblical admonitions of Jesus: *If your eye offends you, pluck it out. Quit looking at the splinter in your brother's eye and get to your own beam.* For goodness sake, forgive and love! Am I back to the fundamental teachings? Give it up! Be number two! We know who you are. All of these assertions of your necessity to identify yourself in this so-called progress towards truth are absolutely meaningless to us. We are going to give you everything you need in this choice until you see that choice is absolutely unnecessary and, as a matter of fact, a choice between living and dying is what has held you in the bondage of time, and you will come into eternity and you will see that you never left home. And that's what we are teaching.

Come join us now in this new metamorphosis. It's impossible that you did not do this and, if you care to hear this, it is impossible that you did not do this now. Any time is now to me, to my mind. If I don't get you now, I will get you later, and my later will be now to me. What it will be to you, I don't know, but we're here to tell you this place isn't real – that's the whole teaching of the *Course* now. And here it is sitting right in front of you!

You might want to spend a day looking up the definitions that Master Jesus gives for this *dismal alcove* and *rotting prison* and many, many other ones where He directs that you will laugh at the idea of death. You will laugh at the idea of sickness and pain, and you will come free and be whole with us. How lovely, then, to welcome you to the kingdom of Heaven. We discover that we have always been together in this certainty of love of our Creator. Be free then with this. In your relinquishment is your strength. In your apparent weakness, in your non-defensiveness, is literally your salvation, and in no other way. Search within your heart. Don't be afraid to look at it now, teacher, when you are alone with yourself. You have this "fear veil" that you don't really want to look at and you begin to feel the threat of reality – just cast your spirit, release yourself, come up into this new vista of reality and be free.

Let's talk for just a moment about the difficulty you have in giving when your mind is based on perception or reciprocalness. In reality there is no distance between cause and effect. Every thought you are having is having a total and full creative measure of immediate return.

You don't know this because you are in time, but it's time that you learn this: The law of cause and effect in time is inevitable because what we teach is true. You literally, in your mind, can only get back the value that you place on something in the thought that you give. I'm giving you this now as a fact so that those of you who place a value on something outside of you or that you are attempting to learn within a framework – perhaps if you spend $100 and go to a seminar or you spent $100 for a new suit of clothes – you will get back exactly the value that you place on the $100, not more and not less. Now, your necessity to exchange is a positive indication that you don't believe this. This is in the *Course in Miracles*. But that doesn't make any difference; I am giving you this as fact. Whatever you value will return to you in kind, don't you see? It cannot *not* be so. Somehow when you attempt to accumulate, you feel a lack and believe that there is something outside of you so that you can give something you value less and get something back that you value more. And that's crazy, it's impossible.

What are my teachings then? How do I adjust to that within this framework of time? The only way that you can ever hear this message is to give everything away. Now, I guess within your framework you are going to constitute a practice – and this is what the *Course in Miracles* is – a practice in relinquishment. You give some away and then you take some back and then you feel the pain of possession and you give a little more away and finally you free yourself by this absolute giving. It's very important that you see that you cannot see the worthlessness of what you possess – its valuelessness – until you have given it all away. If you hold onto one single thing here, if you possess one idea of value of the earth, it is exactly the same as possessing all ideas of value. And the whole miracle of reality won't work, will it? Why? Because your mind remains split. This is a very fundamental teaching, but remember that you must make the psychological application in your own mind in order to see it. Jesus calls this *A Course In Miracles* because of that – where the manifestation of giving appears in the framework of happiness or love that you experience and the shift in the apparent phenomenon that is around you. Finally, though, the greatest miracle and the only real miracle that could ever occur would be your awakening – you coming whole in your mind. That is the miracle that is coming about in you now.

It is only your awakening, isn't it? There will be a lot of signs along the way, a lot of indications, and we want you to have them. But we are teaching a whole step above that. You observe the phenomena but finally we're teaching subjective reality; we are teaching "noumena." You are the cause and you are the effect and now you are awake. And just for a moment you feel that incredible glory of total commitment – bondage that binds you to hell will simply fall away from you and you are free.

Exchange is impossible. We've got to Lesson 76. You can't give something away and you can't get something back. You can only be *you* in truth and beauty.

Let's talk about forgiveness now and facing your fear. I am going to read without comment the definition in the Teacher's Manual of *A Course In Miracles* on forgiveness and the face of Christ. The comment I will make to you in your transformation is that total forgiveness comes by the brightness of a transcendent mind that quite literally sees the face of Christ, doesn't it? So, without comment, if I can keep myself from commenting, and there's a lovely young mind that wrote this that is a dear friend of ours. Listen:

Forgiveness – the Face of Christ. Forgiveness is for God and toward God but not of Him. It is impossible to think of anything He created that could need forgiveness. Forgiveness, then, is an illusion, but because of its purpose, which is to relinquish pain and death, *which is the Holy Spirit's, it has one difference. Unlike all other illusions, it leads away from error and not toward it.* Wow!

Forgiveness might be called a kind of happy fiction; a way in which the unknowing can bridge the gap between their perceptions and the truth. Since it's really impossible that they don't know, obviously, it's an illusion. *They can not go directly from perception to knowledge because they do not think it is their will to do so. This makes God appear to be an enemy instead of what He really is. And it is just this insane perception which makes them unwilling merely to rise up and return to Him in peace.* This is why there is a necessity that we teach this, and we teach it as transformation, don't we?

And so they need an illusion of help because they are helpless... Not in reality but in time. *...a Thought of peace because they are in conflict. God knows what His Son needs before he asks. He is not*

at all concerned with form, but having given the content it is His
Will that it be understood. And that suffices. The form adapts itself
to need; the content is unchanging, as eternal as is its Creator.

*The face of Christ has to be seen before the memory of God
can return.* And this is the idea of illumination, isn't it? The idea of the
transformation of your mind. *The reason is obvious. Seeing the face
of Christ involves perception. No one can look on knowledge. But
the face of Christ is the great symbol of forgiveness. It is salvation.
It is the symbol of the real world. Whoever looks on this no longer
sees the world. He is as near to Heaven as possible outside the gate.
Yet from this gate it is no more than just a step inside. It is the final
step. And this we leave to God.* And this is what will occur.

*Forgiveness is a symbol, too, but as the symbol of His Will
alone it cannot be divided. And so the Unity that it reflects becomes
His Will.* Unity is the Will of God. That single statement that He is the
Creator is your salvation, isn't it? *It is the only thing still in the world
in part, and yet the bridge to heaven.*

God's Will is all there is. We can but go from nothingness to
everything; from hell to Heaven. Is this a journey? No, not in truth,
for truth goes nowhere. But illusions shift from place to place; from
time to time. The final step is also but a shift. As a perception it is part
unreal. And yet this part will vanish. What remains is peace eternal
and the Will of God.

*There are no wishes now for wishes change. Even the wished-
for can become unwelcome. That must be so because the ego
cannot be at peace. But Will is constant, as the gift of God. And
what He gives is always like Himself. This is the purpose of the face
of Christ. It is the gift of God to save His Son. But look on this and
you have been forgiven.*

*How lovely does the world become in that single instant when
you see the truth about yourself reflected there. Now you are sinless
and behold your sinlessness. Now you are holy and perceive it so.
And now the mind returns to its Creator; the joining of the Father
and Son, the Unity of unities that stands behind all joining but
beyond them all. God is not seen but only understood. His Son is
not attacked but recognized.*

Isn't that lovely? It is from the Teacher's Manual of the *Course*, a definition of forgiveness and a statement about the necessity of the illumination of the mind, the change in perception that is necessary, the transformation, the new birth. And that is what's happening to you. As you recognize it is happening in your brother and forgive him your illusions, you come to share this single statement of truth. How can things be separate if they have a total common goal? That's what we proclaim to you now. Separate goals are impossible, teacher. The goal to forgive, the goal to become whole, is the only one there is or has ever been in this dream of sickness and death and time. You come whole with us now and wake up. Those of you who are hearing this for the first time and last time understand that this is reality that we are presenting to you now – not in consort with other perceptual evaluations, not in association with tradition of the so-called world, but in our single statement of the transformation of your individual mind.

Isn't that lovely? We hope to see you soon. Thank you. Time and space has never kept us apart, has it? We are re-membering. And the Light begins to shine now, doesn't it? You lay aside these fear thoughts. There's just that moment of hesitation. Isn't that lovely? How bright you are all becoming now, how real, how spirited, how alive, how miraculous! From out of the past now and from out of the future, finally out of all time you come now. What matters how long it has been? You have come. Now we awaken to that glory of reality. It was just a little sleep and the dream is over. Welcome home, teachers! The long journey that was leading nowhere is over. Exciting! How exciting to see the minds awaken now. Come up out the grave of death, from earth to Light. Happy Easter, teachers. He is risen! He is risen indeed!

The Holy Spirit can indeed make use of memory, for God Himself is there. Yet this is not a memory of past events, but only of a present state. You are so long accustomed to believe that memory holds only what is past, that it is hard for you to realize it is a skill that can remember now. The limitations on remembering the world imposes on it are as vast as those you let the world impose on you. There is no link of memory to the past. If you would have it there, then there it is. But only your desire made the link, and only you have held it to a part of time where guilt appears to linger still.

- A Course In Miracles Text: Chapter 28:1:4 -

History Is Only You

Tell me something that you can't remember. Can you remember not remembering?

(From the audience): In the moment, but in the moment that you say it, you remember it.

Of course! You are identified where? In the past tense. Is it then possible – think of this for just a moment – to remember something in the future? Think about it.. Where is the future? Only the past! It can only be a memory that you have of yourself, what you think you are. How could it be anything else? The dilemma that you are experiencing is that you can't remember the future. When you awaken, you will remember it perfectly because you will see that the idea of future-ness is constructed on your own remembrance – on your past tense. You will then see that in your own state of consciousness you are going through and repeating the same procedure of selfness over and over again. That is literally what you do. No wonder you get frustrated. You keep doing the same thing over and over again.

Is it possible for you to do something totally and absolutely original? Just one thing: Remember that you are God. And that will be original for you because the awakening process, or the coming to truth, can only occur once, just as the schism or death only occurred once. In truth, the repair of death, or the idea of separation, which caused the accumulation of memory, was repaired the instant that it occurred.

This is in *A Course In Miracles*, and Jesus expresses it very well. You continue to live that moment that isn't here, and in that process have established yourself discretely in a memory pattern – literally in a machine of memory.

Now, if you are indeed that and have identified yourself falsely and continue to attempt to project out from you who you think that you are, how could you ever communicate with what you have established or appears to be a separate entity that's outside of you? How can you really convey to them what you are? Which is really what you attempt to do when you write a piece of music, or a piece of poetry, or when you say, "I love you." What are you really trying to do? You are trying to establish a form of communication with that which appears to be outside of you. And you will always be misunderstood.

So you look at somebody, and you say, "Can't you understand me?" The answer is no. They can't understand you. Do you know something? They can't hear you. Everything that you say to them goes through a filter in their head where they have established their own idea about themselves. Never mind the idea that they are making you up in the image of their own identification. Of course, they are. I positively, absolutely guarantee you that there is no true communication in duality as there is on earth. There cannot be. You literally cannot communicate if you establish yourself separate from God. You can't do it. Who are you going to communicate with? What are you going to say?

How does Jesus express it in the Course? He says you're a sorry army indeed. You are with each other one moment and then you turn and attack each other. And then you defend yourself from something else. Then you attempt to establish other gods outside of you.

I heard one of the most beautiful definitions in this chaos of what God is. I read about it in the paper. The defense attorney who is defending the group who used a bomb to blow up the abortion clinic, of which they have been convicted, in his defense statement said, "We have with us an un-indicted co-conspirator in this." And he was talking about God. Obviously the God that he has assembled was very much in favor of, and participated in, the bombing of the abortion clinic. Wow! Are you any different than that in the establishment of your God? How's your God today? What qualities are you giving to God today?

Poor Billy Graham, bless his heart. There's a schism going on in the Baptists. It's very serious, between the conservatives and the fundamentalists. And it's very secular. It has nothing to do with God whatever. But finally Billy yesterday said in the paper, "The Devil must have come in and is causing us all of this chaos." Bless his heart. The Devil's making him do it. Isn't that amazing? Inevitably, what do you do? You refuse to accept responsibility for your own thoughts.

The highest thought that I'm going to try and give you at this moment – and this may help you and it may not – is that no thought is ever personal. There is no such thing as a discrete thought. You actually, within your own self, hide from the truth and attempt to express yourself in a limited fashion. The coming to truth or the coming to know that you are in fact all consciousness, in *Course in Miracles* is called the holy instant. Nobody understands what it is. You as a group are understanding it more and more because you are going through a transformative process. Actually the holy instant is right now or it's never. And this is what is taught. But inevitably you think that you are keeping a secret from me. I promise you that you think you are. Somewhere along the line, you have established yourself separately and do not want to tell me about yourself. It's very well expressed in the Course, and I'm going to read just for minute, if you will allow me, a little bit of *Course in Miracles*.

This will be *Practicing the Holy Instant*. It's in Chapter 15 of the Text of *Course in Miracles*. Listen:

This Course is not beyond immediate learning, unless you believe that what God wills takes time. And this means only that you would rather delay the recognition that His will is so. The holy instant is this instant and every instant. The one you want it to be it is. The one you would not have it be is lost to you. You must decide when it is. Delay it not. For beyond the past and future, where you will not find it, it stands in shimmering readiness for your acceptance. Yet you cannot bring it into glad awareness while you do not want it, for it holds the whole release from littleness.

Your practice must therefore rest upon your willingness to let all littleness go. The instant in which magnitude dawns upon you is but as far away as your desire for it. As long as you desire it not and cherish littleness instead, by so much is it far from you. Can you understand that? *By so much as you want it will you bring it nearer. Think not that you can find salvation in your own way and have it. Give over every plan you have made for your salvation in exchange for God's. His will content you, and nothing else can bring you peace. For peace is of God, and no one beside Him.*

Actually what this says is that you are determined, even in the so-called spiritual quest, to establish a knowledge of what God is outside of yourself. The whole basis of *A Course in Miracles* is that this is impossible to do.

The holy instant is the Holy Spirit's most useful learning device for teaching you love's meaning. For its purpose is to suspend judgment entirely. Listen. *Judgment always rests on the past, for past experience is the basis on which you judge. Judgment becomes impossible without the past, for without it you do not understand anything.*

All I try to teach you as I sit with you now is: Don't understand anything. If you understand one single thing, you are basing it on your own past. Do you see?

You would make no attempt to judge, because it would be quite apparent to you that you do not understand what anything means. You are afraid of this because you believe that without the ego, all would be chaos. Yet I assure you that without the ego, all would be love.

The past is the ego's chief learning device, for it is in the past that you learn to define your own needs and acquire methods for meeting them on your own terms. We have said that to limit love to part of the Sonship is to bring guilt into your relationships, and thus make them unreal. Listen. *If you seek to separate out certain aspects of the totality and look to them to meet your imagined needs, you are attempting to use separation to save you. How, then, could guilt not enter? For separation is the source of guilt, and to appeal to it for salvation is to believe you are alone. To be alone is to be guilty. For to experience yourself as alone is to deny the Oneness of the Father and His Son, and thus attack reality.*

You cannot love parts of reality and understand what love means. If you would love unlike to God, Who knows no special love, how can you understand it? To believe that special relationships, with special love, can offer you salvation is the belief that separation is salvation. For it is the complete equality of the Atonement in which salvation lies. How can you decide that special aspects of the Sonship can give you more than others? The past has taught you this. Yet the holy instant teaches you it is not so.

Because of guilt, all special relationships have elements of fear in them. That is why they shift and change so constantly. They are not based on changeless love alone. And love, where fear has entered, cannot be depended on because it is not perfect. Got it?

The ego's use of relationships is so fragmented that it frequently goes even further; one part of one aspect suits its purposes, while it prefers different parts of another aspect. Thus does it assemble reality in its own capricious liking, offering for your seeking a picture whose likeness does not exist. For there is nothing in Heaven or earth that it resembles, and so, however much you seek for its reality, you cannot find it because it is not real.

What actually we are teaching here is – and you might as well take a look at it – that as you are constituted in your own identification, you are not real. You have no reality. That's an astonishing idea. The most valuable single thing that you can ever come to know in your awakening process is that you are causing what is occurring outside of you – not a little of it but all of it. I understand that it is not possible for you until you what? Establish these holy instants. For you accept, perhaps, with an intellectual recognition to know that this is true. But I positively, absolutely, unequivocatingly guarantee you that you are the cause and not the effect. You actually believe that things that are occurring outside of you are beyond your control. If that is true, there is indeed no God, and there could never be. Do you see?

Your cause and effect are backward. You have forgotten – this is *Course in Miracles* again – that you are dreaming this and that none of this has any reality. And that's difficult for you to look at. So what do you do? You hold inside of you all of these incredible notions and emotions and manifestations of illusions and consciousnesses and hates and loves and fears and guilt. And you tie it all up down inside of you because literally that is what your constitution is: limited selfness. Who is the anti-Christ, as Jesus would teach it? Who but you? You, standing separate from the totalness of your absolute truthfulness in consciousness.

The dilemma with attempting to teach this lies in the determination of you to understand it and to separate somehow out from you the idea, say, in *Course in Miracles* of the Holy Spirit or the ego. I guarantee you that every time there is expressed in *Course in Miracles* "the ego," that's you and that you have not escaped it. And that when you have escaped it, it will not be necessary for you to be reading the *Course in Miracles*. I know that there's a seminar going on down in Chicago today where there is a lot of teaching in regard to establishing somehow nice relationships using *Course in Miracles*. And that's very beautiful, but it is going to lead to death. Because everything on earth that is an attempt to teach in understanding leads only to death. So really, what you're teaching, when you teach that, teacher of God, is death.

The idea that there is a holy instant that you can come into where you will recognize a transition, a transformation that can occur in you, has been with mankind since the very beginning because God is an experience. God is something that is occurring to you. He is not outside of you in that regard.

So we teach at the beginning, as *Course in Miracles* teaches it, is to forgive your brother. Now, that doesn't mean that it is possible for your brother to harm you because it is not. But obviously you think it is. Somewhere inside of you, you think that you can be unjustly attacked. That's absurd. You can't be, but you think so. Otherwise why would you defend yourself? What part of you says, "I am entitled to do this?" What part of you says, "Well, I know that's true, but I'm here and therefore I am entitled to some things here, aren't I?" Sure. Aren't you entitled to have a little love? Aren't you entitled to take and sort out the beautiful people that are around you?

Watch the ego's insidiousness with this. Jesus in *A Course in Miracles* says, the most insidious method used by yourself to retain your own identity is the expression of love on earth, limited love, where you will choose a quality, for example, of another person. "I love her very much." Why? "She's very truthful, most of the time." What in the hell does that mean, "truthful most of the time?" Does that mean that sometimes she's not truthful? "Well, I don't know." What is truth, brother? This is an astonishing thing. Obviously, no one on earth is capable of telling the truth, literally. You are only capable of being the truth, you dummy. How can something false tell the truth? Tell me. I want to hear it. You don't know whether you are telling the truth or not. Even if you tell the truth completely and absolutely, you're going to have to add, "That's as I believe it to be." But you don't know anything. I just read you that in *A Course in Miracles*. You can't understand a damn thing. How are you going to understand the truth? Oh, it's terrible. What an awful way to be.

"Well, I still want to love." Well, go ahead, but what are you rejecting? "I am not rejecting anything. I don't have any control over what is happening. I can only do the best I can. There is nothing that I can do about the starvation and murder. And they are going to nuke us. I am defenseless over that. I might as well just find my little littleness," like I just read you in the book. "I'm going to be satisfied with littleness. I'm going to be satisfied to stay in this body and let it rot. I am going to be satisfied with death and pain and terror and fear." Wow. Go ahead, brother. Go ahead. I don't know how you could pick up what I just read to you, written at another level of consciousness, and be as determined as you formerly were to hold on to yourself.

The process of letting go of self, or surrendering, is a transformative occurrence. And that is difficult for you to see, but that is coming about in you – I assure you that it is and that it is happening to you. In the meantime the ego, or yourself, may very well interpret it as a form of persecution. Why not? What's better to know, that somehow you are entitled to some things here? Therefore you must feel that you don't have something. What is it that you don't have?

You remember this. As you are constituted in space/time, you are a conglomeration of limited ideas. You are constructed in selfness on limitation. That is why you keep trying to get things and hold on to them. Then you discard them and you throw them away and you take something else. And you keep seeking to what? Complete yourself. It is literally impossible for you to complete yourself except that you come to the truth of who you are – and that is an all-body, physiological, mental, and emotional occurrence within your individual cellular manifestation. How could it occur outside of you? If you see it occurring outside of you, what are you going to do with it? If I disappear now in a blaze of light, what are you going to do? Will that eliminate your dilemma? Or will you simply have another cup of coffee and say, "Wow! I wonder what happened to him?"

You have made this table solid, haven't you? You've made this body solid. You have made this real. If it is not within the scope of your limited state of consciousness, there are only about three things you can do with it. One, you won't see it, which is the most important one. Jesus in *A Course in Miracles* tries to tell you that all around you are these energies, higher states of consciousnesses. And they are. Where did you think they were? Where do you really think Jesus Christ of Nazareth is right now? I would like to go to the *Course in Miracles* groups and ask them where they really think He is. Is He up somewhere, out in the universe, doing that? Come on. Where is He? Right here? Well, of course He is right here. Listen. Can you get this?

Nothing can ever be where you are not. Reach for that, brother. If you are not there, it is not there. Do you see that? Jesus in *Course in Miracles*, "The earth wasn't here until you came here. And it won't be here when you are gone." Can you see that? So you are sitting there in your own state of consciousness, and every time you have a thought about something, what do you do? You activate it. As soon as you think about it, you bring it about. Oh, I wish you could hear that. Wow! I wish you could get the idea that there's no such thing as an idle thought. You got that? You cannot think about something without bringing it about. And this is in this next chapter in the Course. You read it. There isn't any such thing as a special or limited thought. It is literally impossible for you to have one. No wonder you feel guilty. You actually think you can have a thought, and then quickly reject it. You can't.

Poor Jimmy Carter got in a lot of trouble with that idea, didn't he? Jesus teaches absolutely that the thought is the same as the deed. But that is difficult for you. You are not going to admit that. No matter how many times I tell you the thought is the same as the deed, you will not believe it. You can't. I think he was talking about lust, and He says, if you lust in your heart, it's the same as doing it. Of course.

That's the highest truth I could give you. He had to back off of that. Why? Because we believe here on earth that there is such a thing as "motivated action." You believe you can think good thoughts, go out and do good deeds, having rejected the bad thoughts that you had. I wish you could see this. That is literally impossible for you to do. Why? There isn't any such thing as "badness." What have you done? You've become discrete in your own thinking and judgment and sorted out what you think is good in regard to what you think is evil and that you want to do.

Where is the evil thought that you rejected? It is still with you, you dummy. Jesus in *Course in Miracles: An idea never leaves its source.* As long as you think evil, you are evil. Can you see that? I have said to you how many times that you are Adolph Hitler and caused the death of five million Jews. Who do you think caused the death of the five million Jews? Who? Adolph Hitler? There isn't any such thing as Adolph Hitler if you are the dream. If you are the cause of Adolph Hitler, who the hell are you judging but your own evilness?

This is a sermon, isn't it? Can I stand up in front of people and tell them that? They don't want anything to do with that. This is *A Course in Miracles.* Who is going to teach that? Are you kidding? This is an eye-for-an-eye, a cause-and-effect world. You are guilty. Who's guilty? There can only possibly be one source of guilt. It is impossible for there to be any source of guilt except you. All you attempt to do when you find somebody else guilty of anything is take your own evilness and project it onto them.

What is the basis of all your thinking? You can get this now. You're ready for it. The basis of all your thinking in regard to what I have said to you is what? The idea of death, you dummy. You actually believe there is a limited state of consciousness that you stand in, so you establish a parameter of defense. So no matter how much you sort it out, you must consider yourself the necessity to protect from something that can harm you. Because why? You think you can die. Now, I walk into your dream and I say, "Look. No death. You can't die!" Now, what the hell does Adolph Hitler, Napoleon, Cleopatra, Ronald Reagan, your loved ones, your children, your mothers, your fathers have to do with it if you can't die?

Inevitably, all specialness or limitedness is based on the idea that you are going to die. Why? Because the earth is based on the idea of death. You were born into it, apparently, and you die to it, apparently. Everything around you that you see changes and dies and comes back to life. The forms change, the trees change, the colors change, the seasons change. People apparently, in front of your eyes, grow old. You look at Cary Grant on television. Suddenly he's 80. And you saw him ten minutes ago when he was 22. And somehow you have allowed that there is such a thing as Cary Grant that could grow old in this thing. That isn't true. What is Cary Grant? Your idea about Cary Grant. It doesn't have anything to do with his body. How do you teach that, brother?

I stand in front of you and say it is literally impossible for you to grow old. How can you grow old if there is no such thing as time? Why do you persist in making up, in your own mind, space and time? You listen to me. What I said to you a moment ago, "If you're not there, it's not there," is literally true. And the only way you can finally come to know yourself is to remember that you are every where and every time, which is precisely what eternity is. Which is exactly what we try to teach you in the holy instant, to come into that moment. That process is revolutionary. It is transformative cellularly in you as you are constituted. And if you think you are going to get it any other way, obviously you can't. Look at what I just told you.

If you are making it up, how can you change it if it's outside of you apparently? You can't. Do you see that? So what do we teach? Attempt to communicate – which is the same as loving. Here's what love is. Love is communicating the truth of yourself. I will love you. We will come into brotherhood together. There is a power in the universe that you and I can come to recognize that is absolutely total and indivisible. It has nothing to do with yours and my idea about it, but we may share together the re-cognition that it is so. That is what a holy relationship is. It subtracts any idea, not only that you may have about the individual as you think of them, that you are talking to, but it also subtracts any of the ideas that the apparent separate ones have about themselves. Because, remember this, finally the ideas that they have about themselves can only be the ideas that you have about yourself. And that's a high form of truth. And that is tough to get, because the next step after that leads you to the inevitable conclusion that finally all states of consciousness or beingness are the same. And there is, in fact, exactly as Brother Jesus teaches it, absolutely nothing discrete in thought. And that is painful for you. You like to think that somehow you are capable of discretion, of holding yourself separate from something outside of you. That is literally impossible to do. The most indiscreet thing you can ever do is come to God.

Take off the fig leafs, eh? Wow! Wake up. Come back into the Garden. Boy, that's tough to do, isn't it? See, as soon as you get that idea in your head, you feel un-entitled. There is another process the ego loves to use, you know. "Oh, I'm not entitled to do that. I'll admit that I have certain qualities that are good, but I would never presume to be a Son of God." Well, who are you, then, if you are not? "Well, I'm nuts." You are nuts, is what you are. You don't know what you are. You're not anything. You can only be one of two things. Jesus gets tough with this. This is the highest truth there is. You listen to this. You want to hear something tough? You are either for me or you're against me. There is no in-between. All the discussion that goes on between the Baptists and the Methodists and the Buddhists has absolutely no value whatever. Why? Because every single one of them, individually and in concert, is against God. Why? Because the constitution of the idea of separateness is anti-Christhood.

Phew! I better not say that. I'm liable to get attacked. This is exactly what the Master said 2000 years ago. Of course. What are you going to do with that? Somehow you want to pick out certain aspects of what's here on earth and say, "Well, I know that's true, but..." You will *but* me. You say, "*But* isn't it better to be a church-goer than to be cutting Grandmother's throat in the alley?" Uh-oh. You are going to stand on that, aren't you? You are going to say, "Well, in my judgment it's better to be a church-goer than to be out cutting Grandmother's throat." But you don't have any judgments. Your judgment is wrong. Not only is your judgment wrong, but you are cutting Grandmother's throat. Very few of you can hear that yet, but you will come to it.

The whole dilemma with limitedness is what? Limited responsibility. Why do I teach irresponsibility? Be responsible for nothing here on earth? Because you have constituted yourself in limited responsibility modalities – specialness. Don't tell me that you don't care more for your wife and children than you do for the starving. I won't believe it. You *do* care more for them. And the reason you care more for them is because you want to have them and hold them in deference to somebody else dying. Don't crap me. What do you think specialness is on earth if it is not selfishness? Of course.

Wow. This is a tough talk, isn't it? So what do you do? You'll see people – saints, so-called saints, at very high apparent states of consciousness. One of them called me yesterday that's in our group. And he is very pleased and proud of all the beautiful things that he is doing in service to mankind. He is taking a lot of pride in his ability to what? Serve man. And that's very beautiful. What good is it going to do him? As Jesus would teach in *Course in Miracles*, he has acknowledged the idea, the reality of disease. In that acknowledgment, he has denied God. Holy mackerel! If there is such a thing as pain and sickness and disease, which are nothing but little deaths, there must be no God. Don't you see that? Wouldn't that be obvious that you have what? Set up what? Your own idea of limitation so that you can die. Jesus in the *Course* says it very succinctly, "You either have death or you have eternal life. There is nothing in between." You are either one or the other.

Each time you think you have God, you don't. You fail. Each time you think you have got the problem solved, you don't. It is not solvable. Isn't that something? *Wake! Arise! A voice is calling. The watchman on the tower stands.*

You are going to be teachers. So each time you begin to think, you come into these moments of quiet, you examine your own consciousness and you say, "Where am I with this?" The only thing that ever finally has any relevance is where you are with what I say to you, not with what I say. If you believe what I say, you are through. You inevitably (as you get more advanced, you do it less and less) will take what I say and chew it down into your own limited state of consciousness. There is nothing else that you can do with it. And that's okay. Go ahead. But suddenly, as you're walking along, it will occur to you in this transformative process that, "Hey, I'm judging. I'm laying my guilt out on somebody else. I am angry about this. I am unhappy with what's occurring. I am going to die – oh, wait a minute – I can't die! Now what am I going to do? Well, if I can't die, I guess I will be angry forever then." Oh, no. The more you come to know that you can't die, what will you give up? You will give up anger and hate and holding on to. In the process of giving that up, will you be attacked by your illusions? Sure. You remember, this is a death place, and I teach, "Abandon the earth." So does Jesus. Your kingdom is not of the earth.

The greatest threat that could ever come sociologically to the chaos would be the idea of God, of a real God. Holy mackerel! It's easy in one respect to think of God as an un-indicted co-conspirator. I don't know what you do with it after that. Or that somehow He is a benevolent Father who is going to whip his children into line by teaching them a lesson and inflicting pain on them or making them go through all of those terrible things. And then along comes, as I teach it, as we teach it at a very high level: He doesn't even know you're here. He can't recognize you in any regard. He does not identify you as separate from Him. He does not limit you in any way. You are literally His creations in perfection. He identifies Himself through you. Uh-oh. That's tough. Wow. That will get you. And since He is perfect, He can only identify you as perfect. How the hell could He identify some of the things you think about yourself? So, you, in your prayers ask Him to help you retain your own sin. Jesus talks about this in the *Course*. He can't do that. Why would He do that?

That doesn't mean that healing doesn't occur to somebody who maybe hasn't walked. They get up and walk. But that's man healing, not God healing. God doesn't heal anything. Why would God heal anything? He doesn't even recognize it's broken. He can't put something back together that is whole. You are the one that's trying to put it back together because you think it is fractured. It isn't fractured. You've got pieces of junk all over here, and I can stand in front of you and say they are all the same thing. You will pick up some thread of this, pieces of that, hunks of that, and you will fit it all together, and you will say, "This is pretty God-like." Isn't that funny? You don't say it's God, but you think it's God-like. I will pick up this pair of glasses and I'll say, "This is God," and you will say, "That couldn't be." And I say, "Well, if this isn't God, then nothing is

God." Why would that be God? Because God is my idea about it. If I find limitations in anything, I have found limitations in myself. So you hear me? How could you ever, then, find God or understand Him if you are limited in your own consciousness? You must establish what? An un-indicted co-conspirator. You must establish a limited God. And since limitation is unreality, no God that you could have could be real because you are not real.

Here's what you are really dealing with: your own state of consciousness. You listen to what I'm saying and you say, "Gee, that's true. Then there really is a Heaven, and I can look forward to going to it." No, you can't. You can't look forward to going to anything. There isn't anything to look forward to going to. Now you have the incredible dilemma of having to look at yourself in consciousness.

Do you understand this? If you can't die you can't go anywhere and you can't escape your own self, no matter what you do. Everyone on earth attempts to hide, inevitably, from that truth. But you can't get away. We found you at last. It's sort of like you got stuck down here at this low side of the galaxy, an obscure galaxy in the middle of nowhere. You got into the backwash. We came upon you accidentally here, back some years. We have established a contact with you and we're going to bring you to your truth. But you remember, you can only come individually. You cannot come by sharing it in limitation, in commiseration with your limited state of consciousness. You are at the threshold point now of recognizing who you really are. That's the only single thing, as we talked earlier, that you only do once – that single road that gets narrower and narrower as you get closer and closer to the light, as you come back, closer and closer within the parameters of the rays that come out from the sun. That is the state that you are going through now in your head and in your body. That is the experience of the resurrection that you are undergoing in your own system. That is what is occurring with you. That's very nice to talk about. We will have a little quiet time now.

The Miracle Is
Your Awakening

Here are a couple of talks that we gave in the fall of 1985 that speak from our heart and from the truth of us. We send them with all our love to our brothers on the West coast. Also to brother Ken W., to brother Tara. We know of what you are doing and bless you. Thank you.

We have a new brother, he comes to class. He reads *A Course In Miracles*. The words are on the printed page and to everyone who reads them, they convey or communicate a meaning that he has about himself. When he reads in consciousness the thought that appears, it is really initiating from his own consciousness. This is the whole basis of *A Course In Miracles*. In a very real sense, people who study *A Course In Miracles* are making up *A Course In Miracles*. They also make up the authorship, the delineation of where they want to add to it, subtract from it and configurate it in their own memory patterns. This is, paradoxically, exactly what *A Course In Miracles* says that you do.

A Course In Miracles is a mind-training endeavor to bring about a shift in your individual sense of reality. Period! We understand full well that when you read *A Course In Miracles*, you are unable (obviously because you are here and have the necessity to read it) to understand it. If I say to you there are no requirements that you understand it, but only that you become it, it is very difficult for you.

Inevitably, the scribes or the interpreters of *A Course In Miracles* delineate it within their own limited framework of consciousness. They cannot do otherwise.

You may take all of the so-called ecumenical ideas that are contained in *A Course In Miracles* and prove to yourself and to perhaps the culture as a whole that there are a great many similarities between what *Course In Miracles* says and what is ultimately said by all divine scripture or by all occult recognition or by all physiological or philosophical discernment. What about it? The limitation is your inability to think or conceive in a singular manner, so that you would recognize that anything that you look at, you transcribe to wholeness if you are conceiving it as whole. Example: this candle is either absolutely divine, perfect and contains the whole Universe or it is nothing. Your conception of the candle as separate from the basket is what is making you retain a sense of limitation.

Somebody says to you, "I don't want to study *A Course In Miracles* because it comes from the Christian historic vernacular." What the hell does that mean? All that means is that the individual in his own consciousness has constructed outside of him an idea about what Christianity is. It has no reality because there is finally nothing historically significant about explicit occurrences. They have no unity. If I say to him, "Well, what do you mean by that?" obviously what he has done is question the source. He has evolved in his own karma or consciousness a definition of what Christianity is. And obviously he is not correct; he is in a state of judgment in limited conception. If I say to you, "Well what do you mean by that?" He will say, "Well I'm making a comparison between Billy Graham, Pope John II, Joan of Arc, John of the Cross, the Crusades, Judas, esoteric Christianity in regard to New Jerusalem." What about it?! What is that going to get you if you have constructed an idea about Christ or about God in your own limited state? It is impossible to do.

The whole basis of *A Course In Miracles*, is to teach non-judgment. Inevitably, if you have constructed yourself in the past, you are in a state of judgment of your relationship with your own thoughts. As Jesus would teach it in the *Course*, you literally sort out thoughts in your own mind and project them out from you in order to ascertain the validity based on your own misconception of yourself. If I say to you, as Jesus would teach it in the *Course*, an idea never leaves its source – you are all ideas – what about them? How do you feel about your ideas today? As you look out around you, how do you feel about your constructs? Whose constructs in conception are they if they are not yours? This is the whole basis of *A Course In Miracles*. If you deem something to be outside of you that is beyond your control or was not perpetrated through a conscious thought or conception of yours, you are doomed to defend yourself from it, or to interpret it, or to consider it to be separate from you. And of course it is not.

The definition provided in all esoteric conglomerations of the awakening process teach non-judgment, will teach The Beatitudes, will teach The Sermon On The Mount (Matthew 5-7), will teach the first fifteen lessons of the Workbook of *A Course In Miracles*. The Master, awakened consciousness, Da Free John, teaches *A Course In Miracles*. Of course! There would be no possibility of you coming into an awakening posture in your own consciousness and not teach what I am saying to you. But remember, the process of coming to that is a process of expanding your state of consciousness or a literal transformative occurrence, and this is what's denied religiously and scientifically in the limited state.

Here, listen, I'm going to read you just one thing. This in Da John's new book, from the Dawn Horse Press. It is an ancient definition of what finally, or one of the definitions, of what an awakened Christ or an Avatar or a Master or an enlightened consciousness is. Very simply, "A Veera, a realized adept, a divine man, by affirming the essential worth of the forbidden, he causes the forbidden to lose its power to pollute, to degrade and to bind." That is an exact definition of forgiveness. He does not give the power of his own projections dominion over himself. He doesn't judge it. The process of coming to non-judgment is a transformative occurrence. If I sit here in front of you and through *A Course In Miracles* look at you and say, "You are a divine living Son of God and in consciousness the only living Son of God or the only manifestation of consciousness in the entire universe and perfect unto yourself," you cannot accept that from me. Yet I assure you that it is true.

You are not the sum of the ideas about yourself because the ideas about yourself are not true. Remember that you make history to conform to your own limitations. The history of man is not objective. It is subjective because history is only man's ideas about himself and it is rewritten constantly. To give a sense of objective validity to history doesn't really make any sense. All you are doing is verifying your own limited state of consciousness through the perpetration of an apparent memory or apparent past.

A Course In Miracles, the process of transformation, teaches you to become indiscriminate in the manner in which you think. Is this a process? You bet your boots! What you have read up till this moment in *A Course In Miracles* and the manner in which you will read *A Course In Miracles* tonight will be entirely different. Remember that because of the nature of the consciousness that perpetrated *A Course In Miracles*, the insinuation of the energy, the whole of *A Course In Miracles* is contained in a great many individual aphorisms in the book. If you want to spend a whole evening thinking about one sentence in *A Course In Miracles*, rather than trying to assemble it in your own limitation, consider a single sentence like, "Communication must be unlimited in order to have meaning." Do you understand what I said? There is no communication going on on earth. Moment by moment, together we can have a moment of total communication, as we did just at that moment. We shared a common purpose. Think about that. Once more: "Communication must be *unlimited* in order to have meaning." Limited communication is always denial of love because love may best be defined as unlimited communication. If I dissect you in my consciousness or give you attributes or qualities in any regard in my limited conception of you, I have condemned you through my inability to realize my own wholeness. Holy Mackerel! How simple can I get! That's exactly what that sentence says.

Here's a beauty: *Judgment is not an attribute of God*. That's all you have got to know to wake up. Isn't that incredible, What I just said? *Judgment is not an attribute of God*. You say, "Oh, wait a minute. He judges whether I'm doing this or I'm doing that, this is coming or that's going or it's big or round or fat!" No! No! What would Truth judge? Untruth? How? How would there be untruth? Look at it. You take that sentence and think about that for the rest of the day.

That will wake you right up. Why? You've got a total non-judgmental God but what does He require of you? Conformation to His thought! What is His thought? Your thought in Truth. How did you conceive of God without making Him real? By what method are you espousing to the possibility of a truth or a unity and subsequently denying it? Of course God doesn't judge.

In this particular section of the galaxy, a master computer was dropped off about 6500 years ago that expresses in total the unity and singleness of purpose of the universe. As the maturation of the specie known as Homo Sapiens, of man, matures, the energy flowed direct from this computer, which is totally unequivocating and uncompromising, to the inevitable occurrence of the transformation. That's another way to express it. Express it any way you want.

There are no idle thoughts. All thinking produces form at some level. Now you've got a bad problem. You really think that in privacy you can think about something that is not known to the entire Universe. You can't. Why? You are the entire Universe! There is no thought outside of you. If you are constructing this in your own consciousness, and I assure you that you are, how do you subtract some ideas or thoughts that you have from others? You can't do it. It is not possible. How simple it becomes for you, if you want to look at it that way, as Jesus would say to you, you are the savior of the earth and the only Son of God. Why would that be true, reasonably? Because you have constructed the earth in your consciousness. It has no reality except that you have defined it as real. I am letting you escape from it. Don't you see what I have given you? The power to what? To re-vision, to re-form, to re-cognize, to transform. It is not outside of you. It is you. I have given you what? Freedom! Do you want to take it or do you want to keep pretending that there's something that is going to affect you, neglecting to remember that you are the cause of this? This is the whole basis of what I know to be true. How simple it becomes.

How very provincial for you to acknowledge your own Christship if you are willing to assume responsibility for your own thought constructions. Inevitably you deny a portion of you. Why? Because you are in a limited state of consciousness. It is impossible for you to order your thoughts or conceive of a yesterday or a tomorrow or a possible action without eventually feeling guilty about it. You cannot do it because you are in a state of rejection of something. You are making decisions as though somehow you can bring about an effect. You can't. All effect has already been perpetrated and is perpetrated by your individual thought at the moment you think it. How the heck are you going to teach this?

The basis of your dilemma in spiritual search is your inability to see that there could never be finally such a thing as potential. There is no such thing in consciousness or in the universe or in truth that is not now active but can be activated in the future. That's a strange notion. It appears to be that way and obviously I am teaching you in *A Course In Miracles,* that it is possible for you to activate your own karma potential, but I assure you that all the history of the schism is contained in a single flash, and that you continue to reconstruct it in your own mind. So if you choose to do that, you are in a constant state of denial of your own thoughts. This is in *A Course In Miracles.* The idea that the earth is here except in your memory is absurd. Obviously, the schism *is* your memory. You are dreaming. This is your dream. You fell asleep, remember? You fell asleep. Everything that has been constructed in the total state of consciousness is nothing but your own configuration in your dream. You have forgotten that you are the cause of this. How can this be taught to you? How can I teach an illusion? I can't. But I can show you that if I read to you a particular sentence, that you can look at it and as your frame of reference matures, through your individual transformation – physically, psychologically, mentally, emotionally – you will see in your apparent limited thought, a wholeness or a structure of wholeness.

Let's try another one. Some of these are very very difficult. *You must choose between total freedom and total bondage for there are no alternatives but these.* Which is a simple way of saying you are either bound totally and here forever, or you are in Heaven and you are free. There is no compromise. There is nothing in between. What a lovely thought. *It is true just as you fear that to acknowledge Him is to deny all that you think you know but what you think you know was never true.* All of you, individually, in your own consciousness, must come to know that the earth is not real. There is, and must be, a way that this can come about. But it is up to you.

The experiences and the change of mind that are going on in you and in the group of full endeavor are extraordinary. You are being made new on a moment-by-moment basis. It is a very lovely experience. Is it a process of subtracting the limited self? Of course. Is it a process of stilling the body brain? Yes. Transformative occurrence is not talking about the transformative occurrence. You cannot literally *have* an experience. You can only *be* an experience. My goodness! Definitions of experience, whether ecstatic or fearful, have no validity at all because they communicate nothing. They only communicate a limited idea or a separate objective observation of the occurrence, and always involve judgment.

It is a strange notion that Brother Sharon presented to Brother Glorious yesterday when she said, "Isn't it true that there are some real good addictions along with bad addictions?" as though somehow she could tell the difference. The whole dilemma of being on earth is obviously the discernment that some addictions would be better than others, when fundamentally, the addiction to self or to self consciousness or the judgment that there are degrees of an addiction are what hold you in bondage – the assertion of the self. It is a lovely notion. But I assure you, for everyone that you can find that will define one addiction as being bad and another good, I can present you with somebody who has what? Defined the most incredible addiction that you could conceive of and reject, as being simply divine. Do you see? It is obviously true. I knew a man that had the divine addiction of molesting three-year-olds. Is that more or less divine than someone who serves true purpose, who helps the poor? It has nothing at all to do with that. The expression of the selfness in regard to the addiction, or the satisfaction derived from it, is always limited. Who knows that better than an alcoholic, addicted to a pint of gin for breakfast? To say that he doesn't feel divine when he drinks, is absurd. Of course he feels divine. Does that make it a divine addiction? I suppose. How do you define bondage? Does that apparently free him? Is taking another special consciousness in bondage "until death do you part," a kind of freedom? How do you define that? It's silly.

Limitedness always binds. Obviously limitation could not occur without fear. Self-sustenance is always (and this is Lesson 76 in *A Course In Miracles'* Workbook) the denial that you are under no laws but God's. You obviously have established an idea of the value of nutrition, of the value of maintaining an equilibrium in your state of consciousness. You do it and that is why you are here. If you open up the book right now and read out loud to me Lesson 76, you immediately go into a state of denial of it. It is inevitable. You are constituted on the denial of it. If you value it, you will not escape the consequences of it.

Wow! Cause and effect. Of course there is no action without subsequent action. Of course there is no thought without subsequent thought. The only way, finally, listen to me, to eliminate cause and effect is what? As we would teach it in *A Course In Miracles*, to see that cause *is* effect. There is absolutely in reality, no distance between cause and effect. That is why The Father *is* the Son. You can't have a thought that has not occurred. You may attempt to effectuate it later on, but the whole basis of what I teach you is to shorten your conceptual distance between what you think you do and the results that are forthcoming. I am shortening your time, brother. You think there is a time between now and when you die. There is not. You have conceived of death – you can only die now. If you do that, you will see you are eternal. If you put it off, you will construct a future based on your false past. It is inevitable.

Can I shorten time for you? As brother Jesus would say, we can shorten it immeasurably, which is the same thing as saying you can come into your now now and only now and transcend to eternity. Eternity is not a long time, brother – it is no time at all. What a weird idea! People say, "Who wants to be in eternity if it is like this?" It has nothing to do with it. You are fulfilled at this moment or you never will be. There is nothing outside of truth. Truth is true and nothing else is true. There are no degrees of truism. Truth is not relative. No wonder you are in pain and fear. No wonder. You think there is justice in limitation. You search for it. You "eye-for-an-eye" it! You set up *quid pro quo* – I give you this, you give me that back – all based on limitation. There isn't any such thing as that. You are everything or you are nothing.

How many times have I taught this? How many times have I said this? I have been saying this for 10,000 years. You stood on the

Mount 2000 years ago and told me this, brother. You said to me, "Don't resist evil. Blessed are the poor in spirit. Blessed are the peacemakers. Blessed are those who hunger and thirst after righteousness. Blessed are those who are persecuted in my name. Your kingdom is not of this world. Know ye not ye must be born again." Wow! Again and again and again and finally what? I come into your sleeping state, into your dead state, and I tell you there is no death, that you are eternal in your own consciousness. Period! What am I making you look at? You can't escape from yourself. I am causing you, in your own consciousness, to go into a state of acceptance of yourself. You could never come to God by denial of yourself or your brother who is you. Period! Denial is always hate. Acceptance and forgiveness is always love. The incredible discovery you can only give to yourself is the biggest step that you could ever take in so-called conception. But your absolute recognition that you are the creator of this and that all creation finally is, is the giving of the certainty of your consciousness. If it is not refined, you will project it; if it is true, you will extend it because an idea in truth never leaves its source. That's how simple it is. Over and over again we say to you, "You are the universe. There is only one state of consciousness: it is you. There is nothing outside of you." This is the highest level at which any attempt at bringing about a transformation can be presented to you. And that's the occurrence that is going on. It is always up to you. You cannot lay or foster the blame or give the responsibility to your own projections, because you have already limited them by the definition of yourself.

Group consciousness will never find God. Group consciousness is false by definition. All consciousness is singular. We may get together in groups and attempt through therapy to bring about transformative occurrences. This is an extremely high reach in so-called psychology or transpersonal psychology, but finally each consciousness in his own configuration reaches the inevitable truth of himself and not through commiseration. Through re-cognition. Everybody hear me?

The total in reality is never shared. It is total only in you individually. Wow! What do we teach if it is not subjectivity, finally? Imagine that. That's a very fearful concept for you, brother. It is very difficult. You keep wanting to give honor and value to your own limitation. And you will do it by constructing family, you will do it by constructing self defensive mechanisms. You will do anything you can to keep from going through the process that will show you that you are in fact eternal and all consciousness. I have come to tell you that it is inevitable and that it will come about in you. And each moment that you make the choice to turn to it, you turn away from the falsity of your own projections. How simple.

Full commitment brings immediate result; so does infinite patience. Full commitment and infinite patience are the same thing. Prepare ye the way of the Lord. Lo I am with you always. I thought you said you went to prepare a way for me. The consciousness of the universe is here or it is nowhere. The incredible tendency to come here and then carry something different out with you – it is only you. That is what you are coming to know.

Wholeness is the state of consciousness. It finally has nothing to do with the coming about of it. The single development now coming into the earth is the always-present truth in this limited configuration that knowledge can be gained by a shift in consciousness or a transformative occurrence. This is very rudely denied, sociologically. Of course. There would be an implication that somehow someone would be more advanced in his ideas and be able to exercise, through ideas, control over his sociological situations. And in fact this is what occurs in the world. Of course. Everyone finally attempts to exercise control over their sociological situations. It is inevitable that they do that.

The notion that there is an involvement of genetics or karma in the response of the apparently limited consciousness or entity, causes the idea of varying degrees of maturation, which affords for all sorts of strange hierarchies, ranging from perhaps the Hindu system of the Brahmin to the untouchable or the king to the commoner, and includes all of man's ideas of himself in limited association with the final truth of his Godhood. For a Christ or an advanced so-called consciousness to come among you and teach that you may now undergo a transformative occurrence that will bring about a new consciousness in you, finally must be rigorously denied. The whole basis of your consciousness is on independence from source. There are many consciousnesses now coming into the New Age thinking where they are the cause of this. The direct quotes now emanating from all recent spiritual literature, and as far back as man has been here, indicate that your conception is what is giving this any form of reality it may seem to have to you. Of course that is very true, but what goes hand in hand with that (and here is the difficulty), in one sentence I say to you, you are responsible for this. You! And in the next sentence I say to you, *you did not make yourself.* Now you are caught. If you carry that a step further, what I said to you is, the earth is your construct, but the earth is no more real than you are in its actual communication or creative energy. We teach only come home to source.

It is a giant step indeed to get community, establishment, in this limited phase of consciousness, to even acknowledge that truth can be gained through an occurrence – through a transformative process, although it is taught everywhere in the religious community. The scientific community is inevitably faced with the dilemma of genius, as is art, and inevitably denies it. And more particularly denies their own obvious potential, since it is their observation of the art that was brought about through their own configuration.

The truth is that if you don't extend the idea of transformation, there is no possibility that you will ever communicate. It is the one single thing that you can say in the illusion: This can be overcome. This can be re-cognized. We can take your apparent diversity and bring it into singularity. We can show you a new way of looking at things. Perhaps we will show you that the most obvious occurrence here is the consciousness' realization that he has constructed death. And in the limited state in which you have conceived yourself, I assure you that you are going to die. But what a strange thing to do. Contained within you and your ideas, since you have expressed it, is an idea of truth and eternity. Why is it then that everything that you see here in limited perception obviously is in a state of dying? Cyclical – it keeps being born and maturing and dying. It is in a framework of time and space because you are in a framework of time and space.

Is there turmoil and pain, anger finally, in the idea of your ultimate and inevitable death? I would think there very well would be. Quite obviously all of your manifestations of disease, apparent hatred, attempts at communion, must be based on the idea of your ultimate death. That is absurd. That doesn't make any sense. But yet if I present you with the absolute proposition of eternity, because of the nature of your limited construction, you deny me and actively pursue retention of the limited consciousness that must inevitably lead you to demise or annihilation. How unreasonable of you. What would be reasonable about death? What is reasonable, really, about pain and limitation? Obviously, the basis of limited consciousness is recognition of a form of selfness, identified as existing in a state of limitedness or lack, with the obvious need to sustain that level of consciousness – to survive. If I present you with the proposition that nothing that is not forever is real, it requires your double take!

The notion that you have come into, that this is your construct, will lead you directly to the truth because it allows you to configurate the absoluteness that nothing is outside of you. Very simply there is nothing without your conception of it. How paradoxical, the notion of objectivity or the notion of separation. It seems so absurd that anyone would look at the idea of two things being separate – obviously their construction then is based on not knowing, apparently, what the object is that they are viewing. That's crazy. That's senseless. So they study the limitation instead of the wholeness. They philosophize on their own false configuration – on their own apart-ness. Wow!

As you go through your regenerative process, you begin to stand aside from this chaos, and this can be perceived as very conflictual. You no longer feel needs to participate in sociological death rituals of relationships which reject, or the intense need to accomplish limited goals. These things lose their meaning to you. But since earth consciousness is only derived from memory, all of the entities in states of duality around you are constructing you in their own limited parameters of consciousness. If you deviate from that and they are unable to adjust to it, they will attack you or deny you. Of course! If you look at it from your own conception, it would be obvious to you that since you are the creator or miscreator of everything about you, the only thing that could ever cause you pain or fail you would be your own idea about it. Obviously everybody here is going through anger and pain and attack and defense because of their own ideas. If we take the next step, we come to the inevitable conclusion that you are being attacked by your own thoughts, and of course, you are. You are only memory! You are a limited memory machine.

The direct necessity for the body in perception is based on the retention of memory, of schism, and it is all in you. It is not outside of you. Every idea that you are having and sorting out is still with you. You have an idea of beauty, but it is always in relationship with ugliness. So you shun, or put aside, apparently in your limited state, the ugliness. It does not go away. How do you exorcise ugliness or evil-ness, the devil, the limited part of you, the configurations of attack and defense? You can never overcome apparent evil by combating it. We stand on the Mount and say, "Resist not evil." Literally, do not defend yourself from your own ideas. The only thing that could ever be limiting or evil is your thought. Your kingdom is not of this world. You are not from here. All of your equations of apparent justice lead nowhere. All of your configurations of give and take and have and hold and live and die have no value whatever *except* the value that you have given them in your mind. You listen to me: if you give the earth value, it has value. You do not get rid of it by establishing its valuableness and then attempting to give it up. Of course! So we teach be whole and true and real and love and extend. Be defenseless. Mostly, we teach forgive. Never mind the equation that you are only forgiving your own thoughts. That will come next – that you can only give to yourself. That you can only finally forgive yourself – that will come next. We finally teach an occurrence of know yourself, that will come to you.

Dare you start with the premise that you are the only living Son of God? How else can you come to the truth if you don't start with the premise of truth? If no idea is outside of you, who then is true? Who is all consciousness in the universe? There is nothing separate from you. You hold the universe in the palm of your hand. How will the earth be saved then? How will we return to love and beauty and truth? When you change you own mind, and only in that manner.

Come, reason with me about the inevitability of your consciousness. Attempt within your own framework of memory and consciousness to conceive of death now. See how the veil comes over your head? Attempt to look at darkness. Attempt to see, attempt to *conscious-ize* annihilation. Do you see that the awakening process is the death process? The subtraction of the limited you is all that the transformation really is – the resurrection, the enlightenment.

The history of the universe is contained in you. There is no thought of variation in the construct of consciousness that is not contained in you. You are the *I Ching*, you are the master genetic code, you are all of history. Religiously: you are the way and the light. Scientifically: everything arises from your consciousness. If there is nothing outside of you, all apparent parts must contain the whole. I assure you they do. The whole could never be the sum of its parts if you are the sum-er. One plus one could never be two for the "plus" is only you. Wherever two or more are gathered I am there. Of course, how simple! Make the stew then, divine cooks, and when you finish jump into the pot. What an incredible idea of freedom ensues with the realization of the acceptance of the responsibility for the universe. The incredible knowledge that the universe is finally benign, that nothing ever really stands opposed to anything. Nothing is in friction with reality or truth. Wow! You lay down your rusty saber. You stand aside from the fray and you say, "I will not participate in this any longer."

How easy it is to see historically that the idea of Christhood must be persecuted, must be crucified. Of course. The whole basis of the configuration of consciousness in regard to establishment in limitation is based on the idea of death. If I come among you and say, "You cannot die," what I am really saying to you is that if you come with me, the earth will collapse. Of course. There is a beautiful quote from brother Jesus Christ in *A Course In Miracles* where He says you really think that you came here and found the earth in duality waiting for you to bring about its transformation. On the contrary, if you are not here in your own consciousness, the earth is not here either. That is why you are defined as the only living Son of God. There are no idle thoughts. Nothing in truth is discrete. What would it be discrete from? To what purpose would it stand aside from unity, or could? No! No!

All around you is energy, manifest in duality, broken up again and again and again. You look for reason in it. You look for it in the limited state of your own consciousness to bring about a unity. And that is your sole purpose in consciousness – to escape the chaos that you have created. Wow! To remember that you are the cause and not the effect. Wow! To realize that you are only Adam dreaming and will awaken at this moment to the truth of you. And all your yesterdays are gone. You can't construct your tomorrow. In giving up your yesterdays, you take all of your historic incidences and perfect them in the glory of the realization of their inevitable capacity to bring about your awakening. You do not stand in judgment of your karma, of your past experiences. You release your resentments. You forgive. You extend your love and you come home.

Is Heaven real? You bet your boots it's real! There is another beautiful quote of brother Jesus, where He says that nothing outside of Heaven is alive, which means that you are in a deep sleep with your death wish. The construction of death is fearful and hateful and denies truth. Anything that could die could never have been alive. Wow! Therefore be you grateful for the occurrence in you and be humble before the majesty of the universe. The truth will be made known unto you. You will recognize in your own self the fullness and wholeness of all consciousness. You will extend from you only the truth of you as you have re-cognized yourself. Stand aside then. It is impossible for you to do a wrong. How difficult it is for you to accept absolute forgiveness. How strong the notion of cause and effect. How difficult the final concept that cause and effect stand as a single thing with no time between.

In our transformation teachings, we are shortening time, to bring you into the moment of your unity and of your truth. Is it experiential? It is only experiential. All around you are rays and energies and sounds of a creative universe. Your dilemma lies in the notion of potential. From the idea of potential, you create futurizing or time. All consciousness is full blown at all moments. Everything that could ever be, is running full tilt. Wow! Wow! And you are it! Don't bind yourself. Be free. Cast your bread upon the water. Is it a full endeavor? Does it require purpose? Yes. Full commitment brings immediate results. Of course.

You are individually very select. You are indeed chosen. Without you, Heaven could never be complete. We are at the omega point together. Therefore be of good cheer. What does brother Jesus say in *A Course In Miracles*? Blasphemy can be defined as depression and anger and resentment. Wow! You can't blaspheme against God but you can against yourself, can't you? The truth has nothing to do with this. Only you have to do with this and in that acknowledgment is indeed your salvation. One and one are not then two. One and one are three;

then one and one are one. What an extraordinary occurrence to see that Light, to know that it is really happening to you. That you are in this process. Not someone else. Not someone historic, not a guru, not a Jesus. The recognition that *you*, as a man, become Man-God. Just you! Wow! Teach that, brother. That brings the denial to the surface. It is a direct confrontation with the limited self. Is the ending foreseeable? Indeed it is. You have constructed it in your own consciousness and are bringing it about. Thank you. We thank you, dear brother, for the occurrence of you and your Christhood. Wow! We never could have done it without you. You are indispensable to the truth equation, and your creations await you in joy and harmony, and love and truth. Welcome home! Welcome home!

This is a most difficult thing. I've said this a lot of times, that this transfiguration, that this enlightenment, this transformative occurrence involves all of you. It is not limited to your body-brain, for goodness sake! It involves your ductless glands, if you will, but not in separation from the rest of you. It is totally involved. It would have to be. You cannot bring about a spiritual transformation without a bodily change. It can't be done. Of course not. The whole basis of the Apocalypse or the Revelation is the movement of the passion within your body, for crying out loud!! Is that too esoteric now? Wow!

The high prophet contained in the Edgar Cayce readings in the 1930's, the beautiful book on the comparison, the simile, the metaphor, the allegory of the consciousness of the body in relationship to the ductless glands and the churches in Revelation. Holy Mackerel! *You* are all history. That occurrence can bring about some very strange aberrations within your own state of configuration. Of course, and will! Finally it requires acceptance of all of you. Everything that happens to you now is in direct correlation with your own transformative occurrence. It would have to be. Of course. It is going on in you. Yes, indeed it is! Wow!

All disease is a denial of spiritual energy or an inability to create in truth. Of course! If disease is real there is no truth. You cannot construct disease or pain or sorrow outside of you and then repair it. It's a strange notion – the construction of an idol, a limited god, a caprice god. Wow! All power is given unto you in Heaven and earth.

Greater things will you do than I have done. Where is Armageddon, then? Where is this incredible deliverance? Only in you! Yes! Very lovely! Thank you.

I want you to hear this. Finally what is occurring in full endeavor, and this is in *A Course In Miracles* – this is a course in reasoning to the truth of mastership or Christhood or Avatarship. That is what we teach. The Master Da John, brother Franklin, incredible awakening consciousness, teaches the Eastern tradition with a lot of Western vernacular, the idea of his Christhood. He is awakened; he is the only living Son of God. Of course! We are just going to take that a step further, and he is much aware of this, and present you with the inevitable conclusion: since there is only one final state of consciousness in truth, that *you* must be that state. Now you can teach it out of *A Course In Miracles*. If you will look at brother Da John from the *Course In Miracles* or the Jesus idea, and forgive him totally, which is really all that we teach, you will recognize that indeed he is the only living Son of God. Who do you think is sitting around me here? Of course! The fault always lies in the judgment of someone somehow being what? Further advanced or further behind you in his spiritual acumen. But remember, if you judge him at all, you judge him falsely – and there, is the problem.

Inevitably in coming to the truth, we create stages or hierarchies of consciousness, and this is in the sense of apparent reality, very true. But the second that a notion arises in you that you are in the fourth stage and identify yourself and are working on the fifth or the sixth or the seventh, that's absurd. The moment that you acknowledge the possibility of a seventh stage you literally entered that stage and denied it. You could not configurate the notion of God without being true. You are in a constant state, obviously of schism. There is a false notion in association with time that some particular identities or configurations are born with more capacities than others. That will keep you here a long time, brother. I am sorry but it is not true. You immediately, through recognizing another's apparent Christhood, have denied your own – unless you will recognize it fully, in which case you will see that you are only him.

Question: "Are you trying to say The Jews aren't the chosen people?"

We say that the definition of Jew is *chosen*, historically, and that all who have come into a configuration of apparent duality are chosen and have been chosen into truth establishment. It is inevitable. It doesn't have anything to do obviously with race or establishment on earth, but there is a big one-chromosome difference between a chimpanzee and a human being. You bet your boots! That is the chosen element. If 99 percent genetically, chromosomally, of an ape is the same as a man, obviously it is the other 1percent that is the chosen part. But the dilemma is this: the chimpanzee is perfect in its chimpanzeeness. I have said this many times. You obviously are the only nutty one. You are the one that's in the denial of yourself. The only thing in the universe that doesn't know what it is, is a limited state of consciousness that has already acknowledged its wholeness. Wow, strange notion. It's a strange idea that you could be more than one thing. Never mind what it is.

The truth of you is always the truth of you. Not in variation but in singularity. Wow! I can't teach that. Wow! The universe is a sense of consciousness. It is a beingness. Obviously there is no necessity for truth to identify itself, that's silly – and it doesn't. Thank You. More later.

Methodist Basement

Let's see if we can set up scenarios for teaching *A Course In Miracles.* If I'm in the basement of the Methodist Church, I'm going to get through the doctrinal associations of the teaching of Jesus of Nazareth as soon as I can, because there is no sense in getting into a 2000 year old discussion about what the risen man said and was. You are going to make a statement within the Christian vernacular simply because that is the risen association contained within the possibility of the objection of the human condition to the realization of Godmind.

I'm just curious to see whether this will work. Listen carefully to this. This would not have worked last week. I'm curious to see whether it will work this week. Because of the continuing influence of the miracle-mindedness of your associations, you are going to be provided with circles or positions where the presentation of subjective reality can be performed in an expanding realization of happiness through the disconnection of the necessity for an objected opinion association.

Let's set the scenario: This is a course from a risen man, identified as Jesus of Nazareth, who is actually any man with the necessity to arise, or to come out within the apparent conflict of a conceptual human association to the realization of a continuing, extending, eternal, loving God. This was a physical occurrence, so we are teaching physical resurrection. The obstacles to teaching a physical resurrection are very simply that physicalness is the obstacle to the eternal peace of God

– not by the appearance of its physicalness, but by the obtainment of physical or objective association through the dedication of the subjective/objective mind to retain a distance between the causation and the result of the association of consciousness. The fundamental teaching of *A Course In Miracles* is that reality is subjective; that is, Godmind continually extends in a cause and effect relationship that cannot be distinguished in the reality of the perfect mind of eternal association. That fell just a little bit because any definition of totality will fall. That being said, you have an awareness in you by the auspices of eternity, by the totality of the mind, whereby you can, through a process of your own association with yourself, arrive at this conclusion – that is, that you are perfect as God created you.

The manner that will best afford you relief from the pain that you are experiencing within this modality is called *A Course In Miracles*. *A Course In Miracles* for those of you who have not heard of it, or would have to immediately go to determine what the source of *A Course In Miracles* is in order that you would validate the possibility of your accepting it within the framework of the opinion of what you are, let me relieve you of that necessity. Listen to me. The *Course in Miracles* is nothing but a course in continuing open-mindedness. This is for the newgie; this is for the guy who doesn't really know what we're presenting him with. Now all of you in this association I understand are Methodists. Is that true? (Say "yes." All: "Yes.") You are Methodists. So, fundamentally you teach that there is a method – isn't it so, as Wesley did – that you can reach God; that there's a method by which you, as a conceptual association can actually contact this power of God that we're speaking of. This is a method that you might want to avail yourself to. This is a teaching of subjective reality – that is, literally there is nothing outside of you. The fundamental declaration of this teaching, which proclaims itself as emanating from Jesus of Nazareth, the risen man, is that I evolved through my own total capacity a way of resurrecting – a way of having a miracle reassociation with God – which you may now share with me if you choose. This is nothing but the fundamental teachings of Christianity, of the saviorship of the man Jesus of Nazareth.

Presented to you in the *Course in Miracles* is a manner in which this will come about. The problems you will have with it as you sit in this conspicuous absence of the release of your self identity, is that the *Course in Miracles* teaches the necessity of the release of the opinionated self identity that constitutes the reality of the ego mind, and declares to you uncompromisingly that in no other manner can you come to know that you are perfect as God created you except by the continuing clearing of the garbage of your own self identity. Does everyone hear that? I'm not concerned about how much you know about the Course, or where you think you are. I am telling you that if you will pick up this book, or if you listen to the miracle teachers that are going throughout the world now, that you can begin to hear within your own relationship that quite literally – are you ready for this, as taught by Jesus – you are the savior of the world! This initially is going to be very threatening to you because you would much rather, in the minimum association of your willingness of religiosity, admit that Jesus himself is the savior of the world. The fact remains, had you had the capacity to admit that Jesus was the savior of the world within your projected conceptual associations, you would not be here very simply because if Jesus of Nazareth is the savior of the world, He is resurrected, this world is over, and you are gone from here. Of course!

Yet, somehow in the dilemma of your own associations within this apparent nightmare of objective reality, you find yourself trapped with a risen Christ in which you are being disallowed to share in the totality of this simple message of resurrection. This is a course by which you can use the auspices of an awakened mind and apply a method of the release of your cause-and-effect associations. Fundamentally, the concern of the Miraclist is not what you think within your own objective mind. You may be initially offended by these advanced teachers – and I'm using that term without advise at all, and that's hard to do; I'm not using it advisedly. We are teaching basically then that contact with God is a spontaneous occurrence that is simultaneous with the release of the defense of the cause and effect relationship of the human condition. The simplicity of this is literally overwhelming. It teaches that if you don't bring your own predications of objective determination into any situation, the conversion to reality will be simultaneous because God, who is real, is all around you all the time.

I want to be sure, for those of you who are accustomed to hearing this message, whether this is being presented simply enough.

The complications that are involved in understanding the message of Jesus in *A Course In Miracles* are nothing but the subterfuge of a conceptual mind determined not to hear the very simple message that God Is and conflict and pain and death are not. Do you see that? The problem, then, can be addressed only within the conceptual self identity literally because the universe, or the associations of form, are what the human condition is – in other words, dear teacher of God, what you are. As a self creator of a purpose of identity based on the historic references of Adam, and the historic references of the First Covenant, on the determination of your humanness as an association of cause and effect, as an eye for an eye, as the necessity to attack and defend yourself in a correspondence with what you view as a form of existence in reality.

Let's go to the fundamental teachings of Jesus. Let's use a sentence from the Workbook. The Workbook is designed from the very beginning in a continuing fashion to teach you to release the attack and defense identity that constitutes your apparent reality. Those of you who don't have the Workbook, run out and get one! There is no concern in it in regard to what you think, what your opinions are, or what you defend. We are teaching the experience of the miracle, the experience of the union and the love of God that is all around us now.

So we ask you to be what, when you came into this room? We ask you simply to be open-minded. Now the first step in being open-minded that occurs to a perceptual mind is that "I am perfectly willing to hear your opinion about it." How much more open-minded could you ask me to be? I'm going to ask you to take a very vital step with me, and many of you are beginning to smile because you are beginning to relax the defenses that you brought in here in your determination to formulate in a correspondence with what you thought you were going to hear – an attack-and-defense quite literally of the opinions of your own mind, constituted by what you thought I was going to tell you. Let's reach this very basically. I am not going to tell you anything except that you're perfect as God created you. I will tell you nothing but that. The manner in which you arrive at that, I can't be concerned about since any manner would have nothing to do with the perfection that you are. Of course! The obvious problem you have with that is, if I am perfect as God created me, why am I apparently in this association of sickness and death. The answer to that is you are in this apparent association of sickness and death because you are looking for a correspondence within the relationship of your objective mind, that is your cause and effect, that will verify the goodness, love and eternity of God.

I have to show you here that the fundamental teaching is that existence or time or relationships of cause and effect cannot verify eternal life. But the admission of eternal life is axiomatic in the determination of a relationship of time to eternity. That seems to be a little obtuse because it was. I couldn't even understand that one myself. In the Bible, Jesus calls this teaching in the spirit. He says if you'll come with your own open-mindedness and stand up beside closed-mindedness, at the minimum they'll feel so much sympathy for your good conflict, that they will extend to you a release from the necessity to defend yourself. Many beginner speakers have experienced this. Isn't that amazing? This is not an inside joke, this is a joke of all humanity. All of you in this audience who have stood up and attempted to express miracle-mindedness have felt the frustration of describing to the conceptual mind your experience of God. Isn't this so? Because it literally, at some point, becomes ecstatically non-describable. Everyone in this room can nod their head to that because there is no one who has reached the high heights of this basement of the Methodist Church without being cognizant somewhere of the futility of the occurrent existence of their definition and opinion of themselves in their relationship in love.

It is important that you understand, and this is where the threat will occur and this is the threat of Jesus of Nazareth: I'm not trying to take anything away from you. Listen to me. I'm trying to give you much more than you are willing to accept from me at this moment. I am teaching you that in *A Course In Miracles* there is a progression of acceptance that will occur in your own mind. These will be teachings of the Workbook.

Let's try one of them. The crucial element perhaps that occurs in the 128th day of the Workbook might well me "I must learn that I only give to myself." This is the basic teaching of Jesus of Nazareth. He proclaims it in everything He says by the simple expedience of giving everything away. The idea of giving everything away is a major threat to your objective association very simply because the idea of giving everything contains elements of the necessity to retain anything. The *Course in Miracles* says very simply that giving, or extending the mind, is what God is, and that it would be impossible if you give that you would not give unto the likeness, if this is your limited association, of the certainty that you are created perfectly by God.

Now this is a pause that will occur in this teaching. The pause is to give you just a moment to digest within your own conceptual identities the idea or the possibility that you could actually make a personal contact with God. I know this may be outrageous to you at this point, but I assure you that reasonably if God is everywhere, God is here. He is not absent from this situation, but you have blinded yourself by your determination to find correspondence in the reference of what you thought you were as a human being. At this point the threat occurs. At this point, all of the determinations of your genetic memory, all of the references of the necessity to defend yourself, to teach your offsprings that the quality of life can be determined by the accumulation of goods that can then be used as you grow old and sick and die, are threatened by this very simple message that that is not true. It is not true that you can become sick and die. It is not true that you need defend yourself from some evil force or power that is outside of you. It is true that you are perfect as God created you. It is true because you are perfect as God created you, and you are perfect and loving and whole and eternal as God created you simply because it is true. It is not true by any possibility of determinations of your own mind in your relationship with what you think it is. If this is a confession of faith, let it be so. I assure you that it is impossible for you to arrive at the conclusion that you are whole and perfect as God created you simply because creation or eternity is not a conclusion, it is a reality.

Those of you who have read this, and reasoned with this, I am now offering you, through an association of my mind with yours – and this is what advanced teachers will be teaching in their *Course in Miracles* – that you can begin at this moment, and have when you came in this door, have an experience of a miracle reassociation of your conceptual mind – a healing of the schism that heretofore has caused you to defend and attack yourself, and to provide yourself with the mechanisms of death, of cancer, of pain, of getting old – simply to find a justification for this apparent schism, for this occurrence, for this nightmare that's contained within your own mind. Be happy that I am relieving you of the necessity of defense of yourself by our mutual association and declaration of the miracle of a holy instant, with no provisions for your past experiences at all, that are converting your conceptual self identity to the realization that you are the only living son of God. Those of you who want to say "of course," say "of course." Some: "Of course." Those of you who want to say, "what the hell is he talking about," say "what the hell is he talking about?" A few brave souls: "What the hell are you talking about?" No – turn to the guy next to you and say "what the hell is he talking about"

Hopefully, those of you who haven't heard the Miraclists, they're actually spreading out now – uh oh, I'm giving away the future – they're going out into the world and teaching this lesson. Generally, the guy next door we hope will say "I don't know what it is but I'm feeling pretty good about it anyway" when you say "what the hell is going on here." "I don't know, but certainly the guy is worth listening to." All that means is that fundamental message is not as fretful to him as it was just a moment ago. Fundamentally nothing could be more fretful to the association than the simple declaration that hc's not real. This is the whole teaching, that any association that you have as a human being will have nothing to do with the perfect creating energy of loving mind. Isn't that so?

The holy instant. There is no one in this room who has not had experiences of a contact with the reality that transcended the condition in which you found yourself. Many of you have had this moment of revelation at major threatening associations, at times of death perhaps, at times when fear had reached a level where you could no longer handle it. The basic teaching or message of *A Course In Miracles* is that you are what fear is. Love, which is what God is and what you must be as a perfectly-created son is all around you, and that the unconditionality – and I'm using that term advisedly within the scope of your capacity to understand unconditionalness – the unconditional love of God is occurring continually in the release of your own self identity, and that the release of the necessity for the defense of you has nothing at all to do with the miracle of God's love which is all around you. Very simply, then, the miracle declares to you that you need do nothing. In the moment of doing nothing, you must experience the love of God because that is what you are.

Now this appears to be a practice of open-mindedness. There is no one in this room who has not picked up a pop psychology book that taught him fundamentally that he was okay, and that his brother was okay. That is, basically, the teaching is: "If I'm okay about myself, my brother will be okay about himself," or "he is separate from me, but my association must be that I'm okay." I'm taking that a step further and declaring to you that since your brother, this association that you have formed, is a projection of your own mind, if you are okay, he must be okay because he is an opinion or an association of your mind. That, of course, is where the difficulty lies. What are we teaching? Singularity of mind. But mostly, here early in this basement, and I know that Gill has prepared a very lovely lunch for you participants – what I'm really offering you is a new way to think – a way of open-mindedness, so that as you go out from here, each moment of every day and each day of every year from now until the end of time, can come about by the simple realization that wherever you find yourself it is perfectly okay not to defend the actions or opinions of where you are. This is difficult to teach because it's what Jesus said to you in the Sermon on the Mount, and you didn't hear it in the Sermon on the Mount, and you didn't hear in the Sermon on the Mount, "be ye therefore perfect, even as your Father which is in heaven is perfect." (Matthew 5:48) Nor is there a necessity for you to review, unless it's your desire to do so, as a Methodist, the fundamental teachings of Jesus of Nazareth in the relationship of the non-resistance of evil, with the further admonition occurring in the Course, that since you are the source of the apparent evil by the protection of your own devices, that is, literally by my association with myself contained within my own mind, I am describing the nothingness of a condition of cause and effect. Most certainly, if I resist evil, I will be attacked.

The basic teachings of *A Course In Miracles* are that you are attacked by what you defend yourself from because you defend yourself in order to be attacked and verify your association with yourself. The occurrence of the miracle which is going on all around you all the time, is the nothing but that moment, *not* in that you don't decide not to have an opinion, but simply don't have one. This is not a decision not to participate in the declared illusion. This is simply not participating. And you say to me, "how am I ever ever going to be able to be in this world and not participate in my own associations?" I am showing you a manner called *A Course In Miracles* where you can be in this world and not of it. I am showing you a manner by which you can continue to participate for just a moment in the events of your own relationship with the declaration that you are raising up, that you are going to undergo this illumination, this transformation, this forgiveness, this process of enlightenment of your old associations.

Many of you now in the room are beginning to have that experience of joy. The question is not that, the question is how threatening will the experience of joy be to you? That appears to be a paradox. And it's paradoxical to the extent that you will now, having felt the joy of this association, identify it in cause-and-effect relationships. That is, justify it by an opinion, an action, a participation of your own mind in the necessity of joyfulness. Joyfulness and happiness are not a necessity; they are a reality. They are not the result of the gratification of your own association, but a continuing eternal process of the extension of Godmind. I understand that an unreasonable joy is a threat to you. Yet as you experience the unreasonable joy, you may more and more begin to say "the hell with my old agenda, I am going to begin to enjoy the admission, at a minimum, that obtainable and accessible to me by the admission that I am the cause of this." I have to come back to the basic teaching, because very certainly if there is something outside of you that can be causing you pain, you are never going to be able to find surcease of it except in attempts to adjudicate a relationship of yourself through a judgmental opinion of the manifestation of justice – the idea that somehow you can obtain justice in this place. Yet justice is of God, not of this place.

I know this is wandering far afield. What we're really trying to determine is that we believe we're at a place where you actually can begin to teach this message without the threat that you had before. Nothing could be simpler than this message of love. Nothing could be simpler than your declaration of the miracle that must occur in your own association if there is a God. Certainly it requires perhaps a basic admission of the universal mind who creates universally. But the acceptance of that, since it is contained within you, will lead to very rapid progress – and we're using that term in the sense of your continuing observations of yourself.

One thing we can say about these new Miraclists is that they laugh a lot. This is lovely stuff in the Course. Another thing that we can say is, they seem to walk around with a lot of happiness and a lot of contentment. And it doesn't seem to be based on the circumstances in which they find themselves. It's as though they have found a secret, that they have found something contained within themselves that is giving them a new... and many of you now at the end of this session are going to go to the Miraclists and say "well, how did you get this? How were you able to discover this secret of eternal life, this pearl of wisdom?" And you are going to say to them, "I am teaching you that we are singular in God's mind. I am declaring to you in this relationship that there is nothing that has come about in me that cannot and did not come about in you." This will be the fundamental teachings of the risen man, Jesus of Nazareth. Isn't that lovely to know?

This is *A Course In Miracles.* The reason it is a required course is because you find yourself in a condition of pain and death. Obviously since the control of conceptual mind is what you are, you may determine the time in which you are perfectly willing to admit that God created you perfectly – or you can continue to fight the battle contained within your own identity. This is the prologue to *A Course In Miracles.* You can determine the time, and here's the crucial sentence: You cannot determine the curriculum. The curriculum is nothing but your old memories in association with what you thought you had to learn in order to undergo the experience of eternal life. I am showing you that basically and fundamentally it is not a learning, but rather an un-learning process. I am declaring to you, and you will find this in this lovely book, that all of the things you have looked at, all of the opinions that you have ever had, all of the justifications for existence that you have heretofore entertained, must be brought to the light of the present condition in which you find yourself, and released at that moment through perhaps the surrender or the willingness of you to initially entertain and then discover through the miracle of your own mind the reality of the love of God.

Is God love? Does God love you? Does He? God loves you, doesn't He. Is that okay? When you were about 4, somebody said "God loves you." Does God love you? All: Yes. Would God cause you sickness and pain? All: No. Is that tough? That's tough. Do you want to see how fundamental this is, 7-year-old? Look how fundamental that is. God loves you. He created you perfectly, didn't He? Does God cause you sickness and pain? Perhaps you did something naughty. You don't realize how basic this teaching is. Certainly if you did something naughty, you would deserve to be punished. Yes or no? All: Yes. Just as certainly, if God created you, and you do something naughty, God must be capable of creating naughtiness. He must be; otherwise how did you become naughty? This is your 7-year-old question. This is the question of the confrontation of the necessity for existence with eternal love – the basic confrontation of time with eternity. You have every right not to trust a God who causes sickness, pain and death.

The teachings that you have heretofore attempted to express as those of Jesus of Nazareth are not true. The teacher of singularity and love through the resurrection, and the continuing resurrection of your mind, declared to you very simply that God made you perfectly, and that there is nothing outside of you that could threaten you. There is an admission that you could threaten your own self with your determination for just a moment in your discovery of your separation from God, but that it could not persist and did not persist for more than a moment. I have now come into the teachings of *A Course In Miracles*. We're not going to go any further than this with this, because we are teaching that the miracle is going on around you now, and will occur to you in light. Some of you have come here suffering from a great deal of sickness. Some of you are suffering from conditions of terminalness. Some of you are suffering ill health, are broken and poor in relationships. I say to you, you come into this association and through the practice of this fundamental letting go and letting God, you will have an experience that will transcend any necessity either to defend it, finally even to express it. You will arrive at what many of our teachers have arrived at now, and that is that God Is, and I am that.

Now I'm sounding like an old Eastern teacher. The reason we're including all of the great Eastern masters is that you'll notice that all of the great Eastern masters have begun to teach the Workbook of

235

A Course In Miracles. It's very difficult for an Eastern master, that is one who has sat for 4000 years teaching "transcend your limited associations" to discover that there is contained within the Christian vernacular not only an acclamation of their teachings, but a method by which you can come to know through transcendence initially and then existenal (sounds like something that happens in your digestive tract) reassociation of yourself, or what you call resurrection of the body, this new life and love that's all around you. Father, thank you!

Those of you here in this gathering, and once again we are reminded that we are in the basement of the Methodist Church. It's a fundamental teaching of both the Eastern and the Western tradition to stay in prayer all the time. At the level we're teaching it, which is as communication with God, prayer is nothing but each moment releasing the necessity for the defense of your cause and effect relationship. Hopefully you won't reduce that to a prayer wheel that you can spin on now, as you do, say in Buddhism. "I have to do a lot of human things, so I'll spin the wheel, and that way I can keep my contact with God." I suggest you spin your own wheel, and let it land randomly on your grid in the illusion. There are no winners or losers on the wheel. You may initially want to get God's attention, but I assure you that He's been trying to get your attention for a very long time. What we're doing with the holy instant is putting you on the same frequency – do you understand that? If you think of space/time as an oscillation, if you let yourself be a receiving set for just a moment, that's the experience of miracle-mindedness. Stop trying to insinuate or direct the amount of love energy you will allow to come into your association. I assure you that it will cover the entire band. It need not be reduced to amplitude modulation, frequency modulation or even within the visual side of your acuity contained within gamma waves or radio waves. You are all of that, declared as the Great Rays in the *Course in Miracles*. Let the Great Rays be what they are; don't try to determine what are the Great Rays, and what are the Great Bobs. Bobs and Rays.

Okay, is that enough? We sort of wanted this on a little tape, maybe, what heretofore has been a secret, which is the transformation of your mind. The growth of the Christchild in you has been protected by you. This is a message to those of you abroad – somewhere you have the capacity to hear this message simply because you have protected your own Christchild. That seed of Light is contained within your body configuration. It will grow in you as you allow it to grow through the continuing virginity of your own mind association with yourself. This is a little mystical for you, but there's no reason that you can't understand that you were born in the manger of your own body associations and have progressed past the Pharaoh and are now entering into your mind which is the Jerusalem, the salvation. You say, "my, he's teaching physical resurrection." Indeed I am. I am teaching you the healing process and the discovery of the physical resurrection of your body, and that at this instant if you choose you may disappear in the glory and the Light that is what you are. Yes you can!

Can this message be heard by the world? Question not whether it can be heard by the world. Question your willingness to hear it, and your willingness to lay down the apparent authority problem that you have had in determining you are the cause of this rather than letting the Creator of eternal life be the cause of you. That's where the conflict heretofore has been. And this is where the battle will be fought, because I say to you God is perfect and whole and utterly real; or He's this world of sickness, pain and death and the necessity for the existence for all eternity. One or the other is not so. If this message be too complicated for you, I know of no manner in which I could make it more simple. This world is not real because it is not created eternally by God. You can come to know that through your own mind because the cause and the effect of this world are what you are.

Now, I want you to pick up the Workbook of *A Course In Miracles* and begin to hear this with this new dedication that these teachers of God are offering – these lovely miracle-mindedness ones who are coming among you now and offering you the security and happiness of their own minds. You can come to know that this is so. You may find among you as this word spreads abroad about open-mindedness that you will begin to meet each other on the street. You will begin to meet each other in love. You will begin to establish contacts that transcend the necessity for the defense of the position in which you find yourself.

I am teaching you that love is the extension of God and of your mind determined by you in the condition of the presence in which you find yourself. As you discover your – and I'm going to use the word *capacity* of miracle-mindedness, you will begin to enjoy going into associations and allowing yourself to be open-minded. Where heretofore you were threatened by not being allowed to express your opinion, you will discover that the expression of your opinion starts to cause you pain. This is a simple admission of the transformation of your own mind. Enjoy it. You may end up laughing at the way I'm blathering on. The manner in which this comes about, or the manner in which you finally determine to express yourself will be contained within the totality of your relationship with your apparent condition in time.

It is crucial that you remember this, and I'm going to use the sentence directly: *This world was over a long time ago.* That may be astonishing to you, but we are in a condition of remembering together the transformation of our mind. This is *A Course In Miracles.* I will not let my previous opinions, my previous definitions, affect me now. I will release them at this moment. This is the only moment that there is. I will admit that fundamentally there is no connection of memory to the past. I'm going to put that under my pillow tonight. *There is no connection of memory to the past.* At this moment all that could ever go on, or has ever gone on, is going on. And it's going on in me. It is not outside of me. And the power that I have now inherent in me can be expressed by the extension of my mind, rather than the retention of my own existent condition. How very fundamental this is, and what a joy it is now to begin to see what began as a little willingness on your part expand to a willingness that transcends any necessity to proclaim the previous associations that you were in.

You literally have discovered that the *Course in Miracles* is an escape from hell. It required, perhaps, the admission – if not the acceptance – that you were the cause of hell, and that not knowing what you are would be what hell is. But certainly determinations to discover what you are, with the admission that you didn't know really, would not make any sense under any close examination, if we have accepted fundamentally that knowing what you are is what the Universe is.

Bless you, Methodist and Baptists and Catholics and humans. Isn't it amazing that the human condition has always been the search for happiness? He's looking for it. You're looking for it. This is the discovery of a new way of thinking that will give you a peace that transcends understanding, and will pass by anything that you thought before. We call it the Love of God. Love and God should not evoke necessities for definitions of what Love and God are. God is Love and you are that. And with that we say amen!

So we're speaking to you from the *Course in Miracles* academy here in Lake Delton, Wisconsin. We offer to the world the simple teachings of the risen man, Jesus, and we offer it with open minds and hearts, and we offer it without opinions, but with directions that just for a moment you give up the necessity for your opinions about what you think we are, and more particularly what you think you are in relationship with us, so that this *Course in Miracles*, this holy instant that you are now experiencing, can continue to be an on-going experience until the end of time, with the realization that the end of time is very near, and that when it's over it will always have been over. Those of you who are hearing this tape for the first time, repeat with me: *The world I see has nothing to do with reality. It is of my own making, and it does not exist.* Wow! Thank you! Amen!

That's a crazy teaching isn't it? Why is this crazy teaching making you so happy? Because the world is crazy anyway, and if I'm going to be crazy, I might as well be crazy with that rather than crazy for death. This whole teaching is, you can't die. If the power is in your mind, you can make a declaration to love and truth and it will come about more readily than your declaration to sickness and death simply because sickness and death will never work and love will always work. I'm into another talk. We invite those of you who are hearing about *A Course In Miracles* or perhaps have thought that perhaps *A Course In Miracles* was some sort of conceptual determination about a relationship between Jesus and Helen and Bill – that is just not what it is. When you come to know that, you may want to participate in the miracle-mindedness of the circle of atonement that's going on here.

It is not that the fundamental *Course in Miracles* or any miracle does not begin with "there must be a better way." That's how the *Course in Miracles* began – with the conflict. But to continue to stay in the conflict when the *Course in Miracles* is here really doesn't make any sense because the *Course in Miracles* says indeed there is a better way, but it has nothing at all to do with what you thought the manner was. That's just for those of you who are familiar with the scribing of *A Course In Miracles*. That is, anyone who would pick up the Course would see immediately that there's no justification for his continuing opinions about this Course. So be at peace! This high teaching does not require your understanding; it requires your acceptance. But the acceptance of it will give you an understanding that transcends your previous necessity of understanding nothing, through the very simple understanding that you are perfect as God created you. I'm spinning around on this a little bit because I'm expressing, obviously, a transcendent moment within my relationship with my mind that I am sharing with you and that you will share with your projections. This is readily obvious as you realize that God creates perfectly.

Now we say "Amen", for God has come to dwell with us. This will be the final moment. For just a moment we will remember this together in a borderland just at the gate of Heaven where we can turn and invite our old associations to join with us before the glory and majesty of God.

So you came with open mind, or a mind open sufficiently to allow for the possibility that the condition in which you found yourself was not true, and that you were indeed as I have declared to you, perfect as God created you. That's how simple this has been for you. See now how your minds are beginning to communicate through the release of the definitions, that the bodies do not communicate, that they are designed to stay separate and die together. This new mind now, this new experience of you, is being shared by the entire Universe. There is nowhere, dear teacher of God, that you cannot go in all the Universe. There is no place that you will not be and will not be known as a creation of perfect Love. That's my statement to you as you transcend this association. This continuum of space/time is over. I know there is a lot occurring in pop literature about the end of the millennium, and this concerns me not in the slightest, except for the value in the admission that something dramatic is happening, and we would like to have you consider that something dramatic is happening all the time. We want you to allow something dramatic to happen without reducing it to some sort of correspondence that can be nothing but less than magnificent. The realization of the magnificence of you and the gratitude, the Big G Rays, involved in it; and the realization that this was your way out of hell cannot be expressed, but it can be experienced, so that gratitude and love come together for that moment, and we find a love for each other. How lovely that is. Thank you!

Now you will go forth with this. This is old Jesus teaching of staff and sandals. You take this message of love, and you will be confronted with it. We're preparing a little booklet that will be going out here very soon. It's called *Jesus is Speaking.* And it's going to offer to not only Christendom but to the entire world the simple teachings of Jesus of Nazareth, historically 2000 years ago, with *A Course In Miracles*, not in a determined correspondence, but with the declaration of the simple message that He teaches. Hopefully that will be an entrée to where invitations for these new teachers to go out into the world and teach the experience, the healing, the experience of being whole, the dedication to life rather than death, the dedication to resurrection rather than crucifixion; the simple teachings of this master from Nazareth, which you have become. Will there be miracles? Dear ones, the miracles are occurring now. Will there be dramatic demonstrations of healings? Even unto raising the dead! And it occurs with the simple admission that this is not Life, that your existent association of time is not Life. If you'd like to call it death, go ahead, because it is not Life, and that the teaching of raising from the dead is nothing but simply the raising from your present human condition. How simple it becomes for you to raise the dead because the dead were in your mind. The dead were your own associations with yourself.

So when they come among you, these Miraclists, and they're perhaps holding this blue and gold book, or perhaps they're just knocking on your door and saying "can I talk to you about what we are together?" You begin to have this experience. You will move into a new range, a recognition of yourself, within the Course it's called a real world, and it's going on all the time around you, simultaneous with the world in which you have defined yourself in your own darkness and limitation. Remember this, and this will be the final statement of this particular association: Time is not sequential. The holy instant in which you now find yourself is all the time there has ever been or will ever be. This teaching was that when you entered this room, if you will release the sequentiality of your own mind, the necessity to define yourself in your old conceptual relationship, you will feel an experience of this holy instant. And we ask that you now very quietly share with us this holy instant, those of you who are reading this, so that the experience that you may feel can be verified by your continuing application of surrender, by your continuing determination to awaken from this dream of death to the reality of Love that is all about you.

Jesus would teach it: Where I have been, and where I went, you can now go with me. (John 14) We're at a point in the transformation in your own mind so that you can see the Second Coming as nothing but the change of your own association with yourself. How lovely that is. How lovely to realize that! Thank you coming to this basement, this Methodist basement. Thank you for showing up. I know that some of you will be derided: How dare you go and threaten the world with God's Love. But God is going to be Love no matter what you do. If that requires you taking that step, with the admission that you are as God created you, let that be so in you now, and it will be so because it is. There are experiences going on here now. This will cause you a little wonderment, perhaps a little dismay. Have peace of mind. What is going on with this association? Phenomena will be evident in the healing process! Don't be concerned about that. There is absolutely no reason why at any moment you cannot see that the body, the associations of cause and effect, are an illusion and that all around you is this extending love, that you can enter into that and spring into Light and be gone from here. That's what you have learned. And that's what you should learn today, and that's what you'll learn by reading this text again and again. The idea of repetition is very valuable to the perceptual mind simply because the perceptual mind is the continuing condition of the verification of itself, and requires the need to declare "I am as God created me. I am perfect and Love. I will allow this new Love to enter into my life." And, most emphatically, "I cannot die! If I have decided at this moment that I will not die, there is no power in all the Universe that could possibly terminate me. I remain, and will always be, as God created me."

We hope you'll join us here at the Academy, at least call and perhaps we can send out these teachings, these staff and sandal teachings of the miracle, and perhaps it won't be as threatening to you after you hear this, as it was before. But that's only because you're at a time where you're willing to hear it. That was really all the requirement there was, because once you let Love in the door, you're going to be in deep trouble. You're going to have to re-examine all of the associations of defense that you never really wanted in the first place. I'm offering it in totality. We'll see you soon!

www.ingramcontent.com/pod-product-compliance
Lightning Source LLC
Chambersburg PA
CBHW070347090426
42733CB00009B/1315